Ozone Discourses

NEW DIRECTIONS IN WORLD POLITICS

Helen Milner and John Gerard Ruggie, General Editors

NEW DIRECTIONS IN WORLD POLITICS
Helen Milner and John Gerard Ruggie, General Editors

Ozone Discourses

Science and Politics in Global
Environmental Cooperation

Karen T. Litfin

Columbia University Press
New York

Columbia University Press
New York   Chichester, West Sussex
Copyright © 1994 Columbia University Press
All rights reserved

Library of Congress Cataloging-in-Publication Data
Liftin, Karen.
Ozone discourse : science and politics in global
environmental cooperation / Karen Litfin
p. cm.—(New directions in world politics)
ISBN 0-231-08136-7 (alk. paper)
ISBN 0-231-08137-5 (pbk)
1. Ozone layer depletion—International cooperation.
2. Environmental policy—International cooperation.
3. Science and state—International Cooperation.
4. International relations.
I. Title. II. Series
QC879.7.L58 1994
363.73'84—dc20   94-8867
                                              CIP

Casebound editions of Columbia University Press books
are printed on permanent and durable acid-free paper.

Printed in the United States of America
c 10 9 8 7 6 5 4 3 2 1
p 10 9 8 7 6 5 4 3 2 1

Contents

List of Figures

List of Tables

Acknowledgments

Many people have offered their insightful comments on portions of the manuscript, including Richard Ashcraft, Susanna Hecht, Sheldon Kameniecki, David Lake, Ronnie Lipschutz, Gordon MacDonald, John Odell, John Ruggie, Arthur Stein, Richard Turco, Hartmut Walter, and Oran Young. Special thanks are due to David O. Wilkinson and M. H. Peterson for persevering through the entire manuscript, and also to Sarah St. Onge for her editorial assistance. Conversations with Peter Haas and Edward Parson were helpful both in formulating the research questions and in locating participants in the ozone negotiations. And, of course, this work would have been impossible without the many hours of time contributed by the dozens of scientists and other individuals involved in the policy process. Finally I am grateful to the Institute on Global Conflict and Cooperation at the University of California in San Diego and the American Association of University Women for their financial support.

Ozone Discourses

1 • Science in World Politics: The Need for a Discursive Approach

While most studies about science and world politics focus on military and economic issues, and some work has been done on science and domestic environmental politics, precious little is available on how scientific knowledge functions in international environmental negotiations. Yet the expanded temporal and spatial perspectives implicit in large-scale environmental problems make the analytical skills of scientists especially important in this area. In general, uncertainty increases as the causal chain of events moves further into the future, thereby empowering a new class of scientific policy elites.

Beyond the environment, scientific culture may be seen as a driving force in the politics of postindustrial society.[1] Indeed, with the end of the Cold War and the emergence of new sorts of challenges to national security, many theorists of world politics are seeking alternatives to the traditional ways of conceptualizing power (Rosenau 1990; Nye 1990). A host of new issues, including the AIDS epidemic, drug trafficking, and the environment, require cooperative endeavors among states while simultaneously involving a diffusion of power away from states to nonstate actors. Technical experts are frequently drawn into the policy process for these issues, becoming important political actors in their own right.

Conventional approaches to international relations tend to depict power as a material resource, a tool wielded by nation-states to further their own interests. The kind of power most clearly relevant for many of the so-called postindustrial issues, including international environmental problems, diverges from conventional definitions in three respects. First, because it is so deeply connected to scientific and technical knowledge, power is not reducible to material resources like wealth and military capabilities.[2] Second, because a nation's interests are often unclear under conditions of scientific uncertainty, knowledge may become a significant source of power as it facilitates the clarification of states' interests. Third, the determination of state interests entails various subnational processes, so structural approaches that "black-box" the state are rendered woefully inadequate in the face of challenges raised by the new issues. Thus, issues that highlight the role of technical expertise require a threefold revision of the dominant theoretical assumptions: power must be conceived in terms broad enough to encompass knowledge-based power; interests must be problematized as arenas of political struggle that should be formulated in light of contending knowledge claims; and the study of domestic political processes must be given greater emphasis.

The two dominant theoretical approaches to the study of international relations in the United States, neorealism and neoliberal institutionalism, are objectivist: they take goals and interests as given. For neorealists, state interests are determined by a state's position in the international system, the structure of which is defined by the distribution of capabilities (Waltz 1979). Neorealist scholars have paid little attention to transboundary environmental problems, perhaps because the relationship of these problems to international military and economic structures is unclear. These new problems, however, may soon increase the level of conflict in the international system, making them more acceptable research topics for neorealists (Homer-Dixon 1991).

Like neorealists, neoliberal institutionalists maintain that states pursue their given interests, but they are more concerned with the institutional factors that temper the effects of anarchy in the international system and facilitate cooperation. Institutions are regularized practices consisting of recognized roles and clusters of rules that constrain activity and shape expectations; changes in them may alter the costs and benefits of cooperation. States modify their preferences and behavior on the basis of the changing institutional context of decision making, a context that is external to the actors' self-identities and mutual understandings. Thus, like neorealists, institutionalists focus on the objective sources of interests and behavior. The institutional approach to international environmental regime formation suggests that states cooperate in order to reduce uncertainty and transaction costs; the question of interest construction is not central (Bucholtz 1990; Young 1989a).

A reflectivist approach, in contrast, focuses on the subjective understandings of state and nonstate actors as the source of interests and action. Like neorealists, reflectivists study social structures, but they insist that structures, constituted by identities and interests, cannot exist apart from process. Even anarchy, the defining feature of the international system, has no inherent logic but is rather "what states make of it" (Wendt 1992). Institutions, reflectivists argue, are expressions of intersubjectively shared norms, ideas, and knowledge (Wendt 1992; Dessler 1989).

Until recently, the dominant theoretical approaches to international relations have downplayed the role of subjective factors, focusing instead on structural and material explanations of state behavior. Norms, ideas, and knowledge have been viewed by both realists and Marxists as epiphenomenal expressions of material interests (Carr 1964; Cox 1987). A new trend, however, highlights the influence of cognitive factors on foreign policy-making and international politics (Goldstein 1989; Hall 1989; Kratochwil 1990). Implicit in this new tendency, and perhaps reflecting the recent major changes in the world system, is the view that the main impediments to cooperation lie in malleable beliefs and conventions rather than in the comparatively solid structures of the neorealists and institutionalists (Jervis 1988:340).

International environmental policy coordination, which typically entails an evolution of perceived interests on the part of state and nonstate actors, is well suited to a reflectivist approach. Environmental policy is heavily dependent on such cognitive factors as scientific knowledge, philosophical ideas, and public opinion. Reflectivist approaches to international environmental politics include the epistemic communities literature (Haas 1989, 1992b), studies of social learning processes (Clark 1990), and negotiation-analytic modeling (Sebenius 1992).

None of these reflectivist approaches, however, makes a concerted effort to analyze the influence and substantive content of discursive practices in international environmental politics. By *discourse*, I mean sets of linguistic practices and rhetorical strategies embedded in a network of social relations. In particular, the distinctive role of scientific discourse in regime formation has been undertheorized. This work seeks to establish a groundwork for filling that gap.

Reflectivist approaches, including those emphasizing discursive understandings, do not replace structuralism and institutionalism altogether; bureaucratic and interest group politics—institutional and systemic obstacles and incentives to international cooperation—do not disappear once we acknowledge that policy is also driven by subjective factors. These other approaches, however, are often mechanical, focusing on the pushing and pulling of nation-states and their agents around interests. By contrast, reflective approaches understand policy-making as a problem-solving activity with important intersubjective dimensions. They may focus on a range of cognitive factors, including belief systems, ideologies, and consensual knowledge.

The few theoretical frameworks that have focused on the role of expert knowledge in international relations suffer from an implicit assumption that scientific consensus tends to generate political consensus. The prevailing approaches, including variants of functionalism and the literature on epistemic communities, tend to work from a simplistic view of science as standing outside of politics, of knowledge as divorced from power. These approaches are part of the "rationality project" (Stone 1988:4), albeit to a lesser extent than many other methods in political science, a project that attempts to "rescue public policy from the irrationalities and indignities of politics" (Stone 1988:4).

Yet, contrary to the implications of these approaches, the cultural role of science as a key source of legitimation means that political debates are framed in scientific terms; questions of value become reframed as questions of fact, with each confrontation leading to the search for further scientific justification. Paradoxically, the demand for legitimation results in a process of delegitimation. Moreover, facts must be expressed in language, and they require interpretation. Facts deemed relevant are always chosen selectively, depending on the interests of the communicator and the audience. This is where knowledge brokers come in—as intermediaries between the original researchers, or the producers of knowledge, and the policymakers who consume that knowledge but lack the time and training necessary to absorb the original research.[3] The ability of knowledge brokers, who typically operate at low or middle levels of governments or international organizations, to frame and interpret scientific knowledge is a substantial source of political power. Knowledge brokers are especially influential under the conditions of scientific uncertainty that characterize most environmental problems.

The argument that knowledge and interests are mutually interactive is most effectively demonstrated through detailed contextual analysis; an intensive case-study approach is the best way of exploring such complex sets of interactions. Of course, a single case study cannot prove that a given set of dynamics is the rule, but it can provide a heuristic device for exploring possible conjunctions. The Montreal Protocol on Substances that Deplete the Ozone Layer, along with its subsequent revisions, provides an excellent case for contextual analysis because of the pivotal role of science in its framing. Although an agreement was the ultimate outcome, international cooperation was not the straightforward consequence of consensual knowledge.

The Montreal Protocol, negotiated in 1987 under the auspices of the United Nations Environment Programme (UNEP) as the first international treaty on a global ecological problem, was the result of close collaboration between scientists and policymakers. It was amended in 1990 and then again in 1992. Superficially, this landmark ozone regime appears to have been the result of a rigorous process of risk analysis and adroit diplomacy, with sophisticated atmospheric models serving as the scientific basis of the negotiations. This is essentially the thesis of Ambassador Richard Benedick, the chief negotiator for the Unites States during the negotiations (Benedick 1991). Peter Haas offers a similar but more refined account, based on an epistemic community composed primarily of atmospheric scientists (1992a).

I, too, began my research with the tentative hypothesis that the ozone regime grew out of efforts by an epistemic community to forge a political consensus on the basis of science. International environmental problems, I believed, were inherently science-driven, and scientific knowledge could provide the common ground that was otherwise lacking among competing nations. Knowledge could furnish the means for reorienting actors' conceptions of their own best interests. In short, like others, I was beguiled by a faith in the ability of science to make politics more rational and cooperative. Given the intuitive appeal of the epistemic cooperation thesis and the superficial resemblance of the Montreal Protocol process to the procedures of risk analysis, my delusion is not surprising.

Had my original hypothesis been confirmed, I could have at best told an interesting story with little theoretical value. The Montreal Protocol is a "most likely case," meaning that it would be expected to conform to the epistemic cooperation hypothesis. Consequently, no reliable generalizations beyond this individual case could have been made. My study might have answered the question, "*How* did an epistemic community operate in this particular instance?" but it would have been of little service in ascertaining *whether* the application of science to political problems tends to precipitate more cooperative solutions.

Most-likely case studies, a special instance of crucial-case studies, are especially tailored to invalidating hypotheses. The logic is that if a case is most likely to fit a theory and does not, then the theory is probably wrong. Conversely, least-likely case studies, the other form of crucial-case study, are tailored to confirmation. Crucial-case studies are the most apt to produce generalizable conclusions. At the other extreme, configurative-idiographic case studies are descriptive explanations of unique cases couched in idiosyncratic terms (Eckstein 1975; George 1979). These would be the eqivalent of telling an intersting story.

As I interviewed the participants and read the source documents from the international negotiating process, however, I began to suspect that more complicated dynamics than epistemic cooperation were involved. It became increasingly evident that "knowledge" was not simply a body of concrete and objective facts but that accepted knowledge was deeply implicated in questions of framing and interpretation and that these were related to perceived interests. Although the range of uncertainty was narrow, atmospheric science did not provide a body of objective and value-free facts from which international cooperation emerged. Rather, knowledge was framed in light of specific interests and preexisting discourses so that questions of value were rendered as questions of fact, with exogenous factors shaping the political salience of various modes of interpreting that knowledge. In particular, the discourse of precautionary action, not itself mandated by atmospheric science, moved from a subordinate to a dominant position. The disconfirmation of my initial hypothesis required some psychological adjustment on my part, but in the end it gave me a far more theoretically interesting research agenda.

The evidence against the epistemic cooperation thesis in the ozone case study is convincing. Had I stopped at that point, my research would have challenged the dominant theoretical perspectives on the role of scientific and technical knowledge in world politics, but it would not have offered an alternative. I chose to press on with the further question: if the epistemic cooperation thesis is deficient, then what other theoretical tools might be more useful? The study cried out for a more interactive and multidimensional conception of knowledge-based power, one that I have begun to develop through a discursive practices approach. Thus, the purpose of the case study shifted from testing the epistemic cooperation thesis to forging an alternative theoretical approach. In other words, my research began unintentionally as a crucial-case study, with the Montreal Protocol being a most-likely case for an epistemic communities approach, and developed into a heuristic case study tracing the outlines of a discursive practices approach. Heuristic case studies are "used deliberately to stimulate the imagination toward discerning important general problems and possible theoretical solutions" (Eckstein 1975:104).

A word of caution: a discursive practices approach, with its resistance to unidirectional causal explanations, offers little in the way of methodological tidiness. With outcomes dependent upon interdependent variables and idiosyncratic contextual factors, universally applicable generalizations are not to be expected. Sometimes scientists can shape policy, and sometimes they cannot; sometimes consensual knowledge engenders a policy consensus, and sometimes it does not. Only a detailed contextual analysis can explain how a particular discourse comes to be accepted for a given problem.

The Montreal Protocol process, including the ensuing treaty amendment process, provides a rich source of detail for analyzing the complex sets of interactions between science and politics. Precisely because it looks like an example of epistemic cooperation, or consensual knowledge generating political agreement, the ozone case is an excellent vehicle for the study of other, more counterintuitive possibilities. The ozone deliberations offer an opportunity to formulate a multidimensional account of the interaction of science in politics. Finally, because that treaty is widely considered a prototype for future agreements, an understanding of its evolution is important for making any inferences about policy-making under conditions of global ecological interdependence.

Chapter 2 is largely deductive, proceeding from the question, "If knowledge were to be considered as either a source or a kind of power, how would power need to be conceptualized in order to be broad enough to encompass knowledge?" The chapter's purpose is to provide a conceptual background rather than to erect anything resembling a universal theory or model. The chapter, which constitutes the theoretical heart of the book, builds upon the works of a wide range of thinkers in making a case for an interactive conception of power and knowledge. I argue that agent-centered and physicalist conceptions of power, which dominate the international relations literature, ignore or downplay issues of legitimacy, consensus, and interpretation. Because these dimensions are essential to knowledge-based power, conventional accounts must be expanded to include a discursive and productive conception of power.

Poststructuralism, particularly the later works of Michel Foucault on power and knowledge, emphasize the neglected communicative, generative, and systemic dimensions of power. For Foucault, power is generative yet inherently conflictual, and its dynamics tend to be much more subtle that simple domination or repression. His notion of disciplinary power is fundamentally linguistic, not material. Although Foucault and other poststructuralists seem to banish social agents altogether, I reject this move and argue that such a maneuver detracts from a coherent theory of power. The decentering of the subject, however, is a useful strategy in that it highlights the constitution of identity through discursive practices, a key process in knowledge-based power.

In light of the preceding discussion on power, chapter 2 provides a conceptual analysis of scientific knowledge that seeks to avoid the twin epistemological perils of objectivism and relativism. While recognizing that science is an inescapably social process, my approach also grounds scientific knowledge in the world of empirical objects and structures. Science, I argue, is much more closely related to a Foucaultian conception of disciplinary power than it is to conventional notions of power as control by specific agents through material means. As a cornerstone of modernity, scientific knowledge delimits the boundaries of legitimate discourse. Regimes of truth define not only what can be said, but what can be thought: to define is to control. As political problems have become increasingly entwined with questions of scientific evidence and proof, the ability to interpret reality has itself become a major source of political power.

Chapter 2 also takes up the more practical question of how science interacts with politics in light of the preceding theoretical discussion. The dynamics of expert advice dominate the power-knowledge nexus for transscientific problems, of which environmental problems are a subset.[4] In many respects, policymakers and technical experts inhabit different worlds and speak different languages. Yet they interact with one another in complex networks of power, with the authority of each group being highly circumscribed by the authority of the other. At various turns, the fact-value distinction, commonly believed to divide the two worlds, breaks down. Knowledge is framed in light of specific interests, so that information begets counterinformation. Interpreting and framing knowledge become crucial political problems as information is mustered to achieve policy objectives.

Many contemporary analyses of science in politics misconstrue the relationship between knowledge and power. In considering the more specific question of science in world politics, with the added dimension of international anarchy, a skeptical attitude seems especially appropriate. Yet the only three theoretical approaches that have specifically taken up the question—functionalism, neofunctionalism, and the epistemic communities literature—have all adopted a rationalistic stance, emphasizing instead science's potential to contribute to global unification.

International environmental problems provide an ideal terrain for tracing the interactional dynamics of science and politics. Particularly as temporal and spatial scales assume global and intergenerational proportions, these problems are characterized by conditions of high risk in the face of scientific uncertainty. Scientists are often important political actors because they are the first to discover the problems and are therefore instrumental in defining both how the problems are conceptualized and what policy options should be addressed. Through such methods as risk analysis, both policymakers and observers have sought to delineate science sharply from politics, with the goal of identifying the objective knowledge from which policy decisions can rationally be made. But such strategies rely on a strict fact-value distinction, a distinction that is suspect in the abstract and of even more dubious practical value for trans-scientific problems. Nonetheless, because science is a primary source of legitimation and because scientists help to define environmental problems, the language of international environmental policy debates can be expected to be flagrantly scientific.

The material in chapters 3, 4, and 5 contains the case study of regime formation around the stratospheric ozone problem. Because of the contemporary nature of the case, many of the actual participants were available for personal interviews, allowing me to ask specific questions that I might not have been able to answer through archival research alone. These interviews were crucial in determining the beliefs and discursive orientations of the participants, information that is not readily accessible through publications and documents. As Paul Sabatier (1987) argues, it is easier to identify beliefs than it is to ascribe interests. In this sense, a reflective approach has some methodological advantages for empirical research over structural and institutional approaches, which base their analysis on interests.

Chapter 3 serves two purposes. First, it provides a technical and historical backdrop for the case study; key terms are defined, and the origins of the relevant scientific and political networks traced. Second, it demonstrates that certain modes of framing the available scientific information had important political implications even before the international negotiations for control measures got under way. The scientific and political networks in place before the Montreal Protocol negotiations, as well as the dominant modes of framing scientific knowledge, were all instrumental in formulating a precautionary discourse, enshrined in principle with the 1985 Vienna Convention for the Protection of the Ozone Layer.

Chapter 4 is a detailed case study of how scientific knowledge and political processes interacted in the international negotiations leading up to the Montreal Protocol. The 1987 agreement called for roughly 50 percent reductions in chlorofluorocarbon and halon consumption by the year 2000. It was immediately hailed as "the first truly global treaty that . . . seeks to anticipate and manage a world problem before it becomes an irreversible crisis" (UNEP 1987c). Clearly, scientific knowledge was a necessary precondition for the treaty's negotiation, and the prominence of scientists at key international meetings attests to this fact. But it was far from being a sufficient condition. It is one thing to focus on how knowledge facilitated cooperation, and another thing entirely to claim that scientists themselves were the precipitating force behind the agreement. Yet the prevailing interpretations dodge this distinction, attributing the political consensus either to a scientific consensus or to the atmospheric scientists themselves (Benedick 1991; Haas 1992b).

My own analysis, based primarily upon original source documents and personal interviews with participants, focuses on the contending discursive practices during the negotiations and seeks to trace how the discourse of precautionary action shifted from a subordinate to a dominant position. The capacity of scientific knowledge to facilitate international cooperation on the ozone layer was mediated by two crucial factors. First, the science was framed and interpreted by a group of knowledge brokers with strong ecological beliefs who were associated with UNEP and the U.S. Environmental Protection Agency (EPA). Second, the context of the negotiations, defined largely by the discovery of huge ozone losses over Antarctica, determined the political acceptability of various modes of framing the available knowledge. Science did not offer a set of objective facts from which a policy consensus evolved.

Despite its narrow margins of uncertainty, the international scientific assessment that served as the informational basis for the negotiations (NASA/WMO 1986) was amenable to a wide range of interpretations.

Not surprisingly, what was accepted as knowledge was tightly linked to the political and economic interests of the principal antagonists, the USA and the European Communities (EC). Yet the outcomes were not based primarily on either material interests or material power, for scientific discourse, shaped by distinctive contextual factors, was crucial in defining the range of acceptable policy outcomes. The international policy process that led to the Montreal Protocol was not a linear movement from scientific consensus to policy coordination. Typical of trans-scientific problems, the process was far more multidimensional, defined by an interactive relationship between knowledge and power, science and politics.

Chapter 5 extends the analysis of science in politics into the post-Montreal period. The discourse of precautionary action, concretized in the Montreal Protocol, was strengthened and expanded in two sets of treaty revisions, the 1990 amendments in London and the 1992 amendments in Copenhagen. Once the Antarctic ozone hole was definitively linked to anthropogenic sources of chlorine and bromine and once ozone losses were observed over the Northern Hemisphere, a consensus emerged in support of a stronger treaty. Yet, as before, scientific consensus did not automatically beget policy consensus; rather, certain discursive strategies helped to frame the available knowledge in ways that defined the range of policy options.

Chemicals that only a few years before had been considered irreplaceable were now targeted for elimination, precipitating an unprecedented search by producer and user industries for substitute chemicals and alternative technologies. Yet the availability of substitutes and alternatives was not simply dependent on the status of scientific and technical knowledge but was itself associated with discursive practices and psychological proclivities. Without substitutes, parties to the Montreal Protocol would have been extremely reluctant to adopt measures to phase out CFCs, halons, and other ozone-depleting substances. Scientific discourse, based on the alarming findings of the atmospheric scientists, confirmed the desirability of stringent regulations; sensing the air of crisis, industry moved rapidly to develop new technologies; these new technologies, in turn, expedited the international regulatory process for ozone-depleting substances. Thus, atmospheric science, industrial technology, and political decision making were all interconnected.

One important contrast between the deliberations before and after the Montreal Protocol was the enormously expanded role of the developing countries. Despite the differences some developing countries had with industrialized countries, for the most part they did not frame those differences in terms of scientific knowledge—even when the scientific arguments were there to be made. This fact, I argue, testifies to the nearly universal appeal of the discourse of precautionary action. But precautionary action on a global scale required the participation of the developing countries, many of which resisted until they were assured that it would not be economically damaging. Developing countries, framing their arguments in terms of equity and sovereignty, were successful in persuading the parties to establish an innovative mechanism to finance technology transfer from north to south. More than anything else, however, it is technical knowledge (not physical technology) that is being transferred, indicating yet again the extent to which the ozone problem is an informational phenomenon.

The final chapter, chapter 6, examines the implications of an interactive conception of power and knowledge for international relations theory. Conventional theories of regime formation, at either the systemic or the national level of analysis, cannot account for the processes and outcomes in the ozone deliberations. The fundamental problem with all these approaches is that they fail to account for the central role of scientific knowledge in shaping processes and outcomes. Moreover, they overlook the importance of cognitive factors in shaping actors' conceptions of their interests and identities.

Recalling the earlier discussion about knowledge and power, I argue that the epistemic communities literature, which represents the most recent attempt to theorize about the place of scientific knowledge in world politics, represents an important contribution to a reflectivist approach. Yet this literature focuses on scientific consensus as a source of more rational and cooperative political processes. Just as interesting, and perhaps even the norm under the conditions of uncertainty so prevalent in environmental decision making, is epistemic dissension. Epistemic community approaches downplay—almost to the point of neglect—the ways in which scientific information simply rationalizes or reinforces existing political conflicts. Questions of framing, interpretation, and contingency are glossed over in an effort to explain politics as a function of consensual knowledge. In failing to consider the nature of discursive practices and strategies, the epistemic communities approach grasps neither the dynamics nor the full significance of the convergence of intersubjective understandings.

To the extent that the power and perceived interests of social actors are rooted in how they frame and interpret information, then a discursive practices approach can make a valuable contribution. As determinants of what can and cannot be thought, discourses define the range of policy options, thereby functioning as precursors to policy outcomes. A discursive practices approach is sensitive to the interactive dynamics between knowledge and power, as well as the contextual factors that enable certain discourses to prevail in the policy process. An emphasis on discourse, rather than on states, bureaucracies, or individuals, interprets international regimes as loci of struggle among various networks of power/knowledge. Environmental problems may be viewed primarily as informational phenomena or as struggles among contested knowledge forms. The Montreal Protocol process, for instance, is essentially the story of how a dominant antiregulatory discourse was supplanted by a new regulatory discourse. This discursive shift occurred both domestically within the Unites States and internationally during and after the Montreal Protocol negotiations. A discursive practices approach focuses on the contextual factors, such as the discovery of the Antarctic ozone hole, that empowered a subordinate discourse.

More generally, a discursive practices perspective on international regimes provides a valuable alternative to both liberal and realist approaches. Ultimately, both schools of thought tend to reduce power to material factors in the possession of specific agents. Only a discursive practices approach offers an understanding of regimes as crystallized embodiments of power and knowledge. If those scholars who discern a trend toward a postindustrial or informational world order are correct, then this argument has important implications not just for environmental issues but, more generally, for the nature of power in the emergent global system. One trend may be the diffusion of the sovereign power of nation-states to nonstate actors and the proliferation of disciplinary micropowers. Consistent with this diffusion would be the displacement of power toward those actors most proficient at controlling and manipulating informational resources.

There are good reasons to believe that, as environmental pressures become more severe and other international problems become increasingly technical, the terms of political discourse will become ever more scientific. Yet the prevalence of scientific discourse should not delude us into the common misconception that politics will therefore become more rational and less conflict-ridden, whether through functional cooperation or through epistemic communities. A profusion of information may, in fact, lead to greater confusion as the world becomes a ubiquitous market for discourses. The "scientization of politics" may well devolve into the "politicization of science" (Weingart 1982:73).

2 • Power and Scientific Discourse

The present physical interpretation of power is but a manifestation of the larger process of turning everything into an object, generally an object of manipulation.

Henryk Skolimowski, "Power: Myth and Reality"

In this chapter, I analyze my key theoretical concepts—power and knowledge—and explore some of the complex sets of relationships between them. Rather than providing parsimonious but oversimplified definitions, I draw eclectically on existing conceptualizations. This approach is particularly suitable for a discussion of "essentially contested concepts" (Gallie 1956), a label that applies well to power and knowledge.

My interest is in the intersection of knowledge and power in international environmental politics. Hence, I highlight notions of power that include legitimacy, consensus, and access to information, sketching the limitations of the structural and materially based conceptions dominant in recent international relations theory. Likewise, I focus on the social and pragmatic aspects of knowledge and its political application. I do not deny the usefulness of other definitions; I merely claim that power and knowledge must be conceptualized in terms broad enough to include a more subtle and interactive understanding of both. Otherwise, one risks falling prey to the modernist fallacy that power and knowledge can be neatly sequestered from one another. In the realm of policy studies, this fallacy becomes part of the "rationality project," with its mission of "rescuing public policy from the irrationalities and indignities of politics" (Stone

1988:4). The modernist fallacy wrongly assumes that scientific and technical knowledge can provide an objective body of facts from which policy can be rationally generated.

I begin with conventional notions of power and work toward a more comprehensive conception that can accommodate the complexity of power that is knowledge based. The prevailing conception of power in the study of world politics is truncated, largely confining power to its physical and manipulative aspects. In contrast, knowledge-based power is productive and discursive, not merely repressive and materialistic. Such an approach makes an important contribution to the study of science in policy decisions, especially for environmental issues. A discursive approach to science in policy emphasizes the rhetorical nature of scientific evidence, argumentation, and persuasion. Information does not emerge in a void but is incorporated into preexisting stories to render it meaningful. Information is framed and interpreted in ways that bolster certain policy positions.

The dominant perspectives on the role of technical expertise in international politics, namely variants of functionalism and the epistemic communities literature, lack the richness and depth of a discursive approach. First, they tend to overstate the ability of scientific knowledge to generate political consensus. Second, because these approaches are agent-centered, they downplay the content and context of discursive practices, thereby obscuring the primary sources of persuasive competence. If, as I argue, discourses are important power centers, then an approach that delves into their inner workings is absolutely essential to understanding science in politics.

Aspects of Power

Power is probably the most elemental concept in the study of politics, yet there is no consensus on what it is, much less how to measure it. If we want to say, for instance, that experts exercise power, we need a notion of power that includes access to knowledge, the value of consensus, and persuasive competence. Power here has positive, capacity-giving dimensions beyond the negative dimensions of domination and control. Experts may disavow their political role, so we need a definition that includes the covert and unintentional exercise of power. Moreover, knowledge-based power is not solely a property of social agents; ideas and discourses themselves may be powerful entities.

Beginning with the most rudimentary notions of power, we may build a conception broad enough to encompass knowledge-based power, and in so doing we may discern its distinctive traits. Power may be defined generically, from the Latin *potere*, as "the ability to produce an effect," a definition that includes everything from the power of a steam engine to a nation's ability to fight and win a war. Yet the effects of power, like those of gravity, are tangible in a way that power itself is not.

In general, the emphasis has been on the ability of actors to exert intentional control over the actions of others through material threats and incentives, an emphasis consistent with the premises of methodological individualism and behavioralism. Robert Dahl's definition is widely accepted among American political scientists, and certainly influential among international relations scholars: *A* has power over *B* to the extent that he can get *B* to do something that *B* otherwise would not have done (1957:203).

The issue of unintentional consequences of action, however, is fundamental to structural notions of power. Marxists, for instance, claim that a society's class structure shapes all behavior and thought, regardless of individuals' intentions. In his structural theory of international relations, Kenneth Waltz (1979) rejects Dahl's definition on the grounds that assessing power in terms of compliance overlooks unintended effects and, hence, much of what political processes are about. Whatever its flaws, structural realism is based on the valid observation that conventional behavioral and individualistic notions of power omit consideration of how acts and relations are shaped by social structures.

Structural theories in general make a small contribution to an understanding of knowledge-based power. The ability of experts to affect policy decisions derives from their location within institutionalized structures of knowledge production.[1] They may consciously impact policy—recent history is replete with such cases, from Albert Einstein's famous letter to President Roosevelt to Edward Teller's vocal support for space-based defense—or they may exercise power unintentionally by identifying problems with policy implications or by conveying information at critical junctures in the policy process. In the context of the ozone negotiations, many of the atmospheric scientists involved believed themselves to be totally apolitical. Yet, though guided by the canons of scientific reasoning rather than political convenience, they did exercise power.

While neorealists' structural notion of power moves beyond an agent-centered worldview, in another respect it is entirely conventional. Waltz's view of power is ultimately not very different from that of other realists, with the addendum that it may be exercised unintentionally. Among realists, power is typically taken to entail domination and control by states, it is measured in relative rather than absolute terms (Grieco 1988), and it is usually materially based (Knorr 1975). Such a notion is of limited utility in constructing a conception of knowledge-based power. First, if one changes one's behavior on the basis of new information, it is not clear that one has been dominated or controlled. Second, while some experts may be more influential than others, whether because of their superior professional reputations or their close relations with policymakers, the relative power of states tells us little about the application of knowledge to policy choices. Third, while some states and individuals may have access to more and better information, the intangible nature of ideas means that knowledge-based power is not easily quantified and does not fit easily into a distribution-of-capabilities framework. A major consideration in exploring knowledge-based power is to assess not so much to what degree actors are affected but in what way. As I shall argue later, fundamental nonmaterial factors such as identities and interests are themselves implicated in knowledge-based power.[2]

To contrast further knowledge-based power with realist conceptions of power, consider how the two treat questions of domination and interest. Hans Morgenthau, perhaps the most articulate proponent of realist thinking, identifies power with domination and control (Morgenthau and Thompson 1985:11). While this definition no doubt covers many power relationships, it does not so obviously apply to the power of persuasion. Morgenthau states, "realism assumes that its key concept of *interest defined as power* is an objective category which is universally valid, but it does not endow that concept with a meaning that is fixed once and for all" (Morgenthau and Thompson 1985:10; emphasis added). In the abstract, this definition seems broad enough to cover knowledge-based power, but only if persuasion is considered a subtle psychological method of control. Perhaps a starting point for a revised realist conception of power might be E. H. Carr's notion of power as control over opinion (1964) or Arnold Wolfers's distinction between power and influence (1962). Both of these, however, place knowledge-based power in a decidedly secondary position relative to physical power, particularly military power, so that it remains an underdeveloped concept.

The identification of power as the capacity to realize interests is even more problematic. Morgenthau, for instance, claims that any theory of world politics must be grounded in the concept of "the national interest" (Morgenthau and Thompson 1985:204). Those who argue that states, by definition, pursue their interests run the risk of post hoc reasoning. In this view, interests are surmised by observing the behavior of states.[3] But instrumental action implies goal-oriented behavior, and only a contextual analysis can reveal what goals are being pursued and why. Realists neither explain adequately how interests are formulated nor provide a method for determining when states pursue long-term rather than short-term interests. This dilemma is especially relevant for global environmental problems, where interests in the two time frames are typically pitted against one another. The fundamental insight of reflective approaches is that interests—and even identities—are socially produced and not given in any straightforward way.

In sum, the conventional association of power with domination and control is problematic in situations where an actor is persuaded to revise her conception of her interests through evidence or reasoning. One would want to say that power operates in such a situation, yet one would also want to question the repressive, even malevolent, connotations implicit in most definitions of power.[4] Rather, power should be conceived as potentially generative and rooted in the self-understandings and interactions of people.

One can imagine a spectrum of power relations, ranging from those most rooted in domination and control to those characterized by mutuality and intersubjective understandings. At one end, we would find *force*, where a powerful actor removes the effective choice to act otherwise. Following force might be *coercion*, where one actor threatens another; then *manipulation*, where some level of deceit is involved; then *authority*, where an actor is recognized as having either a legal or a moral right to impose decisions. Finally, the knowledge-based power of *persuasion* relies upon evidence and argumentation.

The notion of legitimacy, which is vital to authority and persuasion, crops up frequently in the literature of political theory and domestic politics, but it seems somehow misplaced in the study of world politics. Realists link power with domination and characterize the international system in terms of the principles of anarchy and self-help (Waltz 1979; Grieco 1988; Knorr 1975; Smith 1984). In this view, the normative consensus prerequisite to the possibility of legitimate international institutions does not exist.[5] The Grotian tradition, a minority position until recently, holds that the international system functions according to the norms, beliefs, and rules held in common by national actors (Bull 1977; Rosenau 1973). But theorists rooted in the Grotian tradition typically focus on norms of diplomacy and international law and do not address the issue of scientific knowledge as a source of legitimation. A key question, then, is the extent to which knowledge can serve as an instrument of legitimation and a springboard for consensus in world politics. If confidence in science is a hallmark of the modern era, then scientific knowledge can be expected to facilitate cooperation. But if the production and interpretation of scientific knowledge is an unavoidably political process, then knowledge may feed into new or existing arenas of contestation.

The legitimate exercise of power requires that the relevant actors share certain understandings, whether these be cultural norms, legal structures, perceptions of empirical reality, or deductive logic. While Weber refers to the "legitimations of domination," the very legitimacy of this sort of power relation makes it difficult to accept fully it as domination. Moreover, the mechanisms of legitimation that Weber proposes (tradition, charisma, and rational legality) do not explicitly include scientific knowledge, although any of these mechanisms may apply to science in certain contexts. What is important, though, is that the power of knowledgeable experts, inasmuch as they do not directly determine policy, is rooted in the normative beliefs of policymakers. This observation holds not just for policy issues but for any situation involving expert advice. My doctor, for instance, may be exercising a form of power when he prescribes a medication for me, but this is not domination in the common use of the term. In this sense, scientific and political legitimacy are similar, and neither has much in common with power as overt domination. Related to this, and challenging the coupling of power with agency, is the potential for ideas and beliefs to influence agents and change their senses of self-identity. Social movements may be inspired by the power of an idea, just as individuals may be moved by a powerful conviction.

Another aspect of power that has little in common with overt domination is empowerment, a process by which a group gains an understanding of its best interests and collaborates to achieve them (Fay 1987:130). Social empowerment often involves knowledge-based power, as people are educated to reconceptualize their interests, and even their identities, as they were in the civil rights and women's movements. Scientific knowledge can inspire collective action, as it has in the environmental and consumer movements. In these instances, power entails neither mutually exclusive interests nor physical manifestations but is rooted in intersubjective understandings and "generated" collectively within a social system (Parsons 1967).

Yet it would be a mistake merely to reiterate at the systemic level the traditional teleological concept of power, e.g., the capacity to realize goals. What is lacking in interest-based models, according to Hannah Arendt (1970) and Jurgen Habermas (1977), is a communicative model of action. For Arendt and Habermas, power is more the ability to act in concert through consensual communication than the ability to obtain goals by mobilizing resources. Knowledge production is itself a fundamentally consensual activity, although Arendt and, to a lesser extent, Habermas downplay the pervasive element of struggle in discursive practice.

In the context of international relations, aspect of social life, for that matter, an important question is whether the conditions of communicative rationality proposed by Habermas and Arendt can ever be attained. For science, such communication blocks inhibit the rationality of scientific consensus, and more serious blocks can distort the translation of knowledge into policy decisions. The concept of communicative power might serve as an ideal toward which both science and politics can strive, but it does not shed much light on actual processes.

The notion of power as generative and systemic is also elaborated by Michel Foucault, yet his conception is not nearly so optimistic.[6] For him, power is omnipresent; one is never outside it (1980:141). Foucault rejects the modern belief in the possibility of emancipation from power relations, a belief he attributes to both liberals and Marxists. He speaks of the "productivity" of power, "networks" and "webs" of power, and a "microphysics" of power (1979, 1980, 1983). Spurning the conventional emphasis on the most visible expressions of power, he focuses more on its subtle workings than on its aspects of repression or domination. He asks: "If power were never anything but repressive, if it never did anything but say no, do you really think one would be brought to obey it? What makes power hold good is simply the fact that . . . *it traverses and produces things, it induces pleasure, forms knowledge, produces discourse*" (1980:119; emphasis added). Yet he does not disregard the reality of domination, noting that it is always exerted in a particular direction, with some people on one side and some on the other (1977:213). Believing that power should be studied at its "extremities," Foucault examines social relations to which the discourse of power traditionally has not been applied, e.g., schools, hospitals, confessionals, etc. To these, I would add the institutions of science and the networks through which science is applied to social problems.

Foucault traces a historical shift from what he terms the "sovereign" form of power as display exercised under monarchy to a more discursive form of "disciplinary" power typical of modernity (1979). He identifies the traditional notion of power as exerted by autonomous agents imposing their sovereign wills as a throwback to premodernity. He is concerned with how "disciplinary power" and other "technologies of power" operate on bodies, how discourse makes the body the object of knowledge and invests it with power. Because individuals are themselves the effects of power, becoming so entwined in networks of power that they are both agents and victims of social control, there is no autonomous subjectivity for Foucault. Knowledge is intrinsic to these networks of power: "between techniques of knowledge and strategies of power, there is no exteriority" (1980:133). 'Truth' is a system of ordered procedures for the production, regulation and circulation of statements.

The Panopticon, Jeremy Bentham's 1791 design for a model prison, epitomizes and concretizes Foucault's notion of disciplinary power. Each inmate is constantly visible from the tower but isolated from other inmates. The effect is "to induce in the inmate a state of conscious and permanent visibility that assures the automatic functioning of power" (Foucault 1979:201). Prisoner becomes jailer; subject becomes object. Thus, the effects of power may be internalized, thereby yielding a form of "contingent subjectivity."

As Foucault recognizes, power need not embody only the negative qualities of the Panopticon; "the productivity of power" entails the construction of knowledge and discourse. These same dynamics of internalization and normalization can be applied to knowledge production and its application to policy decisions. In fact, although Foucault often speaks critically of the workings of power, an agnostic approach is actually more compatible with his general outlook. If power is genuinely productive, then the appropriate attitude should be the suspension of judgment as to its value and significance until one has evaluated the particular situation. If power is truly omnipresent, then, unless one is prepared to adopt a stance of unmitigated pessimism regarding social relations, its effects cannot be universally negative, an observation consistent with Foucault's critique of power as repression. Thus, we may suspend judgment when we examine the power of scientific discourse.

A discursive conception of power may be viewed as part of the larger turning away from materialistic and mechanistic theoretical approaches to social theory. As Henryk Skolimowski observes, power in modern societies has been exteriorized, conceived as an instrument for the domination of nature and other beings (1983). A civilization that views the universe as a mechanical aggregate to be manipulated by technology for the attainment of personal security and comfort, Skolimowski argues, will inevitably reduce power to its physical and coercive aspects. Thus, reflective approaches to world politics, whether consciously or not, may be part of a larger critique of the modern conception of power.

Mark Poster argues convincingly that, as the "mode of information" displaces the "mode of production" in postindustrial society, "knowledge/power" is becoming more relevant than conventional materialist notions of power. He observes:

> Knowledge and power are deeply connected and their configuration constitutes an imposing presence. . . . The form of domination characteristic of advanced industrial society is not exploitation, alienation, repression, etc., but a new pattern of social control that is embedded in practice at many points in the social field and constitutes a set of structures whose agency is at once everyone and no one.   (1984:78)

Without uncritically embracing the amorphous notion of postindustrial society, a notion to be explored at greater length in chapter 6, one can at least acknowledge the importance of a discursive conception of power.

Poster's allusion to the problem of agency, however, points to what many cite as a basic flaw in Foucault's work: a total rejection of the subject is highly problematic (Habermas 1981; Taylor 1984). If the subject is wholly a product of power, then she has no clear interests, nor has she any basis upon which to confront power. As one critic succinctly puts it, Foucault seems to give us "a hermetically sealed unit; a domination that cannot be escaped" (Philp 1983:40) and, consequently, a deep pessimism about the possibility of human emancipation. While Foucault rejects the discourse of liberation, he frequently speaks of resistance, particularly in his later writings. This, it seems, is our sole deliverance from the hermetically sealed unit. Yet Foucault never offers a rationale for resistance, simply asserting its constant coexistence with power (1980:142).

Contrary to the Enlightenment dream of universal emancipation, Foucault's concept of resistance as ubiquitous yet local rings true, while its abstractness raises doubts about the ontological status of the subject. If people are wholly products of power relations, then who can emerge from the "hermetically sealed unit" to perform acts of resistance? Ultimately, with no theory of action Foucault falls into a deep structuralism. Without subjects or interests, Foucault's support of resistance is so blind and undiscriminating as to seem politically irresponsible (Connolly 1983:332). Beyond the failure to advance normative grounds for action lies the larger failure to produce a theory of social agency. Anthony Giddens puts it bluntly: "Foucault's 'bodies' are not agents" (1984:154).

Foucault's own rhetoric, however, is misleading; in fact, his own model of power demands human subjectivity. The Panopticon, for instance, only functions because of each prisoner's consciousness. Even language, probably the most all-encompassing model of power (Foucault 1973), does not determine all of our thought and actions, though it may circumscribe them. Foucault's achievement, I believe, is to decenter the subject, not to eliminate it. Agents exist, but they should be seen as the effects rather than the fountain of power; power resides neither in agents nor objects but in systems. This is the meaning of "contingent subjectivity," a phrase often invoked by Foucault. Discursive practice involves actors, but they do not function as autonomous agents wielding the power of discourse on behalf of transparent interests. Social processes in general, and even Foucault's own texts, are incomprehensible without some notion of power as the "*transformative capacity* of human action: the capability of human beings to intervene in a series of events so as to alter their course" (Giddens 1977:348; emphasis in original). Intentionality and domination may be involved, but they need not be. The effects of power may be either positive or negative, depending upon the context of action and the values of the observer.

Stewart Clegg (1989) has proposed a useful typology of theories of power along two axes. One is the dominant trajectory, which extends from Hobbes and encompasses Marx, Weber, and Dahl. Rooted in analogies drawn from classical mechanics, power here is exerted by a sovereign will over the will of others. At its most subtle, sovereign power defines the thoughts of others, as in Marxist conceptions of false consciousness (Lukács 1971) and Lukes's third dimension of power (1974). Clegg's second trajectory, running from Machiavelli to Foucault, sees power as facilitative, strategic, and contingent. Without abandoning the concept of agency altogether, as some poststructuralists seem to do, I find it useful to draw heavily on Clegg's second axis in formulating a discursive conception of power. Knowledge structures the field of power relations through linguistic and interpretive practices, through organizational strategies, and through the contingencies of particular contexts.

Scientific Knowledge and Discourse

"Science" covers too much ground to be defined concisely. It is a product of research, employing characteristic methods; it is a body of knowledge and a means of solving problems; it is a social institution and a source of social legitimacy (Ziman 1984:1.2). In terms of the overall cohesiveness of this book, there are three reasons to address epistemological issues directly. First, without doing so, the authority of scientists appears to be no different from the authority of either priests or dictators.[7] While these forms of authority may overlap at times, an explication of the nature of scientific knowledge can point to some important differences. Second, I hope to outline an image of knowledge that is consistent with and complementary to my analysis of power in the previous section. And third, if scientific knowledge is inherently a discursive product of power relations, even before it is brought into the policy realm, then science in policy making is all the more embedded in power relations. However, my primary interest is in the political dimensions of knowledge, not in complex epistemological questions per se. Consequently, I allude to many arguments in the philosophy of science without spinning them out in their entirety.

Throughout the modern era, the appeal of science has rested on its supposedly increasing access to objective truth, rooted in the basic conviction that there must be some "permanent, ahistorical matrix" to which we can ultimately turn in deciphering the nature of reality (Bernstein 1985:8). The two primary traditions in Western philosophy, rationalism and empiricism, share a basic commitment to objective knowledge, whether through "universal" reason or "unbiased" observation. Probably the most sophisticated attempt to forge a permanent, ahistorical matrix for objective knowledge has been the "physicalist language" of the logical positivists. They claimed to have articulated "absolutely fixed points of contact between knowledge and reality (Schlick 1959:226). But their physicalist language was fraught with confusion and impracticality. Responding to these inadequacies, Karl Popper (1972) defended "objective knowledge" through his doctrine of falsification, which has been abundantly criticized (see Kuhn 1962; Lakatos 1970; Feyerabend 1975). The strongest criticisms derive from the "theory laden-ness of observation," striking at the heart of the entire positivist tradition and opening the door to relativism since objective knowledge requires the possibility of unhindered observation. Despite the many contortions in its quest for a "mirror of nature" (Rorty 1980), the objectivist tradition has failed to establish any permanent, ahistorical matrix, whether in the realm of observation, language or rationality.

The publication of Thomas Kuhn's *The Structure of Scientific Revolutions* in 1962 precipitated a storm of controversy by studying science as a fundamentally *social* activity.[8] For Kuhn, periods of scientific crisis are characterized by intense debate over conflicting paradigms and are resolved through intersubjective consensus. The ultimate acceptance of one paradigm over another is compared to a "gestalt switch" and is achieved through such "unscientific" means as "faith," "aesthetic grounds," and "persuasion" (1962: 121, 158, 159). Although Kuhn has adamantly, and perhaps inconsistently, denied the accusations of relativism (Shapere 1964; Kuhn 1977), he clearly laid the basis for a mountain of work seeking to contextualize science as a social activity.

While Kuhn fails to locate scientific communities within the larger context of history and culture, others have taken up the challenge to show how external social and political considerations affect not just the context of discovery but also the context of justification. For instance, Paul Forman (1979) argues that Weimar Germany's antirationalist culture nurtured the acceptance of an acausal quantum mechanics there. Others have even interpreted the primary inferential mechanisms of science, deduction and induction, as institutions whose authority is fundamentally social (Onuf 1989:101). Feminist philosophers take this perspective even further, arguing that the very categories of objectivity and rationality on which science is based are themselves conditioned by the socializing effects of gender (Keller 1985; Lloyd 1984). Steven Shapin and Simon Schaffer, among others, have wholeheartedly embraced relativism. In *Leviathan and the Air Pump*, they argue that the debate between Hobbes and Boyle over experimentalism was actually a debate about social order. They reject questions about truth, preferring instead to explore questions of "accepted vs. rejected knowledge" (1985:13–14). Their work may be read as an intellectualized version of "might makes right," conflating knowledge and power.

Scientific communities are infused with power dynamics. Scientists do not independently verify most of what they accept as valid knowledge, nor do they debate it collectively; most of it is accepted on authority, even if that authority is earned by proven competence. Similarly, the scientist gives his allegiance to the "invisible college" of his specialized field, entry into which is usually achieved through patronage (Crane 1972). Publications in scientific journals, the major social mechanism for disseminating and producing scientific knowledge, must bear the stamp of authenticity from editors and referees (Ziman 1968:111). "Contributing" to journals can be analyzed anthropologically as a gift-giving practice, with social recognition as an expected consequence (Hagstrom 1965).9 Sociologist Robert Merton demonstrates that the failure to credit previous work threatens the social system of incentives within science (1957). Thus, power dynamics permeate science as a social institution.

Jean-François Lyotard contends that the goal of scientific debate is *dissension*, not consensus (1984:60–66). As one physicist puts it, "The game is, you try to smash everybody else's theory" (Hagstrom 1965:31). Indeed, this is how new theories come about. Foucault's notion of power applies to science: theories, like other power centers, generate resistance. By erecting locales of resistance, scientific discourse provides the context not only for its progress but also for its delegitimation. The denotative statements of science must ultimately be legitimated in terms of a second-level narrative discourse, which opens the door to struggle around principles of good theory construction. According to Lyotard, "what we have here is a process of delegitimation fueled by the process of legitimation itself. The 'crisis' of scientific knowledge, signs of which have been accumulating since the end of the nineteenth century, . . . represents an internal erosion of the legitimacy principle of knowledge" (1984:39–40). Lyotard reiterates Nietzsche's argument that European nihilism follows from the truth requirement of science being directed against itself. This process of dissension and delegitimation is especially evident in the policy arena, where claims are met with counterclaims and research seems to be self-propagating.

While accepting that science is a social activity, however, I want to avoid a wholesale relativism. For radical social constructivists, science is merely epiphenomenal to social factors. Yet while science is an inescapably social process involving persuasion and power relations, it also can tell us something about how the natural world works. At first glance, this may seem like a precarious balancing act, but such a middle position generates a conception quite consistent with our intuitive understandings of science.

The failure to respect the fundamental distinction between ontology, which studies the nature of existence, and epistemology, which studies the nature of knowledge, has been a major source of misunderstanding between objectivists and relativists. As they talk past one another, the former seem to claim that knowledge faithfully reflects reality, and the latter seem to say that all knowledge is arbitrary. A more balanced view is that objects and events actually exist and that our knowledge has something to do with them. This is the basis of an ontological realism and a hermeneutical, yet pragmatic, epistemology.

Roy Bhaskar argues that every fact comprises both "transitive" and "intransitive" associations (1989). The former derive from psychological, social, and historical factors, and the latter from ontological reality. For example, the assignment of the atomic weight of 16 to oxygen is an arbitrary, or transitive, convention. Once this convention is established, the atomic weight of hydrogen is inevitably 1.008; this inevitability constitutes an intransitive dimension. Scientific progress is marked by an increase in both the transitive and intransitive aspects of facts.

For Bhaskar, recent philosophy of science is paradoxical. While the fundamental assumptions of positivism lie shattered, alternative accounts of science cannot sustain a coherent notion of the rationality of either scientific change or the nondeductive component of theory. He traces this difficulty to an ontology incompatible with recent constructivist accounts of science. The Humean view of causality as constant conjunctions of events rests upon a mistaken conflation of causal laws with their empirical grounds (1989:11–17).

In his alternative ontology, transcendental realism, Bhaskar tells us that in order for experimental activity to be intelligible, the world must contain actual structures. Though he does not presume to say how the world is structured, for that is the scientists' task, he argues that science moves from knowledge of manifest phenomena to knowledge of the structures behind them (1989:20). He challenges both the Humean identification of causal laws with patterns of events and the Kantian (transcendental idealist) conceptual framework (1986:38–50). Rather than being based on constant conjunctions, a priori constructs, or social factors, the laws of gravitation, thermodynamics and electromagnetism are rooted in the structures of nature.

Bhaskar's account of scientific knowledge is neither objectivist nor relativist. While he does not not explore the social dynamics of science in any detail, for he is trying to fill a critical gap in the philosophy of science by constructing a consistent theory of being, he nonetheless is clear that science is a social process. He refers to it as "a produced means of production" and "a practical labor in causal exchange with nature" (1989:21). Yet Bhaskar rejects a pure hermeneuticism, which reduces knowledge to discourse, thereby presenting an anthropocentric view of nature while failing to offer an adequate account of human agency. Such a view, he claims, is not only wrong but socially irresponsible in failing to recognize the real constraints on people's actions (1989:153).

The transcendental realist ontology can be enhanced by an epistemology that explicitly links knowledge with power. Like Bhaskar, philosopher of science Joseph Rouse is troubled by the postpositivist focus on the theoretical dimensions of science, which emphasizes the epistemic success of science rather than its practical success. Instead, Rouse understands the sciences "not just as self-subsistent intellectual activities but as *powerful* forces shaping us and our world" (1987:ix; emphasis added). For Rouse, science is a deeply practical activity that transforms both the world and how the world is known; its power lies not so much in the representational accuracy of its theories as in the functional skills it deploys. The entire planet has been physically transformed by these skills.

While portraying science as a consensual activity, Rouse adopts a much broader Foucaultian conception of power than do the pragmatists, who remain wedded to the idea that power is repressive and partisan, i.e., an obstacle to consensus rather than a facilitator of it. This approach allows Rouse to sidestep their search for a mode of inquiry unconstrained by the effects of power, although he recognizes the repressive effects on science of certain applications of juridical power. Like the new empiricists, Rouse redirects the locus of knowledge from accurate theorizing to the manipulation and control of events. He goes further, however, in linking this ability to power. The reason science can control nature is that it works with the intransitive structures that must exist if experimental activity is to be understood as intelligible. Thus, it is not surprising that laboratory experiments seem to reveal something about the world; scientists work hard to make them relevant to one another.

Rouse regards the laboratory, the distinguishing expression of science as an institution, as an embodiment of disciplinary power. The laboratory is not just a physical space bounded by four walls but "a context of equipment functioning together, which even incorporates nature among that equipment" (1987:107). In the laboratory, scientists labor to create phenomena; the objects they study are less "natural" events than the products of artifice (Latour 1983:166; quoted in Rouse 1987:23). He compares the laboratory to the school, the asylum, the factory, and the prison, all of which are "blocks" within which a "microphysics of power" is developed and reaches out to shape the surrounding world.[10]

At first glance, the power that arises from science seems qualitatively different from more narrowly conceived notions of power; the former is rooted in power over natural phenomena whereas the latter entails power over people. This dichotomy, however, is based upon three misconceptions.

First, it rests upon a rigid and unacceptable dichotomy between nature and human beings. Second, it ignores the productive and generative aspects of power. Third, and more important for the following discussion of the political implications of knowledge-based power, such a dichotomy ignores the profound degree of interdependence between the two sorts of power. The power of scientists to interpret reality has itself become a productive source of political power, regardless of how knowledge gets translated into technology. Scientists' power derives from their socially accepted competence as interpreters of reality. Yet they are not simply powerful agents wielding an arsenal of knowledge; rather, discourse itself is a source of power, facilitating the production of identities and interests.

Experts and Scientific Discourse in Politics

The belief in the power of science to improve human life is perhaps the quintessential hallmark of the modern era. From the sixteenth century onward, and from left to right across the political spectrum, Western thought has been characterized by an overarching faith in science (Bacon 1889, 1974; Condorcet 1976; Saint-Simon 1952; Comte 1986; Popper 1966). Many of modernity's seminal thinkers have located science in a realm outside power relations, hoping that it might someday provide an objective basis from which to supplant or transform political discourse. Even today this belief, with its implicit dichotomy between knowledge and power, is not uncommon. Science is conceived as a realm of objective facts, divorced from political considerations of "tradition, prejudice and the preponderance of power," from which rational and optimal policy decisions can be forged (Kaplan 1964:24). The "estates" of science and politics, oriented toward truth and power respectively, have generally been conceived as utterly distinct (Price 1965).

Yet, in the shadow of technology-related disasters, including this century's wars of unprecedented destruction, the modernist faith in the ability of science to order human affairs is waning. In many ways, the environmental movement is an ironic expression of this skepticism, calling into question the effects of science and technology while at the same time relying upon scientific discourse to make its case. If discourses are themselves power centers, as Foucault suggests, then we should expect to find resistance to the modern faith in science. Thus, there is a tributary diverging from the mainstream that portrays science more dubiously as Frankenstein's creation or Pandora's box. This undercurrent, typified by the nine-teenth-century Romantics, has grown in popularity as the negative effects of science and technology have made themselves felt. Hans Morgenthau, writing at the close of World War II, opens his *Scientific Man vs. Power Politics* with the following: "Two moods determine the attitude of our civilization to the social world: confidence in the power of reason, represented by modern science, to solve the social problems of our age, and despair at the ever-renewed failure of scientific reason to solve them" (1946:1).

The two faces of science are a subspecies of the two faces of persuasion. On one side is the rational ideal, which overstates the purity of information and exaggerates the rationality of those employing it; on the opposite side is the ugly face of propaganda (Stone 1988:249). Yet if knowledge production is a social process and interpretation is more important than fact in the policy arena, then the dichotomy is illusive. Since knowledge is inseparable from power even in pure science, the links should be even stronger when science is implicated in policy problems. Alvin Weinberg states: "Many of the issues which arise in the course of the interaction of science or technology and society—*e.g.*, the deleterious side effects of technology, or the attempts to deal with social problems through the procedures of science—hang on answers to questions which can be asked of science and yet *which cannot be answered by science* (1972:209; emphasis in original).

Weinberg has popularized the term "trans-scientific" for this category of increasingly common policy questions, such as the probability of extremely improbable events and the application of engineering judgment in technology design. (Regulation of ozone-depleting chemicals and greenhouse gases are specific examples of trans-scientific policy problems.) I would argue that trans-scientific discourse derives its influence from three sources: the authority of its agents, the political context in which it is situated, and the cogency of its content. This section examines the first of these, scientific experts as discursive agents in the policy arena, and the following section turns to the second and third, the contextual and substantive constitution of discourse.

The importance of expert advice in shaping policy decisions is nothing new. In the past, advice came from such sources as oracles and prophets, although rational calculation and the equivalent of cost-benefit analysis have existed since ancient times (Goldhamer 1978:129–31). Expert advice has often pertained to military matters, a trend that has continued up to the present.[11] More generally, turbulent political conditions, characterized by complexity and uncertainty, induce decision makers to seek greater clarity and predictability through consultation with advisers. Contemporary turbulence is characterized by an increase in international interdependence and a greater connection among policy issues (Rosenau 1989; Keohane and Nye 1977); thus expert advice is increasingly sought in addressing international problems.

Though my focus is knowledge-based power, I do not want to exaggerate its importance. The influence of experts is limited; they do not replace the existing political process. Information is always relayed and exchanged in the larger political arena—ultimately, experts can be fired or become pawns. They may also become pawns, their prestige used to legitimize policy objectives not directly relevant to their areas of expertise, as when scientists were mobilized in support of the Atmospheric Test Ban Treaty during the Kennedy administration (Uyehara 1966). Disagreement among experts can also be used as an excuse to ignore their advice, as was the case for many years with the acid rain issue and, until the Clinton administration, with the global climate change question as well.

Despite these limitations, the ability to interpret reality allows experts to wield real power. Policymakers who ignore experts or conceal facts risk political embarrassment, particularly in pluralistic societies where scientists speak out publicly. Scientists are likely to find allies in the media, since both science and the media seem to have an innate distrust of political and economic elites (Wood 1964:59). Political leaders also risk embarrassment when their ignorance of important scientific information is exposed, as happened more than once during the Montreal Protocol process. But the most important source of power for experts, even when they disagree, is the fact that without them policymakers are more likely to make bad decisions. In the words of one author, "to assume that technical inputs are unimportant because both sides of a controversy commonly present technical analyses purporting to prove their own side of the issue is a little like a judge deciding the facts of a case are unimportant because the lawyers on each side always present briefs purporting to show how the facts support their own client" (Margolis 1973:51).

The discursive worlds of experts and policymakers are inherently different, leading to the possibility of mutual misunderstanding and mistrust. Experts often deal in abstractions within their narrow specialties, whereas politicians must be attentive to specific circumstances and how various interests will be affected by their decisions. Policymakers may be uncomfortable with experts' neglect of the economic consequences of their recommendations, as often happens in environmental politics. Experts may be uneasy in the world of compromise and pork barreling, and they may be ignorant of their own political influence. Policymakers may be awestruck by technical language, leading them to develop unrealistic expectations of what expert advice can accomplish. They may also resent experts for their occasional pedantry, or they may lose patience with technical detail. Decision makers are also liable to ignore significant aspects of advice, suffering from the general human proclivity to believe that what one does not understand must not be very important (Margolis 1973:50). The two faces of science—overstatement and propaganda—also surface in the policy context; nonscientist policy actors have been known to complain of "the cult of doctor worship" (Wood 1964:43).

A related problem is the different time frames within which experts and policymakers work. Experts can help expand the time horizon to anticipate policy implications. Yet their analyses may be unwelcome in political circles, where the ability to stay in power depends on relatively short-term considerations. This is a major issue for global environmental problems, whose full effects may not be felt for generations.

As with other forms of power, success breeds success for knowledge-based power.[12] Experts do not deal simply with facts; they must cultivate their reputations as sources of authoritative knowledge. In this area, rationality takes the back seat to power and trust. The ability of experts to reduce uncertainty depends in part on whether they are perceived as powerful or trustworthy, particularly during crises, when experts who save the day may modify existing power structures by displacing others. Yet experts also are trusted only inasmuch as they succeed in reducing uncertainty. Thus, power is generated in a circular fashion. A good example is the prestige the National Aeronautics and Space Administration obtained through its successful Apollo program, contrasted to the sharp decline in public trust after the Challenger disaster.

Because of their access to specialized knowledge, scientists are uniquely situated to place certain issues on the public agenda. Scientists were the first to point out the potential to build atomic weapons, the unresolved problems of nuclear waste disposal, the dangers of recombinant DNA research, and the ecological threat of DDT. In most cases, however, they must rely on coalitions with public officials, interest groups, and bureaucracies to implement their policy proposals. But unlike the search for knowledge, which is accepted as a legitimate practice, the search for allies must be disguised by other professional activities (Benveniste 1977:149).

Ultimately, this necessity is rooted in the larger belief that science is objective and value-free, while political life is ideological and value-laden. While that view, as I have argued in the previous section, is faulty because facts are socially constructed, it is nonetheless influential.

But the fact-value dichotomy and the resultant split between science and politics raise other problems in a policy context. First, if the dichotomy were pure, scientists would never call attention to a problem, for to do so would betray a commitment to certain values. But why did Einstein urge President Roosevelt to develop atomic weapons? And why should a researcher point out that a certain chemical might cause cancer? For the simple reason that they care and are committed to specific values. At a minimum, they believe in the value of their own information, and they are concerned with how their recommendations are received. Second, both scientists and policymakers recognize that not all facts are of equal value, for they vary in their interest and productivity, as well as in their internal robustness (Ravetz 1986:421). Third, data does not stand on its own; it must be interpreted, and it is frequently interpreted according to preexisting value commitments.

Further dividing the two worlds are the different modes of factuality involved. Kratochwil's description of "the three worlds of facts" is relevant here (1990:21–27). Scientists generally operate in the world of observational facts, while policymakers deal primarily with intentional and institutional facts. Scientific facts are subject to validation tests very different from those for political facts. If the public believes something to be true, even if science has shown it to be false, that belief remains an important fact for policymakers. Similarly, if the fact-value distinction is fallacious, the perception of its validity can influence the politics of technical advice.

Scientists who perceive their own work as by definition value-free in its approach and beneficent in its results can easily delude themselves about their own political involvement. A better impetus for unfettered political activity can scarcely be imagined than the belief that one's preferences derive from objective reality (Wood 1964:63).[13] The potential for self-deception is consistent with my earlier argument that power is not inherently intentional. Most scientists, even those who work in policy-relevant areas, do not see themselves as seeking power. Nor do their more overtly political counterparts, for the belief in the objectivity of science is deeply entrenched.

Facts must be communicated verbally, and the choice of words is itself a value choice. One example is whether risk is stated in terms of absolute or relative risks. The same exposure to a toxic chemical may be expressed either as a one-in-a-million risk per year or as a 5 percent increase over normal background rates (Wynne 1987). Clearly, the second sounds more serious. As I shall show, certain modes of framing the facts were vital in negotiating the international ozone agreements.

Ideological goals can also be pursued and legitimated through science. Judgment calls are frequently required when technical questions lie at the heart of decision making; more than one solution is usually justifiable on scientific grounds. A good example is how the Reagan administration's political goal of deregulation was implemented by the Environmental Protection Agency (EPA). Decision rules regarding carcinogens included the following: animal studies were not necessarily relevant; benign tumors need not be considered damage; and merely looking at the chemical structure of some substances could suffice to determine their carcinogenicity. These interpretations of scientific rules of inference show that "there is a significant area in which science and policy are not separable—they organically interpenetrate one another" (Wynne 1987:108–9). While all these rules are technically defensible, the outcome is a policy rooted in ideology.

Proponents of risk analysis argue that the so-called scientific functions of risk assessment should be separated from the political process of risk management (*Environmental Forum* 1984). Risk analysis has been attacked on epistemological, ethical, and political grounds.[14] Among other things, it is called to task for reducing all values to economic values, for assuming linearity in calculating risks, and for failing to recognize the value-ladenness of certain techniques such as discounting the future. All these criticisms add up to the failure of risk analysis to recognize that the science of risk assessment is really trans-scientific.[15] If even the purest science cannot be wholly extricated from social and political considerations, then it is unwise to have such expectations for environmental and other science-based policy problems.

Recent research on risk perception and decision making under uncertainty point to major flaws in the rationality assumption. People tend to employ a number of general inferential rules, or heuristics, in evaluating risks (Tversky and Kahneman 1981). One such judgmental bias, "availability," predisposes individuals to overestimate risks resembling ones they have encountered recently and to ignore risks that they have never experienced. Thus, the likelihood of unprecedented environmental change, such as extreme changes in local climate or severe ozone depletion, is often discounted in spite of dire scientific predictions. A related heuristic is the "out of sight, out of mind" bias (Fischhoff, Slovic, and Lichtenstein 1982). People tend to accept that the data in front of them must represent all the possibilities. These heuristics are particularly pernicious because people tend to be overconfident about decisions based on them, a tendency just as prevalent among experts as among laypersons.

The rationality assumption is also undercut by the importance of framing in policy discourse. Frames, which are fundamental in discourse, are analogous to varying visual perspectives on the same scene; the apparent size of an objective, for instance, varies with the observer's distance from it. A frame is also a boundary that cuts off something from our vision (Stone 1988:198). Contrary to experience, rationality requires that changes of frame should not alter one's preferences. Tversky and Kahneman uncover some fascinating instances of the framing problem. They find, for instance, that for most people choices involving gains are often risk averse and choices involving losses are often risk taking, even when a problem can be framed either way (1981:453). Other research reveals that people prefer insurance that covers specific harms fully over policies covering a wide range of harms conditionally, even if the latter would be a more "rational" choice (Kunreuther 1978). Apparently, insurance is "bought against worry, not only against risk, and worry can be manipulated by the labeling of outcomes and the framing of contingencies" (Tversky and Kahneman 1981:456). An action increasing one's annual risk of death from 1 in 10,000 to 1.3 in 10,000 is perceived as far more hazardous when framed as a 30 percent increase in mortality risk (Fischhoff, Slovic, and Lichtenstein 1982:479). These findings have important implications for environmental policy, which is inherently probabilistic. In fact, international environmental treaties have been regarded by negotiators as insurance policies (U.S. Department of State 1986).

Debates about values and norms are typically couched in empirical terms. Seldom does a person rest her case for a particular policy on mere subjective preference; rather, she buttresses her position with facts. For this reason, no matter what values underlie a controversy, the debates generally focus on technical questions; questions of value become framed as questions of fact. Since science is modernity's preeminent instrument of legitimation, all participants can be expected to claim that their positions are mandated by science, even if science alone can never mandate anything. Power hinges on the ability to deploy knowledge, with the result that political values and scientific facts become difficult to distinguish.

The increasing amount of reference to science seems to be accompanied by its decreasing credibility. Policy science is paradoxically a scarce resource, in spite of its exponential growth. When debates are framed in scientific terms, each confrontation may undermine the credibility of the positions and lead to the search for more scientific weapons. Expertise generates counterexpertise (Benveniste 1977:147), particularly in pluralistic societies. Lyotard's epistemological argument that the demand for legitimation results in a process of delegitimation is mirrored in the policy world.

I do not mean to imply that science is so hopelessly mired in political questions that it is of no help in depoliticizing issues; I simply want to claim that the waters are muddier than is generally appreciated. Still, just as I would want judges to read their briefs, I hope that policymakers listen to scientific advice. Science may depoliticize certain issues to some small extent, for two reasons. First, as I have argued above, facts have both fixed and conventional dimensions, and the former are axiomatically apolitical, even if their implications are sources of considerable political controversy. Either chlorofluorocarbons destroy stratospheric ozone, or they don't; the question is not answerable in polemical terms. Second, inasmuch as policymakers believe that science is apolitical, they may be willing to use it to build a policy consensus. But such an outcome is likely only if there already exists a strong impetus toward political consensus.

Neither do I mean to suggest that all forms of power are reducible to discursive power. Scientific discourse is circumscribed by juridical forms of power. While national interests may be shaped by expert advice, once those interests are determined, more traditional forms of state power come to the fore. Science is entwined with state power in another important respect: scientists are also citizens. National governments are often reluctant to accept "foreign science," and despite the cosmopolitan culture of science, scientists do not generally relinquish their national identities.

Environmental issues inject distinctive temporal and spatial understandings into the policy process, tendencies that are amplified as the problems take on intergenerational and planetary proportions. One factor that is both cause and effect of this spatial and temporal expansion is the emergence of new policy actors: a network of scientific and technical experts, including "risk professionals," with access to specialized knowledge (Dietz and Rycroft 1987).[16] Because of the highly specialized nature of much of the relevant "pure" science, another important intermediary category of actors has entered into the environmental policy-making process. These people are not themselves researchers but have the skills needed to understand the work of academics and other researchers. Typically, they also have a flair for translating that work, identifying the policy-relevant angles in it, and framing it in language accessible to decision makers. James Sundquist calls them "research brokers," citing as an example the U.S. President's Council of Economic Advisers (1978:130). I prefer the term "knowledge brokers," because it highlights the broad range of information that is translated and underscores that interpretation is more important than fact. Implicit in the term is the recognition that injecting science into policy is itself a political act requiring a strategy of information transfer (Caldwell 1990:23).

Knowledge brokers can exist at lower levels of government, as did the small group of EPA policy analysts who kept the ozone issue alive both domestically and internationally for years. Nongovernmental actors, including social movements and businesses, can also function as knowledge brokers, framing and translating information not only for decision makers but also for the media and the public. Thus, while scientific knowledge is an important source of power, scientists are not the only ones with access to it; once produced, knowledge becomes something of a collective good, available to all who want to incorporate it into their discursive strategies.

Scientific Discourse in the Policy Arena

As determinants of what can and cannot be thought, discourses delimit the range of policy options, thereby serving as precursors to policy outcomes. The emphasis on discourse calls into question the traditional focus on agents without reverting to structure as the ultimate explanatory factor (Wendt 1987; Dessler 1989). This epistemological shift moves away from the standard schism between subject and object (decision maker and decision situation) toward a recognition that subjects are at least partially constituted by the discursive practices and contexts in which they are embedded (Shapiro, Bonham, and Heradstveit 1988:398).

One should not understand this epistemological shift as a wholesale elimination of the subject, despite the language of some poststructuralists. Rather, what is entailed is the decentering of the subject, engendered by a refocusing of one's methodological lenses on the study of discursive practices rather than agents. Just as power necessarily entails some degree of subjectivity, even if only in contingent form, so too do discursive practices. Discourses could not exist without individuals and groups promoting them, identifying with them, and even struggling with them. Discursive practices are inconceivable without discursive agents, coalitions, and knowledge brokers.

Yet the overarching regulation of the political field by codes, specifically linguistic codes, "transcends the generative and critical capacities of any individual speaker or speech act" (Terdiman 1985:39). The supreme power is the power to delineate the boundaries of thought—a feature of discursive practices more than of specific agents. What becomes important, then, is how certain discourses come to dominate the field and how other, more marginal counterdiscourses establish networks of resistance within particular "power/knowledges" or "regimes of truth" (Foucault 1980).

Discursive power is decentralized, nonmonolithic, and linguistically rooted. All discourses, including hegemonic ones, are, in Mikhail Bakhtin's words, "heteroglot." They represent: "the co-existence of the socio-ideological contradictions between the present and the past, between differing epochs of the past, between different socio-groups in the present, between tendencies, schools, circles and so on" (Bakhtin 1981:291; quoted in Terdiman 1985:18–19). Networks of resistance operate perpetually among dominant discourses and subjugated knowledges. Because counterdiscourses are always intertwined with the hegemony they oppose, the two stand in a necessary relation of "conflicted intimacy."

In much social science research, context is marginalized as a backdrop against which the real drama takes place. But with a turn toward discursive practices, the pervasive nature of context becomes evident. Meanings are shaped by context, and "the frame comes unexpectedly to define the center" (Terdiman 1985:17). For environmental problems, disasters and crises are often the contextual factors that serve as a kind of mold within which accepted knowledge is cast, thereby permitting hitherto rejected ideas to gain a hearing.

Deborah Stone discusses the forms of symbolic representation that characterize policy discourse (1988:108–26). "Narrative stories" are emotionally compelling explanations of how the world works, featuring heroes, villains, and innocent victims (which need not be human). Stone cites two broad story lines: a story of decline and a story of control. The former recounts the undoing of an earlier, superior situation, calling for policy action to reverse this decline. The latter suggests that a problem that was previously seen as inevitable, natural, or accidental is actually solvable through human action. Both story lines are bolstered by facts, and both are compelling in as much as they point to deliverance from decline or the promise of control. The two are frequently woven together, as they were in the ozone negotiations..

Environmental crises, for instance, are not just physical phenomena; they are informational phenomena about decline and loss of control. As one commentator puts it, problems like ozone depletion and global warming are "rumors" (Anderson 1990). As soon as policy-relevant information appears, people incorporate it into stories to render it meaningful. For instance, information about global warming has been embraced by advocates of both nuclear energy and solar energy to support their deeply held beliefs. New information is co-opted into previously existing discursive practices, yet under certain conditions, whether by virtue of an exogenous shock or through the ability of social actors to rechannel discursive practices into a more persuasive story, counterdiscourses can become predominant.

Policy stories, including those told in scientific terms, use rhetorical devices to persuade the audience. Metaphors, which employ a word that denotes one thing to describe another, frequently take a "normative leap" from description to prescription (Rein and Schon 1977; cited in Stone 1988:118). The discourse on nuclear weaponry is rife with such metaphors. The terms "ozone layer" and "ozone hole" are both metaphors, the latter having a strong emotional charge. The term "greenhouse effect" is another metaphor, one with favorable overtones: greenhouses are pleasant places to grow tropical plants (although those who work in them can testify to the oppressiveness of the environment). One climate scientist urges that the metaphor be abandoned because it cannot motivate action, suggesting that it be replaced with a term like "global heat trap" (Schneider 1989:58).

Interpretive repertoires may also employ synecdoche and metonymy, whereby apparently particular phenomena are integrated into a whole or a whole is reduced to one of its parts (White 1978). The global warming problem, as enormous as it is, has been taken by some environmentalists as a symbolic representation of the "end of nature" (McKibben 1989), an application of synecdoche. Attempts to address the climate change problem through partial solutions, whether through CFC regulation or saving the rain forests, are metonymical moves. The discursive strategy to reduce ozone depletion to a skin cancer problem also employs the rhetorical trope of metonymy.

The belief that scientific knowledge can yield policy decisions without the intervention of rhetorical strategies is part of what Stone calls the "rationality project," which attempts to "public policy from the irrationalities and indignities of politics" (1988:4). The misguided identification of science as a tool for ending political dissent is part of that project. Science itself, in seeking to persuade an audience through language, is a rhetorical activity, even when it conceals its rhetorical aim; factual description is a seemingly innocuous and uncontroversial activity. In the policy world, "advocacy science," which proceeds through the "strategic orchestration of scientific arguments," is even more clearly rhetorical (Ozawa 1991).

Framing, heuristics, and other rhetorical strategies are all defining elements of particular discourses. But they are not disembodied phenomena; they require human agents for their initiation, application, and dissemination. Discursive coalitions and knowledge brokers employ their strategies in a web of power relations, and those strategies become implicated in and constitutive of that web.

Conceptions of Science in International Relations: Functionalism, Neofunctionalism, and Epistemic Communities

All the problems inherent in the politics of technical advice are replicated in international policy coordination, with the added complication of interstate rivalry. Earlier I argued that the power of technical experts is proportional to the trust that decision makers have in them. This problem arises with a vengeance in international relations, an arena characterized by inherent distrust. Governments are far more likely to pay attention to studies done within their own borders than those from other countries. International organizations and, in some cases, scientists themselves, have sought to alleviate this problem by conducting studies and evaluations through independent international panels, the United Nations' specialized agencies, and regional organizations. Nevertheless, governments often insist on doing their own studies, and in the end they may not even listen to their own scientists. Too, if the stakes are high, there is even more incentive to disregard the science.

On the one hand, there is some validity in the widespread belief that "science forms the most truly international culture in our divided world" (Brooks 1964:79). International conferences and journals are the main channels through which scientists communicate new ideas and discoveries. Even at the height of the Cold War, scientists on both sides of the Iron Curtain were calling for greater openness, not just for political reasons but to further their own work. In addition, to the extent that scientists are committed to universalism and communality (Merton 1973:263–64), there is reason to see science as a potential unifying force in international conflicts over technical issues. On the other hand, the political dynamics of technical advice indicate that an untempered optimism in the cosmopolitan nature of science may be misplaced. The hope that science can harmonize international politics is not completely groundless; unfortunately, however, it is often accompanied by a naive view of knowledge as separate from power, as well as a poor understanding of the complexities involved in translating scientific knowledge into policy.

In this section, I look at three theoretical approaches to science in politics at the international level: functionalism, neofunctionalism, and the literature on epistemic communities. Unlike the dominant theories of world politics, which focus on military and economics sources of power, these approaches recognize the importance of cognitive factors—knowledge, ideas, and beliefs—in shaping events and outcomes. Yet each of these approaches tends to divorce knowledge from power, and they all fail to appreciate fully the discursive nature of science. They are, to varying degrees, part of the rationality project.

Functionalism has its historical roots in nineteenth-century thinkers as diverse as Saint-Simon (1952), Herbert Spencer (1896), and the Fabian Socialists (Woolf 1916). It is sometimes a descriptive or predictive theory and sometimes a normative theory; it evinces a modern faith in technical rationality. Kenneth Thompson cites the defining characteristics of functionalism: it is nonpolitical, involving social and economic issues, addressed to urgent problems, undertaken in a problem-solving manner, and built upon the cooperation of professionals (1979:96–99). Technical experts are expected to steer the way to a functional world by virtue of their ability to fashion a consensus on means-ends relationships.

Most representative of the recent literature is David Mitrany, who foresees that, as the nation-state's ability to protect the welfare of its citizens decreases because of the interdependence of nations and issues, power will be ceded to functional international organizations (1975). Although Mitrany's focus is economic, environmental problems are also of universal concern and may even fit his theory better, since knowledge in the natural sciences is more consensual than in the social sciences. A major problem, however, is that Mitrany assumes both expert consensus and technical certainty, assumptions that disregard the discursive nature of knowledge. Mitrany, like so many others, portrays experts as above the fray of social and political conflict and has a purely negative conception of power.[17] Ernst Haas criticizes Mitrany on these grounds: "The peace of statesmen, of collective security, of disarmament negotiations, of conferences of parliamentarians, of sweeping constitutional attempts at federation, all this is uncreative. It is so much power instead of creative work" (Haas 1964:12).

Another problem with functionalism is its deterministic assumption of historical efficiency. Mitrany assumes that social processes are rational, holding that a community-building consensus will inevitably develop in a context wider than the specific issue area addressed by a functional organization. Functionalism cannot say how this development will come about; it has no theory of social change because it lacks a theory of agency.[18]

In his first major work, Ernst Haas (1964) attempts to amend functionalism by proposing a more empirically relevant, less ideological neofunctionalism. In his two case studies on the World Health Organization and arms control, Haas finds that the predictions of functionalism do not withstand scrutiny. In the former, he sees no attempt to delineate political and technical concerns clearly. In the latter, experts were important, but they frequently pursued nationalistic, not universalistic, objectives.

Haas argues that functionalism's main shortcoming is that it has no theory of interests and so must resort to the utopian notion of the common good as the motivation for action. Ignoring the role of interests in international cooperation, functionalists attribute cooperation to manipulative experts working for the common good. For Haas, any claim represents an interest, interests need not be consciously shared in order for integration to take place, and integration can occur under conditions of competition as well as cooperation. Unlike Mitrany, Haas provides an account of how authoritative decisions can be made even when experts disagree among themselves. Likewise, he can account for at least some unintended consequences of actions.

Unfortunately, Haas's conception of interest is truncated. If each claim constitutes an interest, then Haas cannot differentiate between interests and delusions. Nor does Haas adequately link his notion of interest to Mitrany's notion of function. In his concern to distinguish his own more "scientific" work from the overly normative functionalism, he offers no basis for the performance of functions other than the growth of organizations. Functionalism, with its normative bias, at least grounds its prescriptions in the desirability of meeting human needs.

Haas also takes issue with the assumption of inevitable spillover effects, pointing out that functionalism offers no theory of how this development comes about. His less deterministic neofunctionalism attempts to solve this problem by using the process of "social learning" to account for international community building. Haas interprets functionalism as a development from gesellschaft to gemeinschaft, or from an elite community to a network of societal associations.[19] Haas's neofunctionalism, like its precursor, evades issues of power. He does not give sufficient credence to the possibility that scientists may constitute an elite class with a monopoly on information. Nor does he consider that expert advice may simply reinforce existing power relations among states, rather than move the international community "beyond the nation-state." Like Mitrany before him, Haas, at least in his early work, succumbs to the modernist fallacy: he drives a wedge between knowledge and power, dislodging expert advice from the realm of politics.

In his later works, Haas is more aware of this problem, though he continues to adhere to the same misconception on a more subtle level. In *Scientists and World Order* (1977), he and his coauthors specifically consider whether the introduction of science into international politics indicates progress toward a more rational and cohesive world order. On the one hand, they recognize that science has not brought about the end of ideology and that it will never be able to do so inasmuch as it cannot settle questions of ends. They admit that scientists suffer from sociological ambivalence. They draw no rigid line between the technical and political but rather propose a continuum from the "purely technical" to the "purely political."

On the other hand, much of their work seems to be rooted in contrary principles, particularly their depiction of knowledge as the independent variable and world order as the dependent variable. While claiming that their taxonomy in a two-by-two matrix is merely a heuristic device, their method belies an underlying commitment to this dichotomy. Figure 2.1

Figure 2.1. Goals versus Knowledge: A Neofunctionalist Reading

Goals vs. Knowledge

	Political goals are	
Expert knowledge becomes	Specific	Expanding and interconnected
More Consensual	Pragmatic world order	Rational world order
Not more Consensual	No new world order	Skeptic world order

Adapted from Haas, Williams and Babai 1977:51

shows their matrix depicting possible world order models as a function of how knowledge and politics are perceived, with the lower left quadrant representing the current world order. While the authors claim that a pragmatic world order represents our best hope, they clearly yearn for a rational world order. "Learning" for them occurs when knowledge becomes more consensual and political goals more comprehensive; movement toward a rational world order, "a technocrat's delight," represents progress (Haas, Williams, and Babai 1977:52).

Although the depiction of world order models is useful for purposes of identification, there are several problems with it. First, the characterization of knowledge in terms of degrees of consensus is misleading, for the authors' discussion is really about the extent to which interdisciplinary linkage is present. In fact, all four world order models, even the most disorderly of them, presume that expert consensus exists at least on single issues, an underlying assumption at odds with our discussion hitherto. As a consequence, Haas et al. ignore decisions made in the face of technical uncertainty, thereby omitting many, if not most, cases.

Second, the authors' method of discerning the potential for various world orders in scientists' beliefs about their own political role recalls the Enlightenment faith that science can engender a world free of conflict. Scientists' beliefs are taken as crucial to determining what kind of world order emerges. In the end, in a tone reminiscent of Saint-Simon, they chastise scientists for adhering to the skeptic's vision of world order, arguing that such a stance subverts the ability of science to bring about a more rational world order. They gloss over the skeptical view, overlooking the many possible avenues by which science might not lead to a more rational world order.

Haas's most recent work, *When Knowledge Is Power* (1990), is an attempt to elaborate and improve upon his earlier ideas about how states employ new knowledge. Of all the analyses of science and international politics examined thus far, this work is probably most consistent with my own argument. Nonetheless, Haas's thinking persists with the tendency to dichotomize knowledge and power and therefore fails to appreciate the discursive nature of science in policy. As in his earlier writings, Haas's primary concern here is with "social learning," or the process through which consensual knowledge influences policy (23). Here, he problematizes interests, arguing that consensual knowledge can be instrumental in defining interests for policymakers. Consistent with my own argument, Haas declares:

It is as unnecessary as it is misleading to juxtapose as rival explanations the following: science to politics, knowledge to power or interest, consensual knowledge to common interests. We do ourselves no good by pretending that scientists have the key to giving us peace and plenty; but we do no better in holding that politicians and capitalists, in defending their immediate interests with superior power, stop creative innovation dead in its tracks. (1990:11)

For Haas, epistemic communities are the most significant agents of institutional innovation, or social learning. After Burkart Holzner and John Marx, he defines epistemic communities as knowledge-oriented groups whose cultural standards and social arrangements revolve around a primary commitment to epistemic criteria in knowledge production and application. He applies this definition to learning in international organizations, limiting epistemic communities to groups of interdisciplinary professionals who share a common commitment to a causal model and a set of political values. They are also committed to truth tests based upon adversary procedures and problem-solving ability. The success of an epistemic community in implementing its preferred policies depends on two factors: its persuasive ability and its ability to ally with the dominant political coalition. Success is most likely during crises, when new knowledge is apt to be solicited. Superficially, at least, the concept of epistemic communities seems consistent with the mutual embeddedness of knowledge and power and a discursive understanding of science in policy.

Although Haas warns against thinking of epistemic communities as "the white knights of expertise . . . arrayed against the forces of darkness" (1990:40), he disregards his own warning at times. Epistemic communities are portrayed as the "enemies of habit-driven institutions"; their inability to achieve their heroic missions is not due to any handicap of their own but to institutional inertia. But by juxtaposing experts with habit-driven actors, Haas neglects the extent to which knowledge is itself institutionalized and routinized. In arguing that experts can contribute to the emergence of shared meanings in opposition to "the drag of institutions," Haas forgets that institutions themselves embody shared meanings. Moreover, his belief that knowledge is the independent variable and politics the dependent variable is implicit in the fact that he only discusses how science influences politics and never how politics affects science. Thus, flying in the face of his earlier caveat that "the line between consensual knowledge and political ideology is often barely visible," Haas concludes that "the language of modern science is creating a transideological and transcultural signification system" (1990:20, 46).

The notion of epistemic communities is both promising and problematic in the context of my argument. Like discursive practices, the concept is intended to elucidate the dynamics of an information society. In addition, it integrates the concepts of power and knowledge into a view of reality as socially constructed. Knowledge is defined as "a communicable mapping of experienced reality" (Holzner and Marx 1979:4) and is inextricably linked to specific frames of reference. Each epistemic community is characterized by particular reality tests to which it subscribes. Empirical reality tests are emblematic of scientific epistemic communities, but other reality tests may be pragmatic, authoritative, rational, magical, or mystical. Only a few epistemic communities are scientific; others could comprise astrologers, witches, beauticians, logicians, mechanics, and bureaucrats. Socialization into an epistemic community requires the internalization of its values and norms, a form of disciplinary power. The relative autonomy of an epistemic community is guaranteed because the larger social system yields to it, on trust, a cognitive monopoly for a certain range of issues. Interest groups differ from epistemic communities yet may actively work to guarantee their autonomy; for example, the American Medical Association's support of the medical epistemic community has served this purpose.

One troubling aspect of this model for understanding science in policy is its overly broad conception of knowledge. Astonishingly enough, Holzner and Marx claim not to be relativists, arguing that "discovering lawfulness" in the various knowledge systems "will contribute to a more general theory of rationality, rather than strengthen a historicist withdrawal into relativism" (1979:93). They do not pursue this task, however, so their claim must be taken as be little more than an article of faith, particularly given the vast spectrum of phenomena that count as knowledge for them. Because their understanding of knowledge bears no relation to ontological reality, it is unclear how Holzner and Marx can escape relativism. Likewise, their notion of epistemic community ignores the ubiquity of dissension; their view of the medical profession as an epistemic community, to say nothing of science, is highly problematic. Moreover, one wonders how a theory designed specifically to illuminate the deployment of knowledge in postindustrial society can also incorporate all other frames of reference. If almost any group can qualify as an epistemic community, then how are scientists unique?

Peter Haas has developed the epistemic community argument in a manner more consistent with the discursive framework of this book. His earliest work is on environmental epistemic communities. He argues that an ecological epistemic community was responsible for negotiating and implementing the Mediterranean Action Plan (Med Plan), a regime for controlling pollution in the Mediterranean Sea. But his conception of epistemic communities suffers from two defects. First, it does not explain adequately the source of epistemic communities' power. Second, it provides no coherent conception of knowledge. Since knowledge is allegedly the source of power for epistemic communities, their power is thereby rendered mysterious.

Epistemic communities are defined in terms of shared knowledge as well as a common political perspective. But the bonding principle of epistemic communities remains vague. At times, Peter Haas refers to their "common perspective," which could apply to bureaucracies and interest groups as easily as to epistemic communities (1989:380). He argues that social learning under the Med Plan took place on two fronts. In terms of foreign policy, marine scientists were able to persuade decision makers of the validity of their consensual knowledge. Domestically, the epistemic community "usurped" decision-making authority through "bureaucratic preemption" (1989:398). It is difficult to see how the usurping of authority, which connotes an illegitimate power move, is compatible with the notion of social learning. Moreover, one wonders why consensual knowledge should be more persuasive in international politics, where the potential for divisiveness is presumably much greater, than it is domestically, particularly given the tendency of governments to mistrust information from outside sources.

The same problem arises in Peter Haas's recent attempt to provide a more comprehensive conception of epistemic communities. Again, he defines them in terms of shared consensual knowledge and political values. But he acknowledges that consensual knowledge alone does not ensure that scientists will maintain group solidarity, citing research showing that "scientists as a group proved no less venal or subject to political temptation than their non-specialist counterparts" (1992b:18). Hence, he proposes that loyalty to an epistemic community derives from a commitment to shared political values). If this is the case, however, then the distinction between epistemic communities and other sorts of more overtly political groups breaks down.

In his work on the Med Plan, Haas explicitly dodges all epistemological issues (1989:401), so that knowledge simply becomes whatever an epistemic community believes. This lacuna raises the question of relativism. In an article in which he explores epistemological questions, Peter Haas seems sympathetic to a hermeneutical stance, but he never commits himself to any position (1992b:20–24). Only a limited range of groups seem to qualify as epistemic communities—all his examples are groups of scientists—so he clearly has in mind a particular sort of validity test as the basis of epistemic communities, but he never explicates what it might be. Instead he dismisses this question by declaring that his primary concern is "the political influence of such groups on collective policy making rather than the correctness of their policy advice" (1992b:22). But if knowledge is the source of that influence, then the failure to examine epistemological questions leaves a big gap.

The epistemological question also arises from the observation that most studies of epistemic communities associate these groups with specific schools of economic and political thought.[20] If the power and the unity of epistemic communities are derived from their shared causal views, it is curious that such groups should be so prominent in disciplines with so little consensual knowledge. Epistemic communities in the social sciences tend to be coupled with the dominant political institutions, whether they be nation-states, classes, or interest groups. Their knowledge may be a form of ideology, and their power may be an epiphenomenal expression of conventional forms of political power. If one finds this reduction distasteful and wishes to understand how knowledge influences policy, then one must be willing to address epistemological questions.

The most recent epistemic communities literature also links power and knowledge through expert advice, but it offers a more detailed and subtle reading of that link and its practical expression. Although these works (see the winter 1992 issue of *International Organization*) suffer from many of the same difficulties as the earlier attempts, they nonetheless come closer to some of the ideas developed in this book. Like the discursive practices approach, the epistemic communities literature responds to the perceived need for a "reflective" understanding of the constitution of institutions, interest, and behavior (Keohane 1989:173). It also recognizes that reality is socially constructed and, unlike neofunctionalism, sees social learning as a deeply political process rather than the rational result of the application of knowledge (Haas 1992b:17). Control over meanings and interpretations, not brute facts, is the point of departure; meanings are "negotiated," not given (Haas 1989:389). The epistemic communities approach also offers important insights into the mechanisms by which knowledge-based actors exert power, e.g., through bureaucratic channels, transnational networks, and "capturing the preponderant power" (Peterson 1992:185).

Despite these insights, the epistemic communities approach has trouble specifying how power is exercised. If epistemic communities influence policy by "usurping bureaucratic decision-making channels," then this approach may be reducible to a bureaucratic politics approach. In that case, power has little to do with actors' persuasive ability or their privileged access to knowledge. To the extent that their power is related to their ability to mobilize resources on behalf of shared normative beliefs, epistemic communities may be indistinguishable from interest groups. Finally, to the extent that the power of epistemic communities is rooted in how they frame and interpret information, then an approach that focuses on discourse may be most appropriate.

Because the epistemic communities approach stops short of discourse theory, it falls prey to some of the flaws of functionalism and its variants. It is fundamentally a theory of agency: knowledge-based experts exert power by virtue of their access to information. Power and discourse are thus properties—rather than constitutive—of subjects; the important dimension of disciplinary power is virtually omitted. In contrast to a more discursive approach, the theory assumes that knowledge and interests are distinct, a distinction related to the separation erected between causal and principled beliefs (Haas 1992b:18).

The notion of knowledge brokers refines the concept of epistemic communities, which neglects the extent to which knowledge, once produced, becomes something of a collective good available to all who employ it skillfully. The notion of knowledge brokerage also underscores the political flavor of expertise, showing its embeddedness in the policy process and thereby mitigating the temptation to adopt a naive modernist perspective. It also problematizes knowledge, stressing the discursive process of translation and interpretation. But to focus only on the agents of knowledge, whether epistemic communities or knowledge brokers, without delving into the content of knowledge, would be to miss much of what is important and interesting in the study of science in policy. This is why a discursive approach, based on a knowledge-based conception of power and oriented toward a rhetorical conception of science, is necessary for a fuller understanding.

Peter Haas contrasts his own approach, albeit very hastily, with poststructuralism. The manner in which he does so suggests that his reasons for neglecting discourse are primarily related to an a priori methodological commitment to agent-centered theory. In a chart depicting the theoretical approaches to policy change, the different units of analysis—experts and discourses—are noted, but no explicit rationale is offered for adopting one rather than the other. Policy is seen as being influenced by "knowledge" in the case of epistemic communities and "usage and meaning of words" in the case of discourse (Haas 1992b:6). But if reality truly is socially constructed and knowledge can only be generated, expressed, and framed in linguistic terms, then this distinction seems artificial at best.

Peter Haas dismisses poststructuralism offhandedly, noting that "Michel Foucault ultimately failed to demonstrate a consistent source of social influences that operated on the development of disciplining beliefs and practices" (1992b:25). Haas seems to want to make two points: that discursive approaches wrongly reduce technical knowledge to social factors and that they have sought to find a single set of social constraints that operate in every instance. Yet both lines of thinking are mistaken. As I have argued above, discourse theory need not be relativistic; a realist ontology is consistent with a hermeneutical epistemology. And Haas's attempt to attribute a universalistic aim to Foucault's work is clearly mistaken; Foucault did not seek to define any overarching set of social influences on knowledge.

Implicit in the epistemic communities approach is a traditional faith that science can transcend politics, that knowledge is separate from power. While proponents of this school are more careful than their predecessors to qualify their remarks about science's ability to make politics more rational and less conflict-ridden, ultimately the differences among them on this score are not so great. As one critic of the approach notes, power and knowledge-dependent joint gains are treated as competing alternatives and as analytically separable, rather than as inherently tied together (Sebenius 1992:324). By focusing on how technical experts can facilitate international cooperation, the epistemic communities approach contributes to the rationality project (Stone 1988). A discursive approach suggests that epistemic dissension, arising from the delegitimation process, may be at least as likely an outcome as epistemic cooperation.

Of all the major approaches to knowledge in international politics, the epistemic communities literature comes closest to an interactive conception of knowledge and power. It also provides important insights into how expert advice influences policy decisions. Yet it falls short on several counts. First, it skirts epistemological questions. Second, it is overly optimistic about the ability of consensual knowledge to minimize political conflict. Third, it reduces the power of epistemic communities to conventional political skills, thereby ignoring the central dimension of rhetorical competence. Each of these shortcomings derives from the larger problem that the epistemic communities approach fails to delve into the discursive nature of the employment of knowledge in policy decisions.

Because of its unrivaled status as universal legitimator, science may facilitate international cooperation. Knowledge is vital in revealing, shaping, and revising nations' conceptions of their own interests. It can also modify the behavior of states through inculcating alternative sets of norms into the practice of world politics. But the path is much more circuitous than one proceeding directly from knowledge to policy consensus. Information is incorporated into preconceived stories and discourses; it is framed, interpreted, and rhetorically communicated. In policy controversies, information begets counterinformation. Knowledge is embedded in structures of power: disciplinary power, national power, and socioeconomic power. The complex web of interactions between knowledge and power makes the study of science in international environmental politics a potentially fruitful one.

This web cannot be unraveled solely through theoretical inquiry; it requires detailed contextual analysis. The relationships between science and policy, technical experts and policymakers, are multidimensional and not reducible to an a priori understanding; indeed, the possibilities of interaction are innumerable. Because of the prominence of scientific knowledge in defining and framing the ozone debates, the bargaining processes that led to the Montreal Protocol and its revisions provide an excellent opportunity for contextual analysis.

3 • Historical and Scientific Background on Human Causes of Stratospheric Ozone Depletion

There just wasn't scientific or economic justification to proceed. How do you trade a possible [environmental] risk for a [business] risk that is real?   —*Joseph Steed, Du Pont environmental manager*

Certain scientific and political events of the 1970s and early 1980s, particular in the United States, spurred later developments that shaped the Montreal Protocol process. Because the United States assumed a leadership role both scientifically and politically, my discussion is not prejudiced by having the United States as a focus. Rather, this emphasis can shed some light on the distinct roles played by specific U.S. agencies, industries, environmental groups, and citizens. This chapter also surveys the evolution of the relevant scientific networks and the varying technical assessments of the ozone problem.

Consistent with the argument in the previous chapter, this chapter confirms that science defined the parameters of the political debate and that certain modes of framing the relevant knowledge had important political ramifications. For instance, the framing of the ozone problem as a human health issue rather than an ecological one conditioned the political context of the entire debate. Moreover, from the beginning, the existence of scientific uncertainty was used by all participants in the debate to support their particular positions.

A Brief Description of the Ozone Layer

Unlike the familiar diatomic compound of atmospheric oxygen, ozone is a rare variant composed of three oxygen atoms. Most atmospheric ozone is concentrated in the stratosphere, a region roughly ten to fifty kilometers above the earth's surface characterized by temperatures that generally increase with altitude (United Nations Environment Programme [UNEP] 1987b:8–9). Figure 3.1 shows how temperature and ozone distributions— influenced by complex photochemical reactions—vary with altitude. The maximum ozone concentration, occurring between twenty and thirty kilometers, is only a few parts per million. Since air at that altitude is about 5 percent as dense as at ground level, the sparse concentrations of ozone are more aptly described as a veil than as a layer or, as one author poetically put it, "a floating network of window panes" (Cogan 1988:1). In fact, if all the ozone in a vertical column were compressed to sea-level pressure, its thickness would be only three millimeters (UNEP 1987b:8).

Figure 3.1. Ozone Concentrations in the Earth's Atmosphere

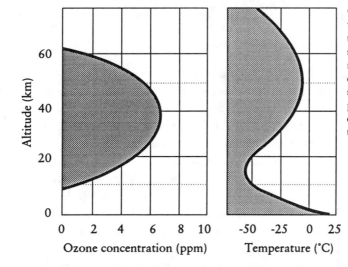

Ozone is found in varying concentra- tions from the Earth's surface to a height of nearly 60km. Its concentration increases sharply in the stratos- phere, which is characterized by rising temperatures.

Ozone is found in varying concentrations from the earth's surface to a height of nearly sixth kilo- meters. Its concentration increases sharply in the stratosphere, which is characterized by rising temperatures.

Source: UNEP 1987b:9

Solar radiation provided the conditions for the emergence of life, but earth's first organisms had to evolve under water, where they were shielded from ultraviolet radiation. Visible light penetrates water much more than does ultraviolet light, and some organisms developed the ability to photosynthesize. With the release of oxygen by oceanic plants billions of year ago, the ozone layer was created, allowing some life forms to leave the protective water and evolve on land. Without this veil, terrestrial life could not be sustained. Ozone absorbs all ultraviolet radiation with wavelengths shorter than about 290 nanometers (UV-C), most of it in the 290 to 320 nanometer range (UV-B), and little above 320 nanometer (UV-A) (Smith 1974:213). While UV-A is relatively innocuous, UV-C is lethal and UV-B is harmful to most life forms (Frederick 1986:121–23).

Ultraviolet rays with wavelengths shorter than about 240 nanometers are sufficiently energetic to dissociate diatomic oxygen molecules, which then absorb energy and heat the upper atmosphere. The single atoms of oxygen then combine with other oxygen molecules to form ozone, which in turn can be split apart by ultraviolet radiation into a single atom and diatomic oxygen again. The principal reactions can be written as follows:

$$O_2 + UV \ (40\text{–}240 \ nm) \longrightarrow O + O$$
$$O_2 + O \longrightarrow O_3$$
$$O_3 + UV \ (240\text{–}320 \ nm) \longrightarrow O_2 + O$$

Ozone is continuously created and destroyed, primarily above the tropics, and carried by winds toward the poles where its concentration is greatest. The rates of ozone formation and destruction are determined by the amount of available solar radiation, which in turn varies with latitude, seasonal variations, and the eleven-year solar cycle (Brasseur 1987:10)

Certain trace gases, such as chlorine (Cl), bromine (Br), nitric oxide (NO), and the hydroxyl radical (OH), accelerate ozone destruction. Recent increases in all of these ozone depleters can be ascribed to human activities (UNEP 1987b:11). Chlorofluorocarbons (CFCs), the primary cause of recent increases in stratospheric chlorine, remain in the atmosphere for about one hundred years (UNEP 1987b:14). This means that stabilizing atmospheric concentrations of chlorine would require not merely a freeze but drastic cuts in CFC production.

The most significant fact about the reactions of these trace gases with ozone is that they are catalytic, meaning that the ozone depleter emerges from the photochemical process unscathed, ready to destroy more ozone molecules. For example, one chlorine atom can destroy as many as one hundred thousand molecules of ozone, so that concentrations in the parts-per-billion-by-volume (ppbv) range may be dangerous (National Aeronautics and Space Administration [NASA]/World Meteorological Organization [NASA] 1986:71). A catalytic reaction cycle can be written as follows:

$$Cl + O_3 \longrightarrow ClO + O_2$$
$$ClO + O \longrightarrow Cl + O_2$$

The net result is:

$$O + O_3 + Cl \longrightarrow O_2 + O_2 + Cl$$

This paints a simplistic picture of an exceedingly complex chain of reactions. Photoche mistry in the stratosphere is quite different from what we find at the earth's surface. Ordinarily stable molecules can be destroyed by the very energetic photons reaching the stratosphere. The rates of the hundreds of subsequent reactions vary greatly with temperature and pressure.

A good deal of stratospheric chlorine is neutralized by reacting with methane (CH_4) to form hydrochloric acid (HCl).

$$CH_4 + Cl \longrightarrow CH_3 + HCl$$

While some methane occurs naturally, much of it is generated from human sources such as rice paddies, cattle raising, and oil fields. The growth in atmospheric methane is expected partially to offset ozone depletion from chlorine sources. But this is a mixed blessing since methane is also a major greenhouse gas (Stordal and Isaksen 1986).

While winds transport ozone throughout the stratosphere and stratospheric ozone sometimes descends to the troposphere, ozone created in the troposphere does not reach the stratosphere, though it will absorb some ultraviolet radiation (interview with Robert Watson). This means that human sources of ozone cannot compensate for losses in the stratosphere, which is perhaps just as well, since ozone at ground level is highly poisonous. Thus, solutions to the ozone problem have entailed curtailing potential depleters rather than inventing schemes to replace what is lost.

Biological Effects of Increased Ultraviolet Radiation

Relatively little research has been done on the health and environmental consequences of ozone depletion compared to the vast quantity of work generated on the physical and chemical processes it involves. One participant in the Montreal Protocol process lamented this dichotomy, noting that "while the U.S. spends about $200 million a year on atmospheric research, the entire world spends less than $1 million on effects research" (testimony of John Hoffman: United States Congress 1987c:136). Whether because of lack of attention or the existence of substantial consensus, the effects literature has not spawned the level of debate seen in the atmospheric sciences. Nor were the biological effects a major source of political controversy during the treaty negotiations. Hence, I will simply summarize the information available to the participants in the negotiations. Three reports issued by the Environmental Protection Agency (Titus 1986; EPA 1986a; EPA 1987a) were the best sources of information available during the Montreal Protocol negotiations.

Most studies of the health effects of ozone depletion have focused on the UV-B part of the spectrum, because, as mentioned, ozone absorbs virtually all dangerous UV-C under all foreseeable scenarios, while UV-A, which ozone does affect, is relatively harmless. Each 1 percent decrease in ozone will allow 2 percent more UV-B radiation to reach the earth's surface, and this is expected to lead to a greater incidence of skin cancer, cataracts, and immune disorders among humans, as well as interfering with terrestrial and aquatic ecosystems (Frederick 1986:130).

Nonmelanoma skin cancer, specifically basal and squamous cell carcinoma, has been definitively linked to the cumulative effects of UV-B exposure (Emmett 1986:138). Every 1 percent decrease of total column ozone (i.e., the total amount of ozone in a vertical column with its base at a given point on the earth's surface) is predicted to produce a 3 percent rise in the incidence of nonmelanoma skin cancer (UNEP/OzL.Pro.WG.II[1]/ 4:7). Melanoma, a far more deadly type of skin cancer, may be associated with acute radiation exposure, but this link is more speculative (140–41). Caucasians living in the mid-latitudes are especially vulnerable to both forms. In the United States, one out of every three cancers is a skin cancer, and one in seven Americans is expected to develop this disease at some point. During the 1980s, increased skin cancer rates may have been caused by the growing popularity of outdoor activities (UNEP 1987b:28). According to EPA estimates, unrestricted CFC growth would result in 180 million new cases of skin cancer and 3.5 million cancer deaths by the end of the next century in the United States alone (:exhibits 7–3 and 7–5 in EPA 1987a). But these estimates may be too low because they are based on linear projections from 1982 data that were later found to be overly conservative (testimony of Darrell Rigel: United States Congress 1987b:70).

Although experts largely agree on their quantitative estimates of health effects from ozone depletion, they differ on their interpretations of the data. Dr. Darrell Rigel, for instance, suggests that the United States is facing an "epidemic" of skin cancer. In a letter responding to his testimony, Dr. Margaret Kripke, who chaired the EPA's Scientific Advisory Board on ozone, questions Rigel's use of the term "epidemic." In her view, the term is "alarmist and conjures up pictures of bubonic plague" (United States Congress 1987b:617). Kripke, herself a cancer specialist, believes that the skin cancer issue has been overblown and that the more serious problems are those involving the human immune system, global food supply, and ecosystems (1989:3; interview).

EPA scenarios also predict that an additional 2.8 million Americans born before 2075 will be afflicted with cataracts, a clouding of the lens that blurs vision (exhibit 7–21 in EPA 1987a:7–26). Each 1 percent total column ozone depletion is expected to lead to a worldwide increase of 100,000 blind persons (UNEP/OzL.Pro.WG.II[1]/4:7). While cataracts are routinely removed by surgery in the industrial world, people in the developing world are unlikely to have access to the operation.

Medical researchers believe that UV-B interferes with the human immune system, lowering the body's resistance to infectious diseases. The few studies in this area have found a link between UV-B and viruses such as leishmaniasis and herpes (Titus 1986:6). Higher UV-B levels might also decrease the effectiveness of some inoculation programs; patients who do not build immune responses to the antigens might develop the disease itself (Shea 1988:15).

Laboratory experiments on two hundred different plant species, including most major crop species, indicate that about two-thirds of them are sensitive to higher levels of UV-B. Increased radiation can damage plant hormones and chlorophyll, leading to retarded growth. Experiments on plants were performed holding temperature and precipitation constant, but if predictions of climatic change are correct, such stability cannot be assumed (Teramura 1986). Some species also exhibit altered chemical composition that could affect their nutritional value (UNEP/OzL.Pro.WG.II[1]/4:7).

The effect of ozone depletion on marine life could also be harmful to humans; fish account for 18 percent of the animal protein that people consume worldwide, and 40 percent in Asia (Titus and Seidel 1986:7). Because it can penetrate to a substantial depth in clear water, UV-B radiation poses a particular threat to the single-celled algae called phytoplankton that live near the water's surface. These algae are at the bottom of the aquatic food chain, and most fish depend upon them somehow for their survival. It is possible that they could move to a deeper level to avoid the increased radiation, but this would decrease their access to the photo-synthetically active radiation on which they depend. Other species would also be affected by increases in UV-B, especially those whose larvae hatch near the water's surface; many of these species are already exposed to as much UV-B as they can tolerate (Worrest 1986).

Other effects of ozone depletion include degradation of polymers and increased urban smog. Ultraviolet radiation is known to stimulate the for-mation of ground level oxidants (smog), a process likely to escalate with greenhouse warming. One study of the damage to polyvinyl chloride (PVC) suggests that for a 26% depletion of the ozone layer by 2075, the undiscounted costs in the United States would be $4.7 billion in 1984 dol-lars (Titus and Seidel 1986:7).

A Brief History of the Fluorocarbon Industry

At the 1930 annual meeting of the American Chemical Society, Thomas Midgely stood in front of his fellow scientists, inhaled the vapors from a cup of clear liquid, and blew out a candle's flame. His demonstration was meant to show that the chemical was neither flammable nor highly toxic (*Washington Post* 1988a). Midgely, who had been hired by General Motors' Frigidaire Division to invent a new refrigerator coolant, had synthesized dichlorodifluoromethane (CFC-12), the first of the miracle chlorofluoro-carbons. In the process of vaporizing within refrigerator coils it absorbs heat, thereby allowing the coils to cool enough to refrigerate food. Du Pont, a cosponsor of Midgely's work, patented the process and began pro-duction under the trademark Freon.[1]

CFCs are produced by reacting simple chlorinated organic compounds (chlorocarbons) with hydrofluoric acid (HF), which is made by reacting fluorospar (calcium fluoride) with sulfuric acid. Fluorospar is mined, typ-ically by the CFC producers themselves, in various locations throughout the world. CFC-11 and -12 plants, with an average annual production capacity of fifty million pounds, generate large amounts of toxic hydro-chloric acid (HCl) which must be either sold as a chemical or disposed as a waste product.

Fully halogenated CFCs are virtually chemically inert near the earth's surface because they lack hydrogen, an element that tends to break apart the compounds and release toxic chlorine into the lower atmosphere. Five fully halogenated CFCs are commercially available: CFC-11, CFC-12, CFC-113, CFC-114, and CFC-115. HCFC-22, the most common partially halogenated CFC, is used as a coolant in large commercial refrigerators and in manufacturing certain polymers. It has replaced some of the CFCs regulated by the Montreal Protocol because it has a lower ozone depletion potential than the fully halogenated CFCs.[2]

Production of CFC-11 and -12 grew rapidly, from about 1.2 million pounds in 1931 to 76 million pounds by 1950 (Chemical Manufacturers Association 1987). By 1945, most ammonia- and sulfur dioxide–based refrigerators had been replaced by ones using CFC-12. During World War II, Dow Chemical Company began using CFC-12 to produce a new kind of insulating foam under the trademark Styrofoam, causing CFC production to nearly double in the five years following the war. CFCs were also used in the war to combat malaria, functioning as propellants in cans of insecticide.

As later advocates of international regulation frequently pointed out, every decade since their invention has seen at least one major new use for these "miracle chemicals." In the 1950s, CFC-11 was used as a blowing agent in flexible polyurethane foams, which became ubiquitous in furniture, carpet pads, and automobiles. By the end of the decade, CFC-11 was also being used to blow rigid polyurethane foams, which eventually overtook fiberglass and other materials to dominate the insulation market (*Washington Post* 1988a:A-18).

The proliferation of air conditioning in homes and public places during the 1960s facilitated the demographic expansion of the United States into the sunbelt. Mobile air conditioners became standard equipment in American cars and trucks, eventually accounting for more CFC refrigerant consumption than all other uses combined. Since vehicles are poorly insulated and their hoses are prone to leakage, the average mobile air conditioner contains enough refrigerant to cool an entire house (testimony of George Kerckhove; U.S. Senate 1987b:499–501).

By 1974, when scientists first linked CFCs to ozone depletion, nearly two billion pounds of CFCs were being produced each year—about ten times the 1951 figure. Over half of this was for aerosol propellants, primarily for personal-care items like hair sprays and deodorants. Even when a combination of legislation and consumer aversion to aerosol propellents in the United States, Canada, and Sweden slowed global CFC production, other applications continued to grow, soon offsetting that decline (see figure 3.2). Aerosols continued to be the major application of CFCs outside the United States, standing at nearly five hundred million pounds worldwide in 1984 (based on Hammitt et al. 1986:18).

CFC-113 entered the market in the 1970s as a solvent and degreaser for electronic components. Because of its high cost, it was first used by the defense and aerospace industries. But when the computer industry began miniaturizing its components, a process requiring a reliable solvent to remove the tiniest particles, American and Japanese CFC-113 production skyrocketed. Annual worldwide production tripled between 1976 and 1987 (based on estimates in Hammitt et al. 1986:60).

Another important class of ozone-depleting chemicals are the halons, which contain bromine instead of chlorine. Although they are produced in much smaller quantities, they are of special concern because their ozone depletion potential per molecule may be ten times that of the CFCs. Halons were developed by the U.S. Army Corps of Engineers after World War II for extinguishing fires in tanks and aircraft. They are most useful under conditions where the use of water might damage expensive equipment or risk people's lives. The military continues to be a primary con-

Figure 3.2. Historical growth of CFC-11 and CFC-12
(reporting countries, 1931–1986)

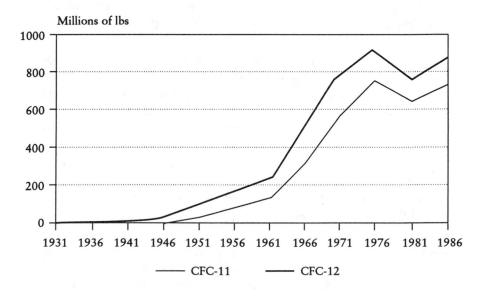

Source: Chemical Manufacturers Association 1987

sumer of halons, followed by banks and commercial airlines. Total global production of the three halons (Halon-1211, -1300, and -2400) in 1985 was about seventeen million pounds, with the United States accounting for about half the total (exhibit 4.1 in EPA 1987a:4.3).

CFCs have other minor uses, among them sterilizing medical equipment, fast-freezing produce, puffing tobacco, and stabilizing whipped toppings. In 1987, the combination of these uses accounted for roughly forty-two million pounds yearly on a global basis (based on estimates in Hammitt et al. 1986)

As of 1986, CFCs in the United States represented approximately $1 billion in sales, or about 30 percent of the world market, by five producers: Du Pont, Allied-Signal, Pennwalt, Racon, and Kaiser Chemical. The principal competitors in overseas markets were Imperial Chemical Industries (ICI) of the United Kingdom, Farbwerke Hoechst of West Germany, and Atochem, a subsidiary of the French Elf-Aquitaine (Jachtenfuchs 1990:265). While virtually all U.S. production was consumed domestically, the EC exported nearly half of its CFCs (Chemical Manufacturers Association 1987). During the international ozone negotiations, this difference in markets may have exacerbated the tensions already present in the relations between the U.S. and European chemical industries. —particularly between Du Pont and ICI, whose mutual hostility went back nearly two hundred years to their competition in the world gunpowder cartel (Taylor 1984).

Generally, the value of CFCs relative to the products containing them is small. For instance, a $1000 refrigerator may contain merely $10 worth of CFCs; the CFCs in the foam and coolants in a $10,000 car may cost only $50. But in 1987 over ten thousand users purchased CFCs from the five U.S. producers, accounting for over $28 billion in goods and services and 253,000 jobs. Servicing of refrigerators and air conditioners adds $5.5 billion in value and 472,000 jobs. The estimated value of American-installed equipment relying on CFCs was over $135 billion (Alliance for a Responsible CFC Policy 1987:V-1). Table 3.1 below shows 1985 global production figures for the major CFCs and halons. All countries except the so-called communist countries[3] reported their production data to the Chemical Manufacturers Association (CMA).

A Brief History of the Ozone Controversy

Initial fears about ozone depletion were unrelated to CFCs. Concern about the ozone layer first emerged in 1970, when the United States, Britain, and

France were planning to build a fleet of supersonic transport airplanes (SSTs). In that year, a German scientist theorized that the oxides of nitrogen emitted in the exhaust of the high-flying planes would catalytically consume ozone (Crutzen 1970). Harold Johnston, a Canadian chemist at the University of California at Berkeley, calculated that the planned fleet of five hundred SSTs would cause a 22 percent depletion of the earth's ozone layer (Johnston 1971). Despite a prominent study study that concluded that ozone reductions from the SST would be insignificant, Congress voted in 1971 to terminate funding for the program (for a history of the SST controversy, see Horwitch 1982).

Several aspects of this controversy were important for later developments. First, this was one of the first times that scientists became involved in environmental policy. It is noteworthy that the original draft of Johnston's paper, which would be considered cautious by today's standards, was rejected by *Science* editors for having too many references to political questions (Dotto and Schiff 1978:65). Second, the SST controversy provided the first major opportunity for atmospheric chemists and meteorologists to spar with one another, a conflict that has abated somewhat but was still evident even after the 1985 discovery of the Antarctic ozone hole. Third, after the U.S. program was defunded and the question of landing rights for British and French SSTs became primary, the Europeans accused Americans of attempting to export their own environmental standards as a veil for their economic interests, an allegation that resounded during the Montreal Protocol process.

Perhaps the most important outcome of the SST controversy was the new interest it generated in atmospheric research. Until then, little was known about the upper atmosphere, and communication between atmospheric chemists and dynamicists was poor. In 1971, the U.S. Department of Transportation established the major Climatic Impact Assessment Program (CIAP) to study the potential impact of the SST. The program's

Table 3.1. World Use of CFCs and Halons in 1985 (in thousands of metric tons)

Chemical	U.S.	Communist	All Other	World
CFC-11	75.0	41.5	225.0	341.5
CFC-12	135.0	78.7	230.0	443.7
CFC-113	73.2	5.0	85.0	163.2
Halon-1301	5.4	0.0	5.4	10.8
Halon-1211	2.7	8.1	0.0	10.8

Source: Hammitt et al. 1986:2.

name reflected early concerns about climate, concerns that later shifted to ozone loss once the skin cancer link gained publicity.[4] CIAP scientists concluded that SSTs would not be as harmful as originally feared (CIAP 1973). By then, a team of scientists working with Richard Stolarski and Ralph Cicerone had determined that chlorine in the exhaust of the planned space shuttle posed a more serious threat to stratospheric ozone, since it destroys ozone far more efficiently than do the nitric oxides produced by the SSTs (Stolarski and Cicerone 1974).

The space shuttle was the first man-made source of chlorine to be studied. Politically, it had important repercussions, for it sparked a great deal of concern within the National Aeronautics and Space Administration. At the time, expenditures on the shuttle constituted one-third of NASA's budget. As the successor of the Apollo project and the only man-in-space program, it was NASA's prestige project. Small wonder, then, that scientists were pressured by NASA to downplay the significance of the shuttle as a source of chlorine and to emphasize volcanoes instead (Dotto and Schiff 1978:127). NASA convinced Congress that it was the best agency to study stratospheric ozone. It quickly became the world's foremost authority on ozone, and it has remained so up to the present. The NASA budget for stratospheric research was between $15 and $20 million annually during the years of international negotiations on the ozone convention, an amount comprising approximately 70 percent of global funding on stratospheric research (interview with Robert Watson).

Meanwhile, James Lovelock, an independent British scientist, had measured CFC-11 in the lower atmosphere. Emphasizing that the compound posed "no conceivable environmental hazard," he viewed it as an indicator of the earth's wind and weather patterns. His estimates of atmospheric concentrations for CFC-11 roughly matched industry figures on cumulative global production, indicating that the chemical was apparently imperishable (Lovelock 1973:194–96).

Two chemists at the University of California at Irvine, F. Sherwood Rowland and Mario Molina, argued that although CFCs are insoluble and chemically inert in the troposphere, "odd chlorine" atoms in the stratosphere could initiate a catalytic chain reaction with ozone molecules (Molina and Sherwood 1974). Their paper defined the parameters of the ensuing controversy, the most important of which, from a policy perspective, was the issue of time scale. Because the atmospheric lifetimes of CFCs are 40 to 150 years, a steady-state concentration would not be reached for decades, even if CFC production ceased immediately. Rowland and Molina were particularly disturbed by the rapid growth in CFC production, which had doubled roughly every five years since World War II. On the basis of 1973 growth rates, they predicted that ozone would be depleted between 7 and 13 percent before stabilizing by the end of the next century. They called for an immediate ban on aerosol propellants, which accounted for half of all CFC usage in the United States.

While the public was shocked by the Rowland-Molina hypothesis,[5] the scientific infrastructure and the federal bureaucracy were well prepared to take up the issue as a result of CIAP and related studies. In the words of Carroll Bastian, who cochaired the federal task force charged with coordinating the scientific assessment, the response to the new CFC-ozone problem was "an unusual (if not unique) example of federal interagency coordination on an environmental regulatory question" (1972:167). The federal study affirmed the Rowland-Molina hypothesis but postponed its policy recommendations until the National Academy of Sciences completed its study (Interagency Task Force on Inadvertent Modification of the Stratosphere 1975). Some states, such as Oregon and New York, were unwilling to wait and passed legislation restricting the use of CFCs as aerosol propellants. These states had access to the same science as did the federal government and other states; they simply chose to err on the side of caution.

Industry called for more research. The international Manufacturing Chemists Association (now the CMA) increased funding for its Fluorocarbon Program Panel (FPP), established in 1972 shortly after Lovelock measured CFCs in the atmosphere. Most scientists I interviewed believe that the FPP did not censor the work it funded, but they also observed that its early grants were for projects that might undermine the Rowland-Molina hypothesis.

Du Pont, the world's largest CFC producer and maker of half of all CFCs in the USA, proclaimed that if studies showed "that chlorofluorocarbons cannot be used without a threat to health, Du Pont will stop production of these compounds" (United States Congress 1974). (As the scientific evidence mounted, Du Pont was frequently reminded of its pledge.) By tying its policy to the effects of CFCs on human health, Du Pont helped frame the issue in a way that focused debate on the health effects of ozone depletion rather than climatic and environmental change. While this mode of framing the issue was probably unintentional, its ramifications were felt throughout the policy-making process. Early on, the problem was framed almost entirely in terms of skin cancer.

Rowland and Molina soon discovered that the photochemistry was more complicated than they had originally believed. They ascertained that chlorine and nitric oxides could combine in the stratosphere to create chlorine nitrate ($ClNO_3$), thereby forming "reservoirs" that would retard the ozone depletion rate by both chlorine and nitric oxides (Rowland and Molina 1976). They concluded that previous estimates of ozone destruction were too high, leading some to accuse the scientists of alarmism (Dotto and Schiff 1978:255). The new discovery prompted the National Academy of Sciences to postpone the release of its final report for several months.

The report, reflecting the new data, cut the estimate of ozone depletion in half, from 14 percent in an early draft to 7 percent. Even so, the report's policy recommendations to defer a regulatory decision seemed flimsy in light of its conclusion that continued releases of CFCs at 1973 levels could reduce ozone in the upper stratosphere by as much as 50 percent (National Research Council 1976). Rowland later lamented that the report "established a debilitating precedent at a crucial time in the whole affair when [it] advocated a delay in regulation" (Brodeur 1986:80). Industry, of course, claimed that the report vindicated its own position.

It is worthwhile to consider the scientific merit of the main arguments used by detractors of the ozone depletion theory in the early years, for these persisted throughout the controversy.[6] The least sophisticated argument was that, because ozone varies greatly under natural conditions, a decrease of several percentage points globally would not be disastrous. The fallacy in this logic is seen clearly by analogy with temperature. While a ten-degree change in one place on any given day is of no great concern, a decrease of ten degrees averaged globally would be catastrophic.

Industry also seized upon reports that ozone had increased over the Northern Hemisphere during the 1960s to undermine the Rowland-Molina hypothesis. There are three problems with this line of reasoning. First, many scientists attributed the increase in ozone to the ban on atmospheric testing of nuclear weapons early in the decade. Second, the increases might have been greater without CFCs during that period. Third, and most notably, industry's reasoning ignored the fact that the effects of CFCs are delayed because of their long atmospheric lifetimes. This point later became immaterial as satellite data indicated declining ozone levels in the 1970s and 1980s.

A third fallacy is the exaggeration of the "self-healing effect." As ozone is destroyed in the upper atmosphere, more ultraviolet light enters the lower atmosphere, where it is absorbed by diatomic oxygen molecules to make more ozone. But each ozone molecule destroyed in the upper stratosphere is not matched by a new one further down. Besides, the computer models had already incorporated the self-healing process, which is why they had predicted so much more depletion at the poles: the self-healing effect drops off as the intensity of ultraviolet radiation decreases with latitude. Furthermore, even if sufficient replacement ozone were produced, there would be no guarantee that it would rise up to exactly those spots where the layer had been weakened. Moreover, redistributing ozone would alter stratospheric temperatures, possibly precipitating dramatic climate changes. With the discovery in 1975 that CFCs are extremely potent greenhouse gases, the link between ozone depletion and climate change became increasingly salient (Ramanathan 1975).

Despite the academy's indecisiveness in its 1976 report, Russell Peterson, chairman of the President's Council on Environmental Quality declared that "we cannot afford to give chemicals the same constitutional rights that we enjoy under the law; chemicals are not innocent until proven guilty" (Brodeur 1986:74). Considering that he had been a Du Pont chemist for over twenty years, his request that federal agencies develop plans to regulate CFCs was remarkable. Peterson's voice was added to an emerging environmental policy discourse premised on what has come to be known as the "precautionary principle," i.e., that, in the face of scientific uncertainty, regulators should act to prevent harm rather than wait until damage occurs (Bodansky 1991).

In its amendments to the Clean Air Act in 1977, Congress called upon the EPA administrator to regulate any substance "which in his judgment may be reasonably anticipated to affect the stratosphere," thereby mandating preventive action based on the best scientific knowledge available.[7] The fact that empirical evidence of ozone destruction need not precede regulatory action later became an important factor in formulating the U.S. position during the international negotiations.

The 1977 legislation also required the United States to try to convince other nations to adopt regulations mirroring its own. Only Canada, Sweden, and Norway, all of which were heavily influenced by the 1976 academy report, followed the U.S. lead in implementing an aerosol ban (Stoel 1983:59). Despite pressure from the USA, the European Economic Community (EC) refused to adopt an aerosol ban. The British and the French were most resistant and remained so during the later negotiations (Jachtenfuchs 1990). The lack of success abroad was one reason that the EPA's proposed reductions in nonaerosol uses of CFCs never went beyond a notice in the *Federal Register*. Other factors included the lack of readily available substitutes and diminished public interest following the aerosol ban.

Despite industry's protests that no substitutes were available, the day after the aerosol phaseout was announced, Robert Abplanalp, inventor of the original aerosol spray valve and a vocal critic of the Rowland-Molina hypothesis, unveiled a new propellant to replace CFCs (Roan 1989:85). The hydrocarbon substitutes were used in the United States after 1978 but were not adopted abroad on a large scale until after the Montreal Protocol went into force.

The events leading to the aerosol ban set a pattern that continued throughout the ozone controversy: industry questioned the science and claimed that no replacements for the risky chemicals were available, but once the regulations were in place, substitutes quickly came on the market. The availability of substitutes, then, has typically been more contingent on the dominant policy discourse, translated into market signals, than on any scientific or technical factors.

Although the CFC-ozone controversy receded into the background politically during the late 1970s and early 1980s, it continued to receive substantial scientific attention. The state of knowledge paralleled the evolution of computerized atmospheric models. Over 192 chemical reactions and 48 photochemical processes are involved in ozone depletion caused by CFCs, but no models reflect all of them (Brasseur 1987:7). The first models in the mid-1970s were one-dimensional, averaging local effects of a single perturbation to yield a uniform global picture (National Research Council 1976:323–31). Later in the decade, two-dimensional models were developed to take into account latitudinal distributions. These models predicted large losses of ozone in the upper stratosphere, calling attention to the possibility of dramatic climate change attributable to ozone depletion. Most modeling since the late 1970s has used two-dimensional models. Three-dimensional models, developed in the early 1980s, factored in wind turbulence and divided the earth into grids. Although they are dynamically more accurate, three-dimensional models are expensive to run and their chemistry is somewhat simplistic, precluding widespread reliance on them (interview with Robert Watson). The models were increasingly refined, and their results tended to converge; disparities in their predictions were more often due to new data rather than differences among the models.

Not only did the models improve, but reaction rates were being revised. In 1977, two researchers found that nitrogen oxides and hydroxides would react forty times faster than previously believed (testimony by Dr. Rowland; U.S. Senate 1987b:5–6). This implied that nitrogen would be inactivated more quickly, thereby decreasing the amount available to form reservoirs of chlorine nitrate. Thus, ozone could be depleted much faster than either Rowland and Molina or the National Academy of Sciences had predicted in 1976.

The 1979 NAS report, taking these findings into account, painted a bleak picture, predicting as much as 16.5 percent depletion by the end of the next century. It also included much more information on climate change and the potential for increases in skin cancer, disruption of the aquatic food web, and crop damage. The report concluded with a sense of urgency, declaring that CFCs should be regulated beyond the aerosol ban already in place (National Research Council 1979).

In the same year, Britain's Department of the Environment released a much more equivocal study (U.K. Department of the Environment 1979). While confirming the 16 percent depletion estimate, this report vacillated by emphasizing that the ozone depletion theory was still a mere hypothesis. It concluded by calling for more research before taking action. (One of the British scientists later admitted that the U.S. report was probably more accurate because it used better models [Roan 1989:99].) Not surprisingly, industry on both sides of the Atlantic stressed the inconsistencies between the studies and endorsed the latter's call for further inquiry (Brodeur 1986:76).

Industry also emphasized that ozone losses had not yet been measured. Du Pont responded to the 1979 studies by pointing out that no ozone depletion had ever been detected and that the depletion figures were merely computer projections based on a series of uncertain assumptions. A vocal minority of scientists, including Rowland and Molina, countered that verifying predictions of future events is inherently impossible. Using the logic of the precautionary principle, they argued, once depletion could be confirmed empirically, it would be too late to reverse the damage. Furthermore, most scientists believed that validating the ozone depletion hypothesis did not require detecting actual ozone losses; finding chlorine radicals (chlorine and chlorine oxide) would be sufficient.

Measurement of changes in ozone, in parts per trillion, presented an array of problems. A few ground-based monitoring instruments, called Dobson stations, had been in place since the 1920s, with many more added after the International Geophysical Year in 1957. Their data, however, was considered unreliable: the stations were not well calibrated with one another, and they are not dispersed homogeneously, there being only a few stations in the Southern Hemisphere and almost none in the tropics. Prior to the Montreal Protocol, about a third of the stations did not report regularly to the World Ozone Data Center in Toronto (UNEP/WG.69/3:5). The stations were also vulnerable to interference from aerosols spewed into the atmosphere by volcanic eruptions. Further, CFC-caused ozone losses could not be distinguished from natural fluctuations, especially those associated with the eleven-year solar cycle. (As sunspot activity decreases, less ultraviolet radiation is emitted, resulting in a drop in ozone.) Finally, while the Dobson stations measured the total ozone column overhead, they could not decipher changes in distribution. Vertical profiles are measured by means of the indirect ground-based Umkehr method, which deduces levels from the differential absorption of light at various angles, and by balloon ozone-scondes, which take measurements at different altitudes. The former method is highly inaccurate because it is susceptible to disruption from aerosol particles; the latter is more accurate but very expensive (interview with Nien Dak Sze).

Until recently, ozone measurements were also gathered by the total ozone mapping spectrometer (TOMS) on the Nimbus 7 satellite, launched in 1978 to replace the Nimbus 4. Satellite data have the advantage of being able to differentiate ozone levels at various altitudes. Because computer models all predicted that the upper stratosphere will be effected most dramatically, this is important. But the satellite monitoring system is also vulnerable to confusion caused by aerosols like volcanic dust, and its instruments were deteriorating with age (Brasseur 1987:39).

Consequently, those who sought empirical proof on either side of the controversy were frustrated by the data itself. In 1981, Donald Heath of NASA's Goddard Space Flight Center, the principal analyst of the satellite data, compared data from the two satellites and believed he found a 1 percent decrease in total ozone during the 1970s. This finding, the first evidence of global ozone depletion, concurred with predictions of computer models. However, Heath's paper was rejected by the editors of *Science* because of questions about the accuracy of comparing data from two different satellites. That same year, the CMA released a summary of data from the ground-based Dobson network. Their analysis indicated that ozone levels had actually increased during the 1970s. Yet a National Oceanic and Atmospheric Administration (NOAA) study found that ozone over North America had decreased by 1 percent between 1961 and 1980 (Brodeur 1986:78). By the mid-1980s, the consensus was that ozone levels had remained essentially stable during the 1970s (*Science Impact* 1987).

While the scientists disputed the data, a bit of diplomatic progress was made. The EC Council of Ministers voted in March 1980 for all members to freeze their production capacity and reduce their consumption of CFCs in aerosols by at least 30 percent compared with 1976 levels (European Communities 1980). At an international meeting in Oslo the following month, delegates from all major CFC-producing nations agreed to reduce emissions from nonaerosol applications voluntarily. Delegates from the EPA went further by offering to freeze annual CFC production in the United States at 1979 levels.

However, changes in the political environment made further regulations in the USA appear unlikely. In the last days of the Carter administration, the EPA honored its pledge and published an Advance Notice of Proposed Rulemaking in the *Federal Register* outlining plans for future regulation of CFCs (EPA 1980). In response to this announcement, a coalition of five hundred CFC users and producers formed the Alliance for a Responsible CFC Policy to ensure that government did not regulate "based on unproven and unverified theory" (Alliance for a Responsible CFC Policy 1987:I-1). The alliance immediately organized an intensive lobbying effort to oppose the EPA's proposal. Then the promise of "regulatory relief" under the Reagan administration made it increasingly doubtful that the rulemaking would ensue. Anne Gorsuch Burford, the EPA's new administrator, made it clear that she did not take the threat to stratospheric ozone seriously (U.S. Senate 1981).

Seeing that further regulation was unlikely, Du Pont stopped its research on replacement compounds for CFCs. In the six years following the Rowland-Molina publication, Du Pont had spent over $15 million to develop commercially acceptable alternatives. Only a handful of compounds survived the tests, and no long-term toxicology studies had been done by 1980 (Du Pont 1980).[8] Clearly, the so-called essential CFCs would not be replaced as easily or as cheaply as the aerosols had been. In explaining Du Pont's suspension of its research program, Joe Steed, environmental manager for the Freon division, remarked, "There wasn't scientific or economic justification to proceed. How do you trade a possible [environmental] risk for a [business] risk that is real?" (*Washington Post* 1988b).

In 1981, a newly released international ozone trends study found no clear evidence of actual ozone loss but predicted that ozone would be depleted between 5 and 9 percent by the second half of the twenty-first century (WMO 1982). The new figures were based on refined chemical reaction rates and better data on the interactive effects of CFCs, carbon dioxide, nitrogen oxides, and methane. The NASA/WMO analysis also painted a more ominous picture of the biological and health effects than had past reports. A year later, the National Academy of Sciences published its third report, echoing much of the NASA/WMO analysis. Despite the bleak forecast, newspapers optimistically proclaimed that the danger was not as great as was previously believed. But this rosy picture only made sense in contrast to the 1979 prediction of 16.5 percent depletion.

A fourth academy report in 1984 seemed to offer even better grounds for complacency. Lowering its estimates for eventual ozone loss to 2 to 4 percent, the study relied on questionable economic data and some new chemical considerations. Ignoring the fact that CFC production was already rising as the world recovered from a recession, the report assumed that CFC output would remain stable. Methane, increasing by 1 percent annually, would also slow ozone depletion. Increasing concentrations of carbon dioxide and nitrous oxide might also counteract some of the negative effects of CFCs (National Research Council 1984).

However, though total ozone loss was expected to be low, the report substantiated earlier forecasts that the vertical distribution of ozone would be greatly perturbed. According to Rowland, this is important because "looking at the total ozone loss minimizes the importance of the issue. No one has yet succeeded in developing a scenario in which the increase of CFC's doesn't decrease upper stratospheric ozone" (quoted in Roan 1989:111).

In addition, while superficially heartening on ozone depletion, the report contained some disturbing news regarding climate change, claiming that the atmospheric concentration of CFCs was growing ten times as fast as carbon dioxide, the chief greenhouse gas. This information was alarming; each CFC molecule was thought to contribute as much to greenhouse warming as fifteen thousand carbon dioxide molecules (Rowland 1987). Combined with other trace gases, primarily methane and nitrous oxide, CFCs could contribute as much to global warming as carbon dioxide would. Moreover, ozone depletion from CFCs is mitigated primarily by rising methane levels, which also increase the risk of global warming. Thus, the 1984 NAS report demonstrated the inseparability of ozone and climate issues, though this was not the message that reached policymakers and the public (Thomas 1986; *Science* 1984). Table 3.2 summarizes the estimates of total ozone depletion calculated in each of the NAS reports.

Interest among environmental groups was all but dead. With little support from his colleagues at the Natural Resources Defense Council

(NRDC) and virtually no visible concern among other environmental organizations, Alan Miller decided to sue the EPA for neglecting to follow up on its Phase Two regulations. He was especially troubled by the fact that CFC output was increasing as the global recession subsided (interview with Alan Miller). Anne Gorsuch Burford had resigned as EPA head amid a storm of controversy in March 1983, providing an opening for a small group of proregulatory EPA staff (interviews with James Losey and Stephen Seidel). After giving William Ruckelshaus, the incoming EPA administrator, a grace period at his new post, Miller filed his suit in mid-1984. The agency persuaded Miller that a lawsuit compelling the USA to act unilaterally might undermine the sensitive international negotiations already under way. Miller agreed to delay the suit. But when it became clear that international regulatory measures were unlikely to be adopted at the diplomatic conference scheduled for March 1985 in Vienna, he filed the suit.

Two things happened at the EPA that would have an impact on the international negotiations. Ruckelshaus resolved a long-standing dispute between two EPA offices by transferring authority over stratospheric pollution from the Office of Toxic Substances, where it had been since the mid-seventies, to the Office of Air and Radiation. The Toxic Substances Office had supported Burford's position that international regulation of CFCs was premature, while officials in the Office of Air viewed CFCs as part of the greenhouse problem and supported international controls (interview with James Losey). The conflict between the two offices was resolved by the switch, with the newly combined office supporting the EPA's Office on International Activities, which felt that the United States should at least back a worldwide aerosol ban. Despite some objections from Burford allies within the State Department, the EPA succeeded in making its plan the formal U.S. policy.

The other important development was the appointment of Lee Thomas

Table 3.2. Estimates of Ozone Depletion

Year	Estimate
1976	2%–20% (7% most likely)
1979	16.5%
1982	5%–9%
1984	2%–4%

National Research Council 1976, 1979, 1982, 1984.

as EPA administrator in January 1985. Thomas, head of the agency's highly visible Superfund/Resource Conservation and Recovery Act programs under Ruckelshaus, was handpicked for the job by his predecessor. Initially, observers doubted that a nonlawyer could operate effectively in such heavily legalistic position. Others questioned the ability of a career bureaucrat to exercise political leverage within an administration whose ideological leanings ran counter to environmental regulation (*Environmental Forum* 1985:23–26). But Thomas, with an educational background in psychology, was also known for his management skills and his ability to work well with politicians. Soon after assuming his new post, Thomas was briefed on the ozone issue by scientists from NASA and NOAA. In his words, "I just took a black-and-white view when I saw the data. I knew we had to get [CFCs] out of process. It didn't appear that even a little bit of them was going to be safe" (interview with Lee Thomas).

The Road to the Vienna Convention

As the science appeared to be softening, the international meetings preparing for an ozone treaty helped to keep scientists' attention on the issue (interviews with Robert Watson and Ivar Isaksen). The United Nations Environment Programme, responding to a statement prepared by the World Meteorological Organization (1976:59), convened a meeting of scientists in 1977 to draft the World Plan of Action on the Ozone Layer (UNEP 1978:190). Despite its grandiose title, the plan simply called for research on ozone depletion and its effects and identified various UN organizations as lead agencies for specific research efforts. The primary international organizations working with UNEP on the World Plan of Action were the World Meteorological Organization (WMO) and the World Health Organization (WHO). The Coordinating Committee on the Ozone Layer (CCOL) was created to make periodic scientific assessments of the problem (UNEP/WG.7/25/Rev.1). According to R. S. Mikhail, a meteorologist and deputy director of UNEP's Environmental Assessment Division, which was overseeing ozone layer activities, UNEP did not intend to push for regulation of ozone-depleting substances. Rather, it saw its role as facilitating an international scientific consensus (Stoel, Miller, and Milroy 1980:276).

UNEP's role as scientific coordinator was surprising at the time, for its staff was small, geographically isolated, and not highly specialized in the relevant sciences. Moreover, its work up until that point was primarily in developing countries, whereas the ozone problem was centered in the developed world, both economically and scientifically. In fact, some observers saw the Organization for Economic Cooperation and Development (OECD) as the logical candidate for international leadership, since the major CFC producers were all OECD members (Stoel 1983).

In 1982, at the request of several Scandinavian countries, UNEP convened the first meeting of the Ad Hoc Working Group of Legal and Technical Experts to negotiate a framework convention on stratospheric ozone depletion. The UNEP secretariat prepared a paper for the working group in November 1982, in which it outlined alternative structures for protocols or annexes to a draft convention (UNEP/WG.78/3). The paper examined fifteen different conventions and protocols from its regional seas program. Following these examples, the group agreed to draw up a "framework convention" to be supplemented by protocols and annexes calling for specific control measures.

The negotiations became polarized when Finland and Sweden submitted a draft protocol, known as the Nordic Annex, calling for an aerosol ban and limits on other uses of CFCs. The EC, Japan, and the Soviet Union strongly opposed the proposal, arguing that the science did not mandate such measures.[9] The Europeans claimed that aerosol reductions and a production cap were sufficient. The United States also refused to back the Nordic Annex, arguing on procedural grounds that provisions for specific controls should not precede a framework convention. American supporters of the Nordic Annex maintained that the general U.S. objection to it sent the message that the U.S. aerosol ban had been a mistake. Eventually, with Burford's resignation, the United States joined the Nordics and Canada in what came to be known as the Toronto Group, after the group's first meeting in that city. Australia, Austria, and Switzerland were sympathetic to the Toronto Group's position (Sand 1985:42).

UNEP's working group met seven times between 1982 and 1985. It often seemed that no agreement would be reached among the fifty participating countries. The EC, bowing to the wishes of Britain and France, supported a cap on production capacity for CFC-11 and -12 and a 30 percent reduction of nonessential aerosol uses. The Toronto group viewed this proposal as self-serving; the EC had already adopted a 30 percent aerosol reduction, and its producers were only operating at about 65 percent capacity, the EC proposal would not require them to modify their behavior at all.

The Toronto group made four proposals in all, any of which would have reduced CFC emissions more than the EC proposal. But they too could be seen as self-serving because they focused on reductions in aerosol uses. The first two proposals were a ban or an 80 percent cutback on nonessential aerosol uses and exports. The third option was a 20 percent reduction of all CFCs within four years. The fourth was a 70 percent reduction of aerosol uses, accompanied by a production cap. The EC also argued that the Toronto Group's proposals did not take into account long-term growth of "essential" uses of CFCs, a conviction that the U.S. negotiators later came to share (interview with Robert Watson). Neither side was willing to accept new constraints on its own industries (Sand 1985:22).

Two legal issues hampered the negotiations: the procedure for settling interstate disputes and the voting status of the EC. After the 1984 World Court's verdict against the USA for mining Nicaragua's harbors, the United States reversed its position in support of compulsory referral to the International Court of Justice and instead insisted on a clause allowing the option of third-party mediation (article 11, Vienna Convention). On the second matter, the EC and other regional economic integration organizations would be permitted to vote on behalf of their states if those states chose not to vote (article 15).

In the end, the framework convention was adopted in March 1985 without any control provisions. Although no CFC controls were instituted, UNEP officials proudly proclaimed that the Vienna Convention was the first legal instrument to protect the global atmosphere. Mostafa Tolba, UNEP's executive director, declared it to be a sign of "political maturity" in that it dealt with a "distant threat," expressly recognizing an "intergenerational responsibility" (Sand 1985:20).

The Vienna Convention, like other treaties negotiated under UNEP's auspices, is careful to avoid the implication that the environmental norm it seeks to establish interferes in any way with the principle of state sovereignty. The second sentence of the preamble cites principle 21 of the 1972 Declaration of the United Nations Conference on the Human Environment, which provides that "states have . . . the sovereign right to exploit their own resources pursuant to their own environmental policies, and the responsibility to ensure that activities within their jurisdiction or control do not cause damage to the environment of other states."

In addition to establishing a general responsibility of states to protect the ozone layer, the Vienna Convention calls for various forms of scientific and technical cooperation among its parties. Despite the vagueness of some of these provisions, they were crucial for negotiating the Montreal Protocol. As early as 1982, it was recognized that the paramount need was for accurate global production statistics for all potential ozone-depleting substances (UNEP/WG.78/6:3). Without good production data, reliable predictions of ozone depletion cannot be made, regardless of the computer models' sophistication. Western Europe, the United States, and Japan report their production data for CFC-11 and -12 to the CMA. Communist countries, however, do not, and they refused to divulge them until after the Vienna Convention was adopted. In many countries, there was no legislation under which the government could compel firms to provide production statistics, especially when a company could show that disclosure would be prejudicial (UNEP/WG.78/6:5). Additionally, the CMA does not compile data on CFC-113 or the halons, so those data were subject to greater uncertainty. A major contribution of the Vienna Convention was that it prompted the gathering and disclosure of critical economic and technical information. In order to ensure some degree of commercial and national secrecy, the convention contains safeguards such as aggregation of data.

The convention also calls for scientific cooperation in developing computer models, monitoring the stratosphere, and developing alternatives to CFCs. The most immediate tangible results of these provisions were greater efforts to ensure that instruments were consistently calibrated.

Most importantly, the Vienna Convention establishes a norm, both in terms of state behavior and the environment itself. It mandates that states have a general obligation to refrain from activities that are likely to modify the ozone layer. No change in the ozone layer is acceptable; the environmental norm is an unmodified ozone layer, and the international norm is behavior that sustains that environmental norm. These norms are fundamentally an expression of the precautionary principle; thus, while no CFC controls were agreed upon, the Vienna Convention was important in that it legitimized a regulatory discourse. Empirical evidence of ozone depletion was not required before states must modify the behavior of CFC producers within their borders. Rather, the probability that certain actions would be detrimental to ozone should be enough, although the responses of states remained purely voluntary. Since this probability can only be known through scientific models, policymakers must look to the scientists. Consensual scientific knowledge becomes the progenitor of state conduct. But, in the face of scientific uncertainty, even actions that are only likely to deplete the ozone layer are unacceptable by the Vienna Convention's standards. In the absence of consensual knowledge, the precautionary principle should guide policy.

All of the participants I interviewed agree that the greatest significance of the Vienna Convention was that it represented the first global consensus that there was indeed a problem. They also believe that the failure to adopt control provisions at Vienna was fortuitous, since any protocol adopted at that time would not have been as comprehensive as the Montreal Protocol that was adopted only two years later.

4 • The Employment of Knowledge in the Montreal Protocol Negotiations

> Where there was uncertainty, they thought we needed more research and I thought we needed to be cautious. We just looked at the same science and came to two different conclusions.
>
> —*Lee Thomas, former EPA administrator*

The Montreal Protocol represents a transition from a regime based on the principle of free access to the upper atmosphere to one based on limited access. This transition articulated the discursive shift toward a precautionary approach to ozone depletion that had begun with the Vienna Convention. That shift was facilitated by the extended time frames embodied in sophisticated computer models, time frames that inevitably clashed with the shorter time frames typical of political decision making. Without a scientific consensus that continued CFC emissions would eventually cause ozone loss, the Montreal Protocol would have been inconceivable. Scientists and, to an even greater extent, knowledge brokers, were powerful political actors simply by virtue of their authority as interpreters of reality. Their power had little to do with control or domination but was instead a function of the perceived legitimacy of their knowledge.

In the most comprehensive history of the international efforts to protect the ozone layer, Richard Benedick, chief negotiator for the USA prior to the Montreal meeting, emphasizes the close collaboration between scientists and policymakers (1990). Superficially, the treaty appears to have been the result of deft diplomacy and a rigorous process of risk analysis; this is essentially Benedick's thesis. It would be a mistake, however, to conclude that science provided a body of objective and value-free facts from which international cooperation emerged. Rather, knowledge was framed in light of specific discourses so that the fact-value distinction on which risk analysis is premised was eroded. Because Benedick is inattentive to the discursive nature of knowledge, he disregards the contextual factors that determined the political salience of various interpretations of the available knowledge—most notably, the Antarctic ozone hole.

Because of the prominence of science and scientists in the ozone negotiations and particularly because there was an actual document that provided an international scientific consensus for policymakers (WMO/NASA 1986), the Montreal Protocol represents a most likely case for confirming the epistemic cooperation hypothesis. Yet while cooperation was achieved, a detailed tracing of the process shows that the treaty was not fundamentally rooted in consensual knowledge. In particular, Peter Haas's claim that the protocol was the work of an ecological epistemic community (1992a) is mistaken on three counts. First, he maintains that the "community" primarily comprised atmospheric scientists. But in actuality these scientists were quite reluctant to commit themselves to concrete policy recommendations before the causes of the Antarctic ozone hole were understood. Almost none of them advocated the virtual ban on CFCs that was promoted by the U.S. delegation. Second, although to a lesser extent than Benedick, Haas downplays the discursive nature of knowledge. The fact is that, although a body of consensual knowledge existed, the wide range of possible interpretations limited its influence. Third, and partly as a consequence of the second factor, Haas underestimates the impact of certain contextual developments, like the Antarctic ozone hole, which conditioned the salience of alternative interpretations. He mentions that the discovery of the ozone hole alarmed the public, and he misleadingly links it to the international scientific assessment (WMO/NASA 1986), but he fails to explain how, despite the negotiators' explicit decision to ignore the hole in their deliberations, it nonetheless contributed to a discursive shift in favor of precautionary action.

The availability of scientific knowledge to the negotiators was a necessary condition for the successful negotiation of the Montreal Protocol, but it was far from being a sufficient one; the persistence of major uncertainties opened the door to contending interpretations. As I argued in chapter 2, an understanding of the interaction of power and knowledge in specific situations cannot be derived through any a priori theoretical exercise but requires contextual analysis of concrete cases. Theoretical inquiry into the mutual embeddedness of power and knowledge, however, does suggest that neither the scientific nor the political context can stand independently. This chapter supports such a judgment, analyzing the events leading up to the Montreal Protocol as a complex interplay between scientific and political contexts, without reducing one to the other. As mentioned earlier, science did not offer a supply of value-free facts from which a policy consensus could be formulated, for knowledge could be framed in light of specific interests so that questions of value were rendered as questions of fact. On the other hand, scientific knowledge was not completely malleable, for it was rooted in an intransitive ontological dimension (Bhaskar 1986).

The acceptability of specific forms and interpretations of knowledge is partly a function of political and economic institutional factors. The domestic structures of the states involved in the Montreal Protocol negotiations influenced the extent to which scientific knowledge was available and appreciated. The nature of relations between industry and government and the structure of the various national CFC industries were also important factors in setting the political context. Another key element was the strength of domestic environmental pressure groups.

One outstanding event that cannot be reasonably classified as either wholly scientific or political, but which had an overriding impact on all aspects of the problem, was the discovery of the Antarctic ozone hole, which not only pervaded the psychological and political milieu by heightening the status of scientific uncertainty but strongly influenced the political acceptability of specific modes of framing and interpreting the consensual knowledge at hand. The hole, I will argue, provided dramatic evidence in favor of precautionary action, evidence that participants could not ignore, despite their conscious decision to ignore it.

The availability of a comprehensive international scientific assessment (WMO/NASA 1986) was another key factor in shaping the context of the debates. The WMO/NASA report was accepted as the most up-to-date and authoritative expression of scientific knowledge on stratospheric ozone and hence as the scientific basis for the negotiations. From a policy perspective, the fact that this document represented an international consensus, rather than the work of scientists from any one country or region, was as significant as its actual scientific content. The process of assembling the study, I will argue, was unmistakably political.

Although the study represented an international scientific consensus with relatively narrow margins of uncertainty, all participants in the policy debates were able to justify their positions according to it—both the United States and the EC found in it support for their diametrically opposed positions. The three-volume assessment also contains a wealth of information, most notably on climate change, that was barely mentioned during the negotiations, largely because the policy debate focused on the effects of increased ultraviolet radiation. This mode of framing the debate had a major impact on the policy process. Thus, while knowledge was indispensable, it was always open to interpretation, and it was never apolitical.

To say that scientific knowledge was critical does not mean that the scientists themselves were the driving force in the policy realm. Of course, they were necessary, for without them there would be no science, but once the knowledge was produced, it became a potential tool for other actors with a stronger policy orientation. In this instance, a group of knowledge brokers was instrumental both in translating the available knowledge into terms understandable to decision makers and in pushing forward specific policy proposals. This group, largely employed in the U.S. Environmental Protection Agency (EPA),[1] was more inclined than were the scientists to employ knowledge on behalf of far-reaching policy recommendations. To this end, the manner in which that knowledge was framed and interpreted became a significant factor. Domestically, these EPA research brokers were able to develop close ties with other agencies and departments, most notably the State Department, and, to a lesser extent, with environmental pressure groups. Likewise, they developed transnational alliances with individuals in foreign environmental bureaus, which were helpful at times in swaying those agencies' governments toward the U.S. position.

The existence of a group of ecologically minded knowledge brokers armed with an international scientific consensus under the crisislike conditions provoked by the discovery of the Antarctic ozone hole was not enough to bring about the Montreal Protocol. Another factor was the relatively neutral atmosphere that could only be provided by an organization with no specific national ties. UNEP provided such a forum and, through its Coordinating Committee on the Ozone Layer (CCOL), disseminated up-to-date scientific knowledge to countries that did not have strong research programs of their own.

While all of these elements were necessary, even the whole package of them might not have been sufficient to bring about the Montreal Protocol. Other ingredients included the strength and idiosyncrasies of individual personalities, the actions of nongovernmental organizations, and perhaps just plain luck.

This chapter is organized roughly in a chronological manner so that it tells a story, but the story is not textually separated from analysis and interpretation. In relating the story, I trace the complex interaction and mutual embeddedness of power and knowledge. Thus, theoretical analysis is embedded in the narrative.

The International Scientific Consensus

In July 1986, just over a year after the Vienna Convention was signed, the most comprehensive international report on atmospheric ozone to date was published (WMO/NASA 1986). This document established a common understanding of the fundamental scientific issues among all participating nations. Building upon a 1982 assessment that was cosponsored by three U.S. scientific agencies and one international scientific agency, the 1986 report was cosponsored by the same three U.S. agencies, three international organizations, and a West German scientific agency.[2] It was generated through a series of thirty focused workshops held in 1984 and 1985, with participation from approximately one hundred fifty scientists from eleven countries. The purpose of the report was "to provide governments around the world with the best scientific information currently available on whether human activities represent a substantial threat to the ozone layer" (WMO/NASA 1986:4). It was an explicit response to the Vienna Convention, which acknowledged the existence of a problem and called for coordinated research and monitoring but had failed to adopt control measures.

Dr. Robert Watson, an atmospheric scientist with NASA and "a master at blending the roles of bureaucrat and scientist," (Roan 1989:159) coordinated the assessment. As a result of his more minor role in the 1982 assessment, Watson, along with a few others, perceived the need for greater international participation. Watson has stated:

> Before 1980, there were several assessments being done periodically in different countries. This just meant that the policymakers spent more time looking at the differences between them rather than at the similarities, even when they said basically the same thing. With one document, even if there was a range of views in it, then the international policy community had a constant base. (interview)

In particular, some of the scientists were "getting very tired of what the British government was putting out" (interview with Ralph Cicerone, atmospheric scientist).[3]

The reasons for including broad representation were more political than scientific. Watson and the other scientists who saw the need for a strong international report "wanted to break down the false skepticism that wasn't based on fact, but rather on things like, 'This is only American research' " (interview with Robert Watson). Watson made a special effort to include British scientists in the workshops but feels that he should have made a greater effort to include scientists from the developing countries and the Eastern bloc (interview). He attracted scientists to the workshops by emphasizing their professional value, stating that "the world's best atmospheric scientists would be there" and that "a document would come out of them that we could all be proud of" (interview with Ralph Cicerone). Some scientists from certain countries were invited to the workshops even if they had little to contribute, in the hope that they might stimulate interest at home. Overall, the rationale for the structure of the assessment was inherently political—to mitigate nationalistic biases. The timing of its publication—just before the international negotiations began—could hardly have been more fortuitous.[4]

The assessment, more than previous ones, concluded that "to really understand the processes which control atmospheric ozone and to predict perturbations, we are drawn into a study of the complete Earth system" (WMO/NASA 1986:2). Consequently, it delved more deeply than did past reports into trends that might modify the impact of the halogenated carbons on ozone, including reactions involving other trace gases as well as tropospheric, solar, and dynamic processes. Also more than past assessments, the 1986 volumes emphasized the issue of climate change more than just ozone depletion and increased ultraviolet radiation (UNEP/WG.151/Background 4). It devoted the bulk of its text to analyzing trends of trace gases and aerosols, tropospheric processes, and changes in the vertical distribution of ozone, all of which are climate issues.

Nonetheless, the policy implications of chapter 13, which modeled predictions of ozone changes, received by far the most attention. On the basis of continued release of halocarbons[5] at 1980 levels, one-dimensional models predicted an eventual global ozone loss by the end of the twenty-first century of between 5 and 8 percent. Two-dimensional models predicted an average 9 percent total ozone loss, with as much as 14 percent loss in the polar regions (WMO/NASA 1986:18). All models predicted that continued release of CFC-11 and -12 at the 1980 rate would reduce ozone by 40 percent or more at an altitude of forty kilometers (18). The report stressed that these predictions were strongly dependent on emission trends for other trace gases, most notably methane, nitrogen oxides, and carbon dioxide, and that these constituted the greatest source of uncertainty for the modeled predictions. The 1986 predictions are a bit gloomier than those in the 1982 and 1984 National Academy of Sciences reports, but not nearly as extreme as the ones made in the late 1970s (NRC 1982, 1984).

Observational data were also reported. Total column ozone measurements using the Dobson network indicated no significant trend between 1970 and 1984, although there was some evidence of losses in the upper stratosphere. These agreed with the modeled predictions. Measurements based on the Umkehr method (see section four of chapter Three) showed negative trends that were consistent with one-dimensional models, but that data was suspect because of interference from aerosol particles (WMO/NASA 1986:21).

Despite the uncertainties, especially with respect to emissions of trace gases, the general tone of the report is one of confidence. No major new chemical reactions had been discovered since the last assessment, many of the reaction rate coefficients had been refined, and the measured observations concurred with the models. In general, the report gives the impression that knowledge about atmospheric ozone had reached a plateau with no new major breakthroughs or controversies on the horizon. The only indication to the contrary is a brief reference to "a considerable decrease in Antarctic total ozone during the spring period since about 1968." Little is said about this phenomenon except that is "presently the subject of further analysis" (WMO/NASA 1986:20).

While the WMO/NASA study was the scientific basis of the negotiations, few if any of the policymakers read the actual document. In hindsight, Robert Watson, coordinator of the assessment, regrets that no executive summary was written (interview). Instead, policymakers had to rely on verbal summaries given by the scientists and knowledge brokers. Many of the technically knowledgeable people involved in the Vienna Convention proceedings continued to participate, including Robert Watson, the EPA's John Hoffman, Ivar Isaksen and Per Bakken from Norway, and Patrick Szell of Britain's Department of Environment, to name a few. UNEP's Coordinating Committee on the Ozone Layer (CCOL) also submitted summaries of the science to the negotiators; these were the most useful to the few negotiators from developing countries who participated in the talks (interview with Guy Brasseur).

Everyone agreed that the 1986 study represented an international consensus that constituted the scientific basis for the ensuing negotiations.

From a political perspective, the most interesting thing about the assessment is that it offered something for everybody. Those who did not perceive the problem as serious could argue that the predictions were not dire and would not come about for quite some time, that no total ozone losses had been detected with any certainty, and that the impact of CFCs would be tempered by rising levels of methane and other trace gases. Those who believed that the problem was grave could point to the fact that the models predicted more ozone loss than they had two years ago and that, consistent with the models, ozone losses had already been measured at certain altitudes and were predicted to become very large by the middle of the twenty-first century. They could also point to the potential folly inherent in relying on increased levels of greenhouse gases to mitigate the impact of CFCs. The 1986 assessment also benefited the scientists themselves. The need to clarify the remaining uncertainties led to a growing research budget for atmospheric scientists; by 1987, the NASA budget for ozone research had risen to about $100 million (interview with Robert Watson).

Those who took a pessimistic view of the WMO/NASA study brought to light an issue that would eventually become hotly debated and even shift the context of the negotiations. The atmospheric scientists, for all their sophisticated modeling, were ultimately dependent on economic projections of CFC growth rates for their own predictions of ozone depletion. These scientists, having little knowledge of economic trends, had arbitrarily chosen 1980 as a baseline date from which to draw their conclusions. A few individuals, particularly a group of ecologically minded knowledge brokers at the EPA, realized that projections premised on 1980 emissions were misleading for three reasons. First, the world had been in a recession at the time, and demand for CFCs is strongly correlated with economic growth. Second, in 1980, the United States had recently enacted its aerosol ban, and other countries did not seem likely to emulate its example, so the figures were artificially low. Third, the figures did not consider the burgeoning demand for CFC-113 in the electronics industry. Since predicted ozone depletion varied greatly with the quantity of CFCs emitted, this group of knowledge brokers took up the task of demonstrating the inadequacy of the 1980 baseline date and showing that the modeled predictions were much gloomier if more reliable economic data were applied.[6]

The political reception of the WMO/NASA assessment evinces much of what has been argued in the previous chapters regarding the discursive nature of knowledge and the interaction of science and politics. First, the very existence of such an international assessment was political, as was the method of assembling it. Second, the atmospheric science itself could not stand alone, for it was fundamentally tied to economic projections, and these were in turn intertwined with interests and values. Third, the complexity and uncertainty inherent in the science allowed the contending political factions to interpret the report's conclusions in ways that bolstered their own preconceptions—in spite of the fact that the science was more refined than at any previous time. Fourth, the purpose of the document, which contained no new science, was to inform political leaders. All this suggests that the WMO/NASA assessment was not merely scientific but *trans*-scientific. The issues addressed, and the manner in which they are addressed, straddle the line between what are ordinarily considered science and politics.

Meetings Preceding the Negotiations

After the international community failed to adopt control measures as part of the Vienna Convention, it was clear that a consensus was needed on critical scientific and economic issues before a political agreement could evolve. UNEP decided that the best vehicle for forging such a consensus would be a two-part workshop focusing on economic issues and a separate conference on health and environmental issues, both of which were held outside the actual negotiating context. The workshops were also part of the settlement of the 1984 lawsuit brought against the EPA by the Natural Resources Defense Council (NRDC).[7] In January 1986, the EPA unveiled its Stratospheric Ozone Protection Plan, to be coordinated by John Hoffman, which called for new scientific and policy assessments and for a series of domestic and international workshops.

During the Vienna Convention negotiations, according to Ambassador Benedick, those who had advocated adopting control provisions "may have put the cart before the horse: [they were] trying, in effect, to make a risk management decision before conducting a risk assessment" (quoted in Roan 1989:154). Though I take issue with Benedick's dichotomy between science and politics, there is little doubt that the atmosphere during the prenegotiation events was less political than that at a negotiating session simply because there was no formal bargaining. Moreover, while science did not provide a set of objective, value-free facts from which a political consensus could be forged, the ontological dimension of the facts was undeniably present. For instance, the existence of the 1986 WMO/NASA assessment made it very difficult for anybody to question whether ozone could be destroyed by CFCs.

The first part of the economic workshop, held in Rome during May 1986, was "a grave disappointment, characterised by bad temper and disagreement" (UNEP 1989:8). Indeed, given the utter lack of concordance at this meeting, it is remarkable that the Montreal Protocol was negotiated in just over a year. There was not even agreement on figures for current production, use, emissions, and trade, much less than on future trends. UNEP had sent out 170 requests for data and had received only 18 responses, which led the most skeptical participants, especially the delegate from France, to question whether anything significant could be said about production. Although most participants agreed that data provided by the Chemical Manufacturers Association (CMA) accounted for 85 percent of all production for CFC-11 and -12, the fact that some countries, most significantly China, had not even begun compiling data added fuel to the skeptics' fire (UNEP/WG.151/Background 1). Those who favored stringent controls pointed out that the CMA figures did not include CFC-113, which was the fastest-growing market.

With such a lack of consensus on current production, the level of uncertainty was foreseeably much greater for future projections. Industry argued forcefully that it had no plans to expand. And while the CMA had recorded 7 percent yearly increases in CFC production for 1983 and 1984, those who had an interest in predicting slow growth, and thus low ozone perturbation, pointed out that two years were not enough to establish a trend (annex I, UNEP/WG.148/2:1). Anticipating industry's position, John Hoffman of the EPA contracted with three separate firms to study the same thing: future growth rates for CFCs. The studies each predicted growth rates between 2.5 and 4 percent, making industry's position untenable after the Rome workshop (interview with John Hoffman).

Regarding costs and effects of CFC controls, the discussion focused on aerosol controls. A study done by ICF and commissioned by the EPA had found that switching from CFCs to hydrocarbons in the United States resulted in savings to both industry and consumers (annex II, UNEP/WG.148/2:2). Those findings were strongly attacked by the British and the French, who declared that European consumers preferred the finer mist produced by CFC aerosols (annex III, UNEP/WG.148/2:3). This section of the workshop concluded that "studies provide no comprehensive basis for estimates of the cost and effects of CFC controls" (annex III, UNEP/WG.148/2:4).

What is interesting from an analytical perspective (though it is not surprising) is that accepted knowledge was tightly linked to the political and economic interests of the principal antagonists, the USA and the European Communities (EC).[8] Representatives from the EPA insisted that trends could be predicted from existing production statistics and that growth would accelerate. As discussed in the previous chapter, the EC's CFC industry was operating at only about 65 percent capacity and was the world's top exporter, while American industry was operating at nearly full capacity and was threatened with further domestic regulation. Thus, the EC opposed strict controls and favored a cap on production capacity. Within the EC was a range of positions, with the British and French protecting ICI and Atochem, respectively, by emphasizing the uncertainties, and the Dutch coming closest to the American position. Because of its dependence on CFCs for its microelectronics industry, Japan tended to side with the EC. China, with its plans to expand its refrigeration industry massively, predictably raised the same kinds of doubts as the British and the French (interview with Michael Gibbs).

Just three weeks after the Rome meeting, UNEP and the EPA cosponsored the International Conference on the Health and Environmental Effects of Ozone Modification and Climate Change. The UNEP/EPA conference, which was attended by scientists and officials from approximately twenty countries, resulted in a four-volume publication (Titus 1986). Dozens of paper were delivered, but, unlike the economics workshop, there was little time for discussion and debate. The topics included atmospheric modeling; the effects of ultraviolet radiation on human health, agriculture, and marine systems; and the impact of global climate change.[9] Although the conference, like the 1986 WMO/NASA report, the conference introduced no new science, it was nonetheless important for providing the most comprehensive compilation to date on a range of issues related to ozone depletion, especially health and biological effects (interview with Stephen Seidel).

One striking feature of the conference is the extent to which the issue of climate change dominated the agenda; nearly twice as many papers were delivered on this topic as on ozone modification and ultraviolet radiation. According to Lee Thomas:

> [Atmospheric] science tells us that ozone depletion and global warming are inexorably interconnected. However, the domestic and international politics surrounding each issue are separate and unique. Combining the two in one conference had the potential to confuse and compound the political

controversy surrounding each issue. Separating the issues would fail to address their physical interdependence. In the end the choice was clear: we resolved this issue by recognizing that this conference is first and foremost a scientific meeting, not a political one, and therefore it should be organized around the science. (1986:27)

For some environmentalists at UNEP and the EPA, the ozone issue was nested within the larger and more complex climate issue, and an agreement on the former could be used as a springboard for dealing with the latter (interview with James Losey). Although the issues were linked, during both the scientific conference and the meetings of UNEP's CCOL, they rarely were coupled in the policy debates. Brief mention was often made of the fact that CFCs would account for almost one-quarter of the anticipated rise in global temperature in the twenty-first century (UNEP 1987b:25), so regulating these compounds would be a partial solution to the problem of greenhouse warming. But otherwise, scientific discourse and policy discourse diverged, with the latter framing the problem of ozone depletion strictly in terms of increased ultraviolet radiation. This is particularly remarkable given that the major scientific studies since 1984 had framed the issue substantially in terms of climate (NRC 1984; WMO/NASA 1986). The issue of ozone depletion, defined narrowly, was perceived as politically manageable, whereas the climate issue was a much greater challenge (interviews with Stephen Seidel and Robert Watson).

At the second session of the economic workshop, held in Leesburg, Virginia, near Washington, D.C., in September 1986, "trust was built up, and for the first time an obvious international will to forge a successful protocol emerged" (UNEP 1989:9). The divergent outcomes of the two sessions are surprising, given that the first session addressed production and emission issues, whereas the second took on the more contentious problem of alternative regulation strategies. Because the modeled predictions of the atmospheric scientists were so tightly coupled to economics, a common understanding had to be reached in this domain before a protocol could be adopted. Moreover, if substitutes and alternatives for CFCs were not feasible in the foreseeable future, then adoption of a protocol might be blocked simply for pragmatic reasons. Thus, the workshop addressed current production data, CFC growth projections, the costs and benefits of regulatory scenarios, and technical control options. It examined these issues not simply as a prelude to international regulation but also because good science had to be based on good economic data (UNEP/WG.151/Background 1).

The second session was characterized by a very strong U.S. presence. At

least in part because of the meeting's location, the USA had fourteen official participants. Britain, with the next largest number, had four. Thirty-
one papers were presented, nearly half of which were from the United
States. While some of these were from industry, eleven papers were presented by the EPA and its contractors, Rand and ICF. It is clear from the
proceedings that the EPA was extremely well prepared; if it did not dominate the meeting, it was certainly the strongest and most well-organized
delegation in attendance.

As in the June UNEP/EPA conference, little new scientific knowledge
was presented, and the few strictly scientific papers agreed on their modeled predictions of ozone depletion (papers 8, 9, and 11, UNEP/WG.151/
Background 2). More important than the knowledge communicated, however, was how the various policy proposals were justified through the science. The papers presented by EPA officials and contractors are particularly interesting; many of them are well-crafted interpretations of science
designed to advance the cause of a strong regulatory protocol. As a consequence of how they framed the issues, the knowledge brokers from the
EPA were able to highlight certain issues and increase the sense of urgency
among the participants. Two papers by John Hoffman, chairman of the
EPA's Stratospheric Ozone Protection Task Force, are especially noteworthy. In one, he focuses on the long atmospheric lifetimes of CFCs, citing
such statistics as that 84 percent of the CFC-11 emitted in 1987 will still
be in the atmosphere by 2000, and 56 percent by 2030. He also broaches
what he called the "chlorine-loading" issue, stating that, given the presence
of past emissions in the atmosphere, stabilizing concentrations at present
levels would require an immediate 85 percent cutback in CFC emissions
(annex I, UNEP/WG.148/3:5). I will argue later that this mode of framing the scientific information was instrumental in shifting the discourse
toward action based on the precautionary principle and that this formula-
tion gained much of its credibility from discovery of the Antarctic ozone
hole.

In his second paper, Hoffman applies Ivar Isaksen's two-dimensional
model (Stordal and Isaksen 1986) to show that global CFC emissions
would need to be lower than 1980 levels in order to limit total depletion
to 2 percent and depletion at 50 degrees latitude to 5 percent (paper 13,
UNEP/WG.148/3). Without explicitly addressing it, Hoffman's analysis
reveals the inadequacy of the EC's proposed production capacity cap,
which would have permitted far greater ozone depletion. Another EPA
paper by Stephen Seidel directly addresses the EC's proposal for a produc-

tion capacity cap in terms of its impact on ozone depletion (annex I, UNEP/WG.148/3:31). Seidel shows that, were the proposal to be adopted, 7 percent total ozone depletion would occur by 2050 and 14 percent by 2075, with far worse depletion at the northern latitudes. Never do Seidel and Hoffman argue against the EC position on political grounds, although it was patently unfair to U.S. industry, requiring it to halt at current production levels while EC industry could have expanded by as much as 40 percent. Rather, their papers simply framed scientific information in ways that supported a strong protocol.

In their papers, two EPA contractors focus on the costs of postponing regulation (papers 5 and 12 of annex I, UNEP/WG.148/3).[10] The first, by James Hammitt of Rand, concludes that immediate controls would be the most cost-effective option if the likelihood that further emission reductions would be required exceeded 0.3 to 0.5. Although the Antarctic ozone hole was not discussed, the implication is that a greater than 50 percent chance that it was CFC-induced should entail prompt regulation. A paper by Michael Gibbs of ICF surveys various control strategies and argues that since only a limited chlorine burden is tolerable, the most prudent policy would be to control the worst ozone depleters first. The implication is that the fully halogenated CFCs should be regulated but that eventually compounds like HCFC-22, methyl chloroform, and carbon tetrachloride might have to be considered.

The EC, unlike the USA, presented its position with little analysis in terms of the atmospheric models, despite the fact that two of the four purely scientific papers were from the Commission of the European Communities (CEC). If the CFC-ozone issue was truly science-driven, as I believe it was,[11] and science is a key source of legitimacy in modern society, as I have argued above, then focusing on economic issues with little scientific support was unlikely to advance the EC position.

The EPA papers, on the other hand, did not promote any particular policy position;[12] rather, they sought to demonstrate the inadequacy of weak proposals and move the terms of the dominant discourse toward precautionary action. In his opening remarks at the Leesburg meeting, Fitzhugh Green, the EPA's associate administrator, urged the participants to focus on the concepts of "inevitability and timeliness" (UNEP/WG.148/3:2). In other words, some ozone depletion was inevitable, and the effects of CFCs would occur long after their emission. Indeed, in one way or another, all of the EPA papers shared one underlying objective: to shift the context of debate by extending the relevant time frame well into the next century. To this end, the EPA and its contractors emphasized the long atmospheric life-times of CFCs and the long-term modeled predictions.

An overview of the science was presented at the end of the workshop by Robert Watson, coordinator of the WMO/NASA assessment. One of his main points was that ozone responds to the total burden of stratospheric chlorine; it does not matter whether the source is CFC-11 or CFC-113, aerosol sprays or refrigerants. This fact strengthened the case of those who favored a comprehensive approach over controls on specific uses. Watson also advised the participants not to allow their awareness of the "Antarctic ozone phenomenon" to influence their approach to the protocol. He suggested that scientists should first complete an intensive one- to two-year investigation, after which the policymakers should reexamine their regulatory policies in light of the new scientific evidence (UNEP/WG.148/3:15). Watson's counsel was accepted by the workshop participants and later was adopted as a premise of the official negotiations.

By the end of the economic workshop, a consensus had emerged that CFC emissions should be controlled, although the degree and timing of regulation were far from clear. The sense of consensus was so great that Fiona McConnell, leader of the British delegation, indicated that the meeting had laid the basis for a new way of thinking and urged the delegates to adjourn two hours early. Industry seemed to recognize the imminence of precautionary action and was beginning to ask that governments "provide clearer signals to the marketplace" (annex II, UNEP/WG.148/3:3). For the first time, the Soviet Union and some smaller nations divulged their production data, adding to the mood of openness (UNEP/WG.148/3:14). In his concluding remarks as the session's chairman, Ambassador Benedick confidently proclaimed that "the ingenuity, good will, and sense of responsibility" that had characterized the meeting would infuse the upcoming negotiations with "the spirit of Leesburg" (annex II, UNEP/WG.148/3:3).

U.S. Industry Shifts Its Position

Within days of the workshop's conclusion, it was apparent that U.S. industry was not immune to the "spirit of Leesburg." Both Du Pont, the world's number one CFC producer, and the Alliance for a Responsible CFC Policy, the lobbying group representing over five hundred U.S. CFC producers and users, announced their support for an international protocol that would limit global emissions (Alliance for Responsible CFC Policy 1987:I-

1). Du Pont also announced that alternatives to CFCs could be available in about five years (Du Pont 1986) Although industry's announcements were cautiously worded and fell far short of endorsing the 50 percent reductions eventually negotiated, they were perceived by many participants as a major breakthrough (interviews with Lee Thomas, Richard Benedick, and Alan Miller). Yet the shift was greeted with skepticism by Europeans and Japanese. They feared that their American competitors were backing controls because they already had CFC substitutes available to fill the market (interviews with James Losey, Guy Brasseur, and Ivar Isaksen).

Du Pont claims that its change of heart was motivated by the 1986 WMO/NASA assessment (interview with Tony Vogelsburg). But since the conclusions there were certainly no more ominous than those in past studies, there is reason to doubt this claim. More important, it seems, was the fact that industry's projections of no future growth had been proven untenable. Once that fact was admitted and the choice appeared to be between domestic and international controls, U.S. industry's shift was not so surprising.

A principal goal of the Alliance, which was formed in 1980 in reaction to the EPA's notice of rule making (see section four of chapter 3), was to ensure that U.S. industry not be placed at a disadvantage relative to the world market. U.S. industry resented the fact that the United States had banned CFCs in aerosol propellants without the rest of the world following its lead. With the threat of further unilateral controls as a result of the NRDC suit and the surge of proregulatory discourse within the EPA, U.S. industry feared that the EPA would "let the U.S. go its own way and commit industrial suicide" (interview with Kevin Fay). Only an international agreement establishing a level playing field could prevent this.

Since U.S. industry supported an international approach and since it had become clear on the heels of the Leesburg meeting that some kind of regulatory protocol would be adopted, the change of heart was neither risky nor drastic. If controls were inevitable, then supporting a limit on worldwide CFC emissions made sense strategically. Although neither Du Pont nor the alliance specified what that limit might be, their position sounds very much like the EC position, the weakest one advanced at the time. Nonetheless, the discursive shift was significant in that it indicated both an acceptance that CFCs posed a potential problem and support for the upcoming negotiations.

Because the absence of alternatives counseled against a strict protocol, Du Pont's announcement that some CFC substitutes would be available within five years was seen as removing one impediment to a regulatory protocol. The controversy surrounding the issue of substitutes provides a good example of how an apparently factual question can actually be a matter of interpretation and politics. As the largest CFC producer and the leading researcher for replacement compounds, Du Pont was a major force in shaping the tone of the policy debates.

As late as March 1986, Du Pont claimed that there were "no foreseeable alternatives available" (interviews with James Hammitt and Stephen Seidel). Rand's report on market trends, published in May 1986, assumes the existence of "no remotely feasible alternatives" (Hammitt et al. 1986:7), and its authors claim to have obtained their data from industry (interview with James Hammitt). Yet within less than six months, Du Pont announced that some alternatives could be available in five years. No new scientific knowledge had been uncovered in the interim; Du Pont's research program for CFC alternatives had lain dormant since 1980. What had changed were perceptions, and these had changed on all sides of the debate.

Dr. Joseph P. Glas, manager of Du Pont's Freon Division, claims that Du Pont never changed its position and never misled EPA. He points out that Du Pont had announced in 1980 the conclusions of its six-year research program: that "seven to ten years may be necessary to reach commercial production for most alternatives, assuming all technical and toxicological programs yield favorable results" (Du Pont 1980:2). Glas also states that "chemistry was never the issue." Du Pont officials had testified before Congress that "without incentives, we couldn't make these chemicals," the implication being that a regulatory decision would spur the development of alternatives (interview with Joseph P. Glas). Put simply, the unavailability of substitutes was simply a function of the absence of a market.

One factor that was linked to Du Pont's apparent shift in policy concerning availability, although whether it was a cause or an effect of that policy remains a puzzle, was the replacement in July 1986 of Dr. Donald Strobach, a thoroughly committed skeptic of the Rowland-Molina hypothesis, by Dr. Joseph Steed as Environmental Manager for Du Pont's Freon Division. Until his departure, Strobach claimed that his company was so confident in the inadequacy of the Rowland-Molina hypothesis that it had abandoned its research on alternatives (Roan 1989:147). Steed was perceived as "more open-minded" by those at the EPA who were working on the ozone problem (interview with Stephen Seidel). When I questioned Steed about Du Pont's policy shift, he said,

There was *no shift in the availability, only in the perception* of the lengths to which people were willing to go to get [the substitutes]. Only regulation would force people to pay three times as much. By mid-1986 *I saw that future regulation was definite.* I concluded that there should be a real push for alternatives and that an international agreement was the only way to go. (emphasis added)

Thus, the issue of substitute availability, which appears to be a straightforward matter of fact, actually hinged on perceptions about market trends, and this in turn hinged on the political question of regulatory policy. Again, knowledge and interests, science and politics were closely intertwined.

The issue resembles a chicken-and-egg situation: without regulation, there could be no substitutes but, at least in the minds of many, without the promise of substitutes, there could be no regulation. However, it was obvious at the Leesburg meeting that an influential minority was intent on pursuing a protocol even in the absence of substitutes. Industry's admission that CFCs should be regulated was important in that it helped the negotiators to focus on the issues necessary to gain a consensus (Glas 1989:148; interview with Richard Benedick).

While the debate over substitute availability can easily be recast as a conflict over perceptions, the controversy surrounding predictions of future growth rates seems to be a more manifest case of deception on the part of industry. Many participants from the scientific and policy communities believe that they were intentionally misled by industry (interviews with Robert Watson, Stephen Seidel, James Hammitt, and Michael Gibbs). The modeled predictions for ozone loss were extremely sensitive to CFC growth rates; a freeze at 1980 levels would not have had disastrous consequences, but a 5 percent growth rate would have (WMO/NASA 1986). At an EPA-sponsored domestic workshop with industry in March 1986, industry representatives argued that low growth rates should be assumed.[13] They claimed that the refrigeration and automobile markets were saturated, while Rand analysts for the EPA countered that this was only true in the industrialized countries. Industry also claimed that it was facing a potential shortage of fluorospar, the mineral from which CFCs are derived. Rand and ICF countered with studies showing that "there was so much fluorospar in the mines that we could never figure out what to do with it."[14]

Working with data provided by industry and making their own economic predictions, the Rand authors predicted annual growth rates for CFCs averaging 3 percent (Hammitt et al. 1986). Industry claimed that these predictions were "wildly optimistic" (interview with Kevin Fay). In my interview with him, Joseph Glas maintained that the EPA-sponsored reports predicted 5 to 10 percent annual growth, which would have caused enormous ozone depletion. But the EPA's predicted growth rates were actually a little less than 3 percent, and these were later borne out (interview with Stephen Seidel). The Rand figure was in the middle range of those discussed at the Rome workshop, and though there never was an international consensus on future growth rates, Rand's estimates were cited frequently during the negotiations.

Notwithstanding U.S. industry's decision to support the talks, it continued to frame the available scientific knowledge in terms most favorable to a weak protocol. It repeatedly emphasized several key statements throughout the negotiations: there was enormous scientific uncertainty; additional research was essential; fears were based on unproven theory; there was no imminent danger; and no total ozone loss had been measured. While these statements were valid, they also disregarded other important facts. Although a great deal of uncertainty existed, much was known, and uncertainty could cut in both directions; reality could end up being worse than predicted, a possibility highlighted by the discovery of the Antarctic ozone hole. Perhaps the threat was not imminent, but it was nonetheless real and would be felt by future generations. And while no total ozone loss had been conclusively measured, losses were being measured in the upper stratosphere, and these were consistent with the models. In essence, all of industry's arguments reflected a short-term perspective, in contrast to the EPA's more long-term outlook. This is consistent with the analysis in chapter 2, which suggests that scientists, environmentalists, and knowledge brokers may be more likely than businessmen to think in intergenerational terms.

The Antarctic Ozone Hole

In May 1985, just two months after the Vienna Convention was adopted and during the final stages of preparation of the WMO/NASA assessment, a paper was published that would transform both scientific and political discourse on the ozone problem. Dr. Joseph Farman and his colleagues from the British Antarctic Survey reported that, for three consecutive years since October 1982, major losses of stratospheric ozone had occurred over Halley Bay (Farman, Gardiner, and Shanklin 1985). Although Farman did not try to explain the "hole,"[15] he stated that "chemical causes must be considered" and included a graph correlating atmospheric concentrations of CFCs, which his group had also been measuring, with ozone losses.

Because the Montreal Protocol negotiators explicitly decided to ignore the Antarctic hole, the causes of which had not been determined, it is difficult to argue that it played a major role in the negotiations. Nonetheless, after many interviews and much analysis, I believe that it did. Despite the fact that the hole had not been predicted by any of the models, it did not undermine the power of the scientists or the knowledge brokers. Instead, it changed the political context in which the negotiations occurred and made certain ways of framing the available knowledge more salient than others. The ozone hole created a sense of crisis that was conducive to the precautionary approach eventually sanctioned in the Montreal Protocol.[16] In the minds of many participants, the ozone losses over Antarctica represented a sudden change in the course of events, a change that indicated a dangerously high probability of ecological disaster. The existence of scientific uncertainty continued to function as a justification for caution, but the meaning of *caution* shifted dramatically. The hole was the clearest evidence that, not the CFC industry, it was the ozone layer that deserved to be treated as a fragile entity.

Farman initially found large ozone losses of more than 20 percent over Halley Bay in the austral spring of 1982, but, suspicious of the peculiar data, he repeated the measurements in 1983 and 1984 with new equipment. During the summer months, the ozone layer recovered almost completely. Farman's measurements, going back to 1957, when the Dobson station was established through the International Geophysical Year, constituted a good historical record for comparison. After recording ozone losses over 30 percent in 1984, Farman decided to publish his data.[17]

The discovery quickly sparked commotion within scientific circles, although it received little immediate attention either in the press or within government or industry (Brodeur 1986:84; UNEP 1989:8). One scientist describes the initial reaction of those who had been immersed in the issue: "It was totally unexpected. We scientists are professional skeptics. We looked at it in an almost perverse sense, filled with joy about something new, something we could learn about. If it was predicted, we wouldn't have learned anything" (interview with Richard Stolarski). Many scientists had reservations about Farman's paper, not so much because of the data, but because they had never heard of Farman and his group.[18] As Ralph Cicerone puts it, "the British Antarctic Survey is not exactly a household word. At the time, most of us had never heard of it [and] had no idea whether these people did good work. You couldn't automatically give credence to the work"(Roan 1989:129).

The first scientists to take Farman's work seriously were those on the NASA team responsible for satellite measurements. It was widely reported that NASA had programmed its computers to reject any anomalous measurements below 180 Dobson units since nothing in that range had ever been recorded. Fortunately, so the report went, the original data had been saved and, when reexamined, confirmed the Farman findings (Stolarski et al.:1986). In actuality, the data had not been rejected but flagged as anomalies and compared to available data from a ground-based Dobson station. The ground station data were later found to be erroneous, but since they were within a normal range, they cast doubt upon the aberrant satellite data (Pukelsheim 1990:542). This anecdote illustrates an important point: by the early 1980s, atmospheric scientists were so confident in their grasp of the ozone issue that they trusted their models implicitly and distrusted any findings that contradicted them (Gribbin 1988:112).

Once the Farman findings were accepted, the race was on to explain them. Although most scientists suspected that chlorine chemistry was involved,[19] "everybody hoped that the solution to such an interesting problem would be right within their field, because then they could explain it and would come out looking very smart" (interview with Richard Stolarski). Three major sets of hypotheses sprang up (*Science* 1986).[20] Of the three, only the first, based on chlorine chemistry (Solomon et al. 1986; Hamill, Toon, and Turco 1986; McElroy et al. 1986), had significant implications for the international negotiations. The papers by the Solomon and Hamill teams argued that "polar stratospheric clouds," formed in the extreme Antarctic cold, could provide surfaces for heterogenous reactions.[21] They maintained that chlorine could be sequestered on the clouds and then released as the clouds dissipated in the spring. The McElroy team suggested that, in addition to chlorine, the bromine found in fire extinguishers using halons could be a culprit. Other theorists sought a dynamical explanation (Mahlman and Fels 1986). And a third set suggested a link to the eleven-year solar cycle (Callis and Natarajan 1986). The journal *Geophysical Research Letters* published a special supplement in November 1986 devoted to theoretical accounts of the ozone hole.

Amid the theoretical debates, NASA's Robert Watson organized the first National Ozone Expedition (NOZE I) to study Antarctic ozone between August and October 1986. Balloon and ground-based measurements were taken of ozone, chlorine, and other chemicals. Susan Solomon, leader of NOZE I, broadcast a statement from Antarctica that chlorine chemistry was the culprit, unleashing a storm of controversy among the dynamicists who felt their theories had been overlooked or misunderstood (*New York Times* 1986). The evidence, however, was against the solar cycle hypothesis. The consensus was that only a second expedition, one that included measurements taken from aircraft, could dispel the uncertainties (interview with Robert Watson). Thus, preparations were being made for the Airborne Antarctic Ozone Experiment during the Montreal Protocol negotiations, but the data from that expedition were not available until after the treaty was signed.

One central fact about the Antarctic phenomenon stood out in stark relief for both scientists and policymakers: *it was not predicted by any atmospheric models.* Among the scientists, this was translated into a heightened sense of humility and a frantic investigative effort (interviews with Ralph Cicerone and Richard Stolarski). In policy circles, it led to a belief that the problem might be much worse than was previously thought and that stricter regulation could be necessary. In recalling the impact of the ozone hole on the negotiations, most of those I interviewed spoke in terms of fear and alarm, confirming that the hole generated some sense of crisis. Industry predictably emphasized that the causes were unknown, but their softened position soon after the publication of Farman's paper was probably no mere coincidence.[22]

Although the hole represented an enormous scientific anomaly, I have found no evidence that it overtly undermined the authority of the scientists. One participant argues that the hole prompted a major change in the scientists' attitudes, and when policymakers saw that the scientists were disturbed, they in turn became more concerned (interview with Alan Miller). The heightened sense of humility among atmospheric scientists helped to shift the policy discourse toward precautionary action. The hole's discovery also increased the prestige of those few scientists who, like F. S. Rowland, had urged strong regulatory measures from the beginning.

However, in a more subtle sense, the Antarctic phenomenon generated suspicion about the validity of the atmospheric models and opened the door to an alternative way of framing the scientific knowledge, one with far more radical policy implications. If it did not undermine the authority of the scientists, it did raise doubts about the science: the models had predicted approximately 2 percent total ozone depletion with constant 1980 CFC emissions (WMO/NASA 1986), and the models were wrong. But there was another way to frame the issue—one that did not rely on any models. As John Hoffman argued at the Leesburg meeting, an 85 percent reduction in CFC emissions would be necessary just to keep atmospheric chlorine levels constant (paper 2, UNEP/WG.148/3). His calculations required no modeling, only knowledge about production data and the compounds' atmospheric lifetimes. If the hole was caused by CFCs, suggesting a radically nonlinear relationship between CFC emissions and ozone depletion, there was good reason to want at least to freeze atmospheric chlorine concentrations.

Hoffman's chlorine-loading argument gained salience from the ozone hole for another reason. Because of the earth's weather patterns, most chemicals penetrate the stratosphere over the tropics. Ozone, however, is much more sensitive to chlorine at the higher latitudes, where at least some of the CFCs decompose because of their long atmospheric lifetimes. Thus, the latitude at which CFCs break apart makes a crucial difference, but there is no clear sense in the models of when CFCs release their chlorine. The extreme losses over Antarctica suggested that much of the chlorine could be released in the polar regions, which would mean that the models' had underestimated the threat. As one modeler explains, "the truth will be between the chlorine-loading perspective and the calculations based on ozone depletion potential, but the ozone hole gave credence to the chlorine-loading scheme" (interview with Guy Brasseur).

Hoffman's simple calculation received a great deal of publicity in congressional hearings and in the press (United States Senate 1987a:61; *Palm Beach Post* 1987; *Science* 1986:928). When the issue was framed in these terms, suddenly a phaseout did not seem like a drastic proposal. The decision to shift the debate from ozone depletion to concentrations was "a strategic one," according to Michael Gibbs. He recalls the decision as follows: "There was no new information here, just *a different way of framing it.* We thought: since the hole may be linked to concentrations, *let's shift the debate.* This also shifts the focus to the warming issue, and in general to the responsibility to the future. It would not have worked one year before; *it only worked because of the Antarctic hole*" (interview; emphasis added). In other words, the hole enhanced the status of a particular mode of scientific framing, one with explicitly political purposes: to promote an environmentalist agenda. Groups like the NRDC used the chlorine-loading analysis to promote sweeping controls; "85 percent became the line in the sand for environmentalists" (interview with James Losey).[23]

The hole had a more direct impact on one aspect of the protocol that was eventually adopted. Because its causes were not known and because it illustrated clearly how quickly both natural systems and scientific knowledge about them could change, EPA administrator Lee Thomas argued successfully for a provision in the text for a periodic scientific update, followed by additional control measures if necessary.

All the individuals I interviewed believe that some kind of agreement would have been reached even without the Antarctic ozone hole. The combination of the 1986 WMO/NASA assessment and the recognition that CFC production was increasing would probably have been enough, they claim, to have led to an agreement. They also believe, however, that the resulting protocol would have been significantly less stringent than a 50 percent cutback and that certain countries might not have been party to it. For most of them, the large amount of press attention devoted to the issue permeated the political milieu during the negotiations. A colorful time-lapse videotape assembled by NASA from satellite data dramatically depicted the hole emerging over Antarctica. That segment, which was shown on national television and in congressional hearings, had a powerful effect on its audiences (interviews with Michael Gibbs and Stephen Seidel). The environmental movement certainly received more media attention, and possibly greater deference, as a result of the Antarctic hole, particularly in the United States where the ozone issue was politically popular (interviews with Alan Miller and Rafe Pomerance). Those who opposed a strong protocol thought it extremely important "not to let the publicity [about the ozone hole] get dragged into the debates" (interview with David Gibbons).

The timing of the Antarctic discovery could not have been much better for it to have a major political impact. The Farman paper was published just after the Vienna Convention had been signed, before the negotiations had resumed, and too late to contribute meaningfully to the 1986 WMO/NASA report. It also coincided with the growing understanding that, with new economic trends, CFC emissions rates would be increasing. Because the hole was expressly ignored, it is something of a wild card in developing an explanation of political events. However, few people can ignore a hole the size of the continental USA, and very few politicians can ignore massive publicity. Despite the lack of a scientific consensus on its causes or, ironically, maybe partly because of that lack, the hole dramatically altered the political context of the negotiations, and it altered the acceptability of various modes of framing scientific knowledge. The hole contributed to a discursive shift toward precautionary action, lending support to those who believed that the consequences of underreacting were worse than the consequences of overreacting. In the face of widespread scientific uncertainty and enormous risk, this mode of framing the debate was a force to reckoned with.

Evolution of the U.S. Position

In November 1986, the U.S. Department of State sent a draft position paper to its embassies around the world to get feedback from foreign governments. During the previous summer, the EPA and the State Department's Bureau of Oceans and International Environmental and Scientific Affairs (OES), had convened interagency meetings to develop the U.S. position, but there was little interest from other agencies.[24] This essentially gave the EPA and OES free reign to devise the position (interview with Richard Benedick). Their draft paper called for a near-term freeze on the consumption[25] of CFC-11, -12, and -113, as well as Halon-1211 and -1301; a scheduled phaseout of these compounds; and periodic policy reviews based on new scientific knowledge (U.S. Department of State 1986).

The U.S. negotiating position grew out of an interesting set of interrelated political and scientific considerations. The EPA was under some pressure to promote stringent controls because of the pending NRDC suit, but the proposed phaseout went beyond what the NRDC had expected and probably further than would have been legally necessary.[26] According to EPA staff who were deeply involved in working out the position, the NRDC suit was only a secondary consideration (interviews with James Losey and Stephen Seidel). More important was the belief on the part of the EPA and OES that, despite the scientific uncertainties, the risks demanded precautionary intervention. During the debates, both domestic and international, they argued for "a prudent insurance policy," even without the Antarctic ozone hole (Benedick 1987). But the hole clearly and dramatically drew attention to those risks.

The State Department's framework protocol, like most draft positions, did not specify numbers and dates; it simply provided the general authority to negotiate for a scheduled phaseout. The decision to call for reductions of 95 percent by 2000 was initially made by two EPA staff members who "just decided to fill in the blanks and the brackets." They thought that "if [they] asked for the whole ball of wax, [they] would be likely to get more" (interview with James Losey).

But the casual revisions of a couple of EPA staff officers could hardly have become the official U.S. negotiating position without the support of EPA administrator Lee Thomas. From the beginning of his tenure in office, Thomas took a considerable interest in the ozone issue.[27] And, having just implemented a phaseout of asbestos, Thomas may have been more amenable to a CFC phaseout (interview with John Hoffman). One of his first actions was to order a major regulatory impact analysis on the protection of stratosphere ozone by means of reducing CFC, which was released in the fall 1986 (EPA 1986a). The extent of Thomas's concern is evident in the fact that he personally addressed the gathering at the EPA's domestic workshop in March 1986, announcing what to many seemed to be the EPA's new precautionary perspective on ozone depletion:

> In the face of all this scientific uncertainty, one might ask why has the EPA embarked on programs to assess the risk and to decide whether additional CFC regulations are necessary? Why not simply adopt a "wait-and-see" attitude and hold off a decision until depletion is actually confirmed? Let me address this question squarely. EPA does not accept, as a precondition for decision, empirical verification that ozone depletion is occurring. . . . *We may need to act in the near term to avoid letting today's "risk" become tomorrow's "crisis."* (quoted in Brodeur 1986:86; emphasis added)

Thomas's decision to press for a virtual phaseout was based on both scientific and political factors, though he tends to emphasize the former in explaining it. The political impetus behind Thomas's decision is evident in a statement he made to me: "It became clear to me that we had to get rid of these chemicals domestically, that either the NRDC lawsuit was going to drive us in that direction, or Congress was going to, or I was going to." Yet he believes that "the scientists were the driving force behind the U.S. position" and recalls that when he looked at the data, he concluded that CFCs had to be banned. Thomas believed that regulation was required despite the scientific uncertainties and that periodic policy reviews should be held as the uncertainties were resolved, a provision that was eventually included in the final protocol (interview).

Thomas's perception that scientists were the driving force behind the U.S. position is somewhat surprising in light of the fact that very few scientists offered any policy recommendations and that most of those who did thought a 50 percent cut would be enough (interviews with Ralph

Cicerone, Nien Dak Sze, and Robert Watson). Watson, for instance, testified before Congress that "the science doesn't justify a 95 percent cut" and
expressed concern that the rush could promote unsafe alternatives (United
States Congress 1987b:90). Dr. Daniel Albritton of NOAA, the other
major U.S. scientist coordinating ozone research, continued to harbor
doubts about the CFC-ozone link (interview with Ralph Cicerone). Since
Watson and Albritton were the two top scientists advising policymakers on
the ozone layer, it is difficult to see how they could have been the "driving
force" behind the U.S. position.

Rather than the science itself, it was Thomas's interpretation of the science and his own philosophical orientation to the problem of risk that
drove his decision. This is clear from his response to my questions regarding his disagreement with William Graham, President Reagan's science
adviser and a staunch opponent of any regulatory measures. Thomas
recalls that, "Graham looked at it from a purely scientific perspective,
whereas I looked at it from more of a policy perspective. Where there was
uncertainty, he thought we needed more research, and I thought we needed to be cautious. We just looked at the same thing and came to two different conclusions" (interview). Thus, there was no clear line between science and politics, and, as I have argued above, all the parties attempted to
legitimate their policy positions scientifically.

When representatives from industry learned of the U.S. position, they
registered their discontent with the Departments of Commerce and
Energy, sparking a series of intense interagency debates that persisted
throughout most of the international negotiations. Recognizing the per-
vasiveness of CFCs in consumer goods, particularly in the import sector,
the Department of Commerce feared that hasty regulation could disrupt
the U.S. economic infrastructure (interview with Ed Shykind). The
Department of Energy was primarily concerned that CFC regulation
would endanger the foam insulation industry, which had grown rapidly
as a result of the oil crises during the 1970s (interview with David Gibbons). The Pentagon entered into the debates to defend its access to
halons, chemicals used to extinguish fires in places where water might
damage equipment or pose a health risk (interview with Ed Shykind).
The Department of the Interior also became involved in the issue, osten-
sibly because of its role as the largest manager of U.S. lands, though most
participants believe the real reasons stemmed from the antiregulatory
ideology of the secretary and his staff (interviews with David Gibbons
and Stephen Seidel).

Once the Department of State lost control of the interagency process, having no substantive expertise on ozone, it could not regain it (interview with Eileen Claussen). Under the auspices of the Office of Management and Budget, David Gibbons convened a series of weekly and biweekly interagency meetings that spanned a period of several months.[28] The meetings were designed to educate political appointees and senior career officers on the scientific and economic aspects of the ozone problem in order to develop "a solid, well-informed presidential decision" (interview with David Gibbons). However, because the fractious interagency meetings paralleled the international negotiations and spilled out into the press, the U.S. negotiating position was apparently weakened by them (Doniger 1988:89).[29]

Throughout the debates, the risk was framed largely as one of increased rates of skin cancer attributable to ozone depletion. Yet this narrow mode of framing the issue ultimately undermined the policy position of those who adopted it.[30] In her presentations at the interagency meetings, cancer specialist Dr. Margaret Kripke emphasized that although skin cancer receives a great deal of media attention in the United States, it was a mistake both scientifically and politically to focus on it. Instead, she argued that, from a scientific perspective, the three most serious issues were the impact of increased ultraviolet radiation on the human immune system, on the world's food supplies, and on aquatic ecosystems. She also foresaw that since skin cancer only affects Caucasians who spend a lot of time in the sun, international cooperation would depend on framing the issue differently (interview with Margaret Kripke).

The turning point in the interagency wranglings may have come with Interior Secretary Donald Hodel's imprudent statement that the administration should consider a policy of "personal protection" instead of international precautionary action. He suggested that a public relations campaign could be launched to encourage the use of sunglasses and sunscreen, without violating the administration's philosophy of minimal government regulation (*Washington Post* 1987c). The public outcry was swift and intense. A *New York Times* editorial lamented that Hodel's "meddling" threatened to undermine the international negotiations and "force the United States from a widely admired position of leadership into humiliating retreat" (1987b). Environmentalists responded to Hodel's proposal by wearing hats and sunglasses at a press conference and calling for his resignation (*Los Angeles Times* 1987 and *Washington Post* 1987d). David Doniger's statement that "fish don't wear sunglasses," which was cited throughout the press accounts, exposed the folly inherent in defining the issue narrowly in terms of skin cancer.

Secretary of State George Shultz temporarily resolved the issue by instructing his negotiators to continue working for an international agreement until the issue could be resolved at the cabinet level (*Washington Post* 1987e:A-13). The original 95 percent position was not revoked, primarily because "it had already been put out on the street" (interview with David Gibbons). But the U.S. delegation received instructions to press only for a 50 percent reduction in CFCs and a freeze on halons (Doniger 1988:90).

Those who opposed stringent controls received one important concession, viewed by environmentalists as undercutting U.S. support for an agreement. At the final meeting in Montreal, the U.S. delegation was instructed to propose that the treaty only take effect when countries representing 90 percent of all consumption had signed it. The purpose of this stipulation was to ensure that the United States would not have to reduce CFCs faster than nonsignatory countries. It was also intended to put public pressure on all countries to sign (interview with Lee Thomas). Environmentalists complained that the concession effectively gave both Japan and the Soviet Union veto power over the treaty's entry into force (Doniger 1988:90).

While the final U.S. position was somewhat weaker than that originally proposed, it was also stronger in one important respect. Because of the contentiousness of the American policy process, the U.S. position was personally approved by President Reagan, whereas no other country's position was approved at the cabinet level. Lee Thomas, who led the U.S. delegation in Montreal, claims that this gave him "the strongest position of anyone going into the final negotiations" (interview).

Despite the interagency squabbles, there was one point on which all sides, including U.S. industry, agreed: a global problem required a global solution. No Americans wanted to repeat the experience of the late 1970s, when the United States banned CFCs in aerosols while most of the rest of the world did nothing. Because further domestic regulation was likely, spurred on by both the NRDC lawsuit and the scientific predictions, there was a consensus that a global treaty was necessary so that U.S. industry would not be put at a disadvantage. Just before the second round of negotiations, Senators Chafee and Baucus sent such a message to the rest of world, introducing legislation that would have cut CFC use domestically by 95 percent and blocked all imports containing or manufactured with the chemicals (S. 570; S. 571). On June 5, 1987, the Senate passed a resolution strongly endorsing the original negotiating position and calling for the virtual elimination of ozone-depleting chemicals (U.S. Senate Resolution 226). The bills and the resolution were intended to support the EPA and the State Department in negotiating a strong protocol; they gave Ambassador Benedick, leader of the U.S. delegation prior to the Montreal meeting, "an important bargaining tool" (interview with Richard Benedick).

Thus, the U.S. bargaining position grew out of a complex set of scientific and political considerations. Predictably, since science was the predominant legitimating force, the negotiators emphasize the former in relating their stories. As with the Antarctic ozone hole, the mode of framing the science had important political implications. Those who defined the issue solely in terms of skin cancer became the objects of political embarrassment when they publicized their views, despite the fact that most of EPA's research on the effects of ozone depletion dealt with skin cancer. Beyond the domestic consensus in favor of a global treaty, the nature of the U.S. national interest was not initially obvious. Rather, it evolved through a process of internal debate that blended both science and politics. As that interest was clarified and formulated into a negotiating position, the United States was able to use its economic leverage as a major importer to sway the international negotiations toward precautionary action.

The Negotiations

As the first round of negotiations opened in December 1986, the two principal adversaries were the European Community and what had been called the Toronto Group prior to the Vienna Convention. The USA was the largest and most outspoken member of the latter group, which included Canada, Norway, Sweden, Finland, Switzerland, and New Zealand. A third group, including Australia and some developing countries, was initially neutral, but later moved closer to the U.S. position (Benedick 1989:48).

The EC's position was strongly influenced by industry; in fact, industry representatives sat on the delegations of some EC countries. Britain, France, and Italy, three of the EC's four major CFC producers, endorsed a cap on production capacity, with Japan and the USSR sympathizing with this position. Japan played a relatively passive role, perhaps assuming that the EC position would prevail. The EC argued that significant ozone depletion would not occur for decades, allowing time for further study before cutting production. This group distrusted the motives behind the U.S. position, suspecting that such a drastic regulatory proposal coming out of the Reagan administration could only mean that U.S. industry had secretly developed CFC substitutes (interviews with Guy Brasseur and Kevin Fay). Within the EC, however, was a diversity of opinion. West Germany, the Netherlands, Denmark, and Belgium favored stricter controls, but only Germany was a major producer. Other EC countries were not active participants.

The internal structure of the EC influenced both the pace of the talks and the content of its negotiating positions. The commission itself cannot make binding decisions; only the Council of Ministers can. The environmental ministers, however, only met twice yearly, whereas the negotiations were proceeding at a much faster pace. With no good common denominator among the various positions of its member states, the EC position was vague; the sole area of consensus was on the need for further research (interview with Guy Brasseur). Complicating the matter was the fact that each country was represented at the meetings, but an internal agreement said that the EC would speak with a single voice. From the U.S. perspective, the EC's requirement of unanimity made it "a difficult and inflexible negotiating partner" (Benedick 1989:48).

At the December meeting in Geneva, there was overall agreement dating from the Leesburg workshop that some precautionary action was necessary, but the EC's proposed production capacity cap was very far from the virtual phaseout proposed by the USA. The EC was willing to discuss a freeze but would not move beyond that (UNEP/WG.151/L.4). Both sides acknowledged the need to develop safe alternatives to CFCs, and both justified their positions in terms of economic "knowledge," arguing that their proposals would "exploit the law of supply and demand" by raising the prices of CFCs and forcing producers to seek safe substitutes (*Wall Street Journal* 1986). The United States and its supporters argued that a freeze or a production cap would not accomplish this goal quickly enough and that, if drastic reductions turned out to be required in the future, the social cost would be much higher. Most importantly, the USA argued that, because of the long atmospheric lifetimes of CFCs, a delay in reductions would allow unacceptable levels of chlorine to accumulate. Hence, the debate between the United States and the EC was really over the appropriate time frame to employ in formulating an international regulatory policy.

The United States showed some flexibility in its position at the first negotiating session, but this was interpreted by congressional advocates of a strong protocol as a "backing off." During Senate hearings held in January 1987, Senator Chafee chastised Ambassadors John Negroponte, head of the OES, and Richard Benedick, the lead negotiator, for vacillating. He stated that "when we got to Geneva, the Government of the United States had changed its position. It was no longer a near-term freeze, but it was a meaningful near-term first step to reduce significantly. Step two was no longer a long-term strategy and goals for coping with the problem. Frankly, I think that we have to push you folks and, if this fails, go it alone" (United States Senate 1987a:49).

Benedick shrewdly turned the congressional criticism, along with the legislation introduced by Senators Chafee and Baucus that threatened to ban imports made with CFCs, to his advantage at the next meeting.[31] When the delegates convened in Vienna that February, Benedick was very critical of "other nations [that] were more concerned with short-term economic gains instead of the well-being of future generations" (UNEP/WG.167/2:6). He adroitly depicted himself as a victim of domestic pressure, informing the delegates of the pending legislation designed "to protect our industry from imports from countries which continue to ignore the threat to the global environment" (Benedick 1987:17).

Benedick's use of scientific knowledge to support his position is particularly interesting. In addition to mentioning the predictions of computer models, he claimed that "both satellite and land-based measurements suggest that the process of ozone destruction may already be under way" (Benedick 1987:17). Since the group had decided to ignore the Antarctic ozone hole, the reference here must be to Donald Heath's satellite measurements and the data from certain Dobson stations, both of which were considered highly unreliable (see section four of chapter 3). Benedick's allusion to measured ozone loss also contradicted his later assertion that the Montreal Protocol was a preventive action, "based at the time not on measurable evidence of ozone depletion or increased radiation but rather on scientific hypotheses" (1989:43: 1991:2). In his address to the Vienna meeting, Benedick framed the issue in terms of chlorine loading, citing Hoffman's calculation that an immediate 85 percent reduction in CFCs would be necessary to keep atmospheric concentrations stable. As discussed above, this mode of framing, which does not depend upon computer models, became more salient with the discovery of the Antarctic ozone hole and lent support to the U.S. proposal to phase out CFCs. Benedick's statement illustrates the political employment of knowledge: partial truths and skillful framing of the available information can lend persuasive power to one's position.

The strength of the U.S. position at the second session bore fruit as the EC reluctantly began to consider reductions of 20 percent. The EC's new flexibility, however, arose not merely from the persuasiveness of the U.S. position but from growing dissent within its own membership. West Germany in particular was moving in the direction of stringent controls. The German government, to a greater extent than most other European governments, was supportive of and receptive to the atmospheric science (interviews with Robert Watson and Ivar Isaksen). The 1986 WMO/NASA assessment was cosponsored by a German agency, and several major scientific meetings had been held in West Germany. More important, though, was the growing political influence of the West German environmental movement. After the Green Party's impressive electoral showing in 1986, the government succumbed to pressure to back an aerosol ban and a long-term phaseout (Doniger 1988:90). By the second negotiating session, Germany was planning unilateral cuts of 50 percent and urging other EC members to reciprocate (Benedick 1991:96). France and the U.K., however, remained steadfast in their opposition.

At the February meeting, some countries that until then had shown little concern began to move toward the U.S. position. The Australian representative spoke of the high incidence of skin cancer in his country and the consequent interest in protecting the ozone layer. The delegate from Argentina noted that the ozone losses over Antarctica extended near his country's southern borders and registered his support for control measures. Yet, along with representatives from Thailand and Egypt, the Argentine delegate insisted on a protocol based on the principle that "the polluter must pay" (UNEP/WG.167/2:7).

There was unanimous agreement among the participants at the second session that CFC-11 and -12 should be subject to regulation, but little agreement beyond that. Many permutations were suggested from a list that included five CFCs, carbon tetrachloride, methyl chloroform, and Halon-1211 and -1301. The Japanese delegate maintained that CFC-113 should not be regulated because no viable substitutes were available and it would contribute only 10 percent to ozone depletion. While the Japanese information was correct, others pointed out that CFC-113 production was growing faster than that any of the other compounds.

Another contentious issue was whether production or consumption should be controlled. The EC sought to control production on the grounds of simplicity, since there were innumerable points of consumption and only a handful of producers. The United States, Canada, and others countered that production controls would mean that the EC, which exported about one-third of its CFC output and was virtually the only exporter, would have a near monopoly. This arrangement would be especially unfair to developing countries, which would be prohibited from increasing their own production while the EC could reduce exports to compensate for growth in domestic consumption. This would motivate developing countries to circumvent the treaty and build their own CFC plants. The USA devised a compromise based on "adjusted production" that was intended to satisfy the EC's desire for simplicity and yet give all countries an incentive to enter into the agreement. Controls would be placed on production plus imports minus exports to other treaty signatories (UNEP/WG.167/2:11). This would allow producing countries to increase exports to protocol parties without having to cut domestic consumption; moreover, importing countries would not be totally dependent on one source of CFCs (Benedick 1991:81).

Throughout the first two rounds of negotiations, opponents of stringent controls emphasized the scientific uncertainties, focusing on the points of disagreement among the atmospheric models rather than on the areas of agreement. This became a source of increasing frustration for those from the EPA, State Department, UNEP, and the scientific community who saw the need for decisive precautionary action (interview with Robert Watson). Consequently, U.S. knowledge brokers sought to sway other governments through informal conversations with officials, bilateral meetings, scientific exchanges, and satellite conferences. EPA staff worked extensively with their counterparts in other environmental bureaucracies and were quite influential in several European ministries (interview with Ivar Isaksen). Watson and Benedick conferred with journalists, officials, and scientists from dozens of countries via the U.S. Information Agency's Worldnet satellite hookup. A team of scientists and diplomats from the United States traveled throughout the world, visiting Japan, the Soviet Union, India, Egypt, and most European countries. Two U.S. nongovernmental organizations, the Environmental Defense Fund and World Resources Institute, also undertook "missionary missions" to educate and mobilize their European counterparts (interview with David Doniger).

The most important of these meetings were in Japan, the Soviet Union, and Egypt, where there was "a real exchange of ideas" (interview with Robert Watson). The Japanese grew more receptive to including CFC-113 in the protocol, largely because they became convinced that skin cancer was not the only important issue. The Soviets concurred on the U.S. assessment of the science and agreed to joint scientific endeavors with the United States. The head of the Egyptian Environment Directorate met personally with the delegation and used his influence to garner support from other Arab and developing countries. Many of these meetings dealt only with scientific issues, with the goal of establishing a scientific consensus. Yet, in typical fashion, science and politics were intertwined, even if one was not reducible to the other. The U.S. delegates believed that "foreign policymakers would have more confidence in the U.S. position once they realized that their own scientists agreed with us." While nobody believes that these bilateral communications were the primary inspiration for the protocol, everybody I interviewed agrees that they were an important factor in generating a stronger agreement (interviews with Robert Watson, Lee Thomas, and James Losey).

Despite the increasing degree of both scientific and political consensus, the British and the French continued to emphasize the scientific uncertainties and the discrepancies among the various computer models. Mostafa Tolba, executive director of UNEP, was convinced that the differences were largely illusory. In early April, he convened a meeting of five modeling teams from different countries in Würzburg, West Germany, asking them to use exactly the same data. As Tolba had anticipated, the models produced roughly similar results. The scientists unanimously agreed on the need to control those compounds with the greatest ozone depletion potential: CFC-11, -12, -113, -114, and -115 and Halon-1301 and -1211 (UNEP/WG.167/INF:1). While the scientists I interviewed barely recalled the meeting because there was "no new science" (interviews with Ralph Cicerone and Ivar Isaksen), for UNEP it represented a turning point in the negotiations. For the first time, "it was no longer possible to oppose action to regulate CFC releases on the grounds of scientific dissent" (UNEP/WG.172/2:2). The Würzburg meeting supported the discursive shift in favor of precautionary action.

When the negotiations reconvened in Geneva on April 27, the U.S. position had been both weakened and strengthened: weakened because of domestic interagency dissension and strengthened by the flurry of bilateral interactions, as well as by the Würzburg meeting. At this point, UNEP took on a greater leadership role. Dr. Tolba, a respected Egyptian scientist, personally addressed the delegates, recounting the Würzburg findings and introducing an ambitious proposal for freezing CFC and halon production at 1986 levels in 1990, followed by a 20 percent cutback in production every two years until they were eliminated by the year 2000 (UNEP/

WG.172/2:2). Tolba met individually with heads of key delegations to press his case (Benedick 1989:49).

The EC announced that it would agree to a freeze followed by a 20 percent reduction in CFC production and imports but maintained that "it would be pointless to go further if the possible benefits of doing so were negated by the refusal of significant CFC producers and consumers to sign the protocol" (UNEP/WG.172/2:6). Japan, which was not invited to the scientific meeting at Würzburg, continued to emphasize the scientific uncertainties and to oppose controls on CFC-113, although its opposition had softened somewhat. The United States, while reiterating its original negotiating position, was decidedly less vocal than at previous meetings.

By the third session, it was apparent that the primary issues requiring resolution were not scientific but political. Once the discrepancies in the models could not be used to justify inaction, and once the need for significant reductions was generally recognized, the process came to be dominated by the usual political dynamics of compromise and concession until the treaty was finally signed in September.

During this period, environmental groups again functioned as knowledge brokers. In June 1987, the European Environmental Bureau brought together European and North American nongovernmental organizations at a conference in Brussels on the scientific and political aspects of the ozone problem. That conference was attended by the European Commission's Directorate-General for the Environment. A few days later, the European parliament's Environment Committee called for an 85 percent reduction of CFC production and consumption by 1997 (Jachtenfuchs 1990:266). That figure reflected the conclusion of the chlorine-loading approach; only an 85 percent reduction of CFCs could stabilize atmospheric concentrations of chlorine. Emerging grassroots concern contributed to the EC's eventual decision to back stronger CFC controls.

The EC's shift may have been partly due to the change in the presidency. U.S. negotiators observed that progress in the negotiations was made only after a Belgian replaced a Briton as EC president in January 1987. Britain, however, was in the "troika" (composed of past, present, and future presidents), which held closed meetings with key delegation heads throughout the negotiations. When the presidency rotated again in July, the troika consisted of Belgium, Denmark, and Germany, all of which supported strong control measures (Benedick 1989:48). This fortuitous political event may have helped to erode the EC's opposition to significant reductions.

Other obstacles were surmounted through a process of political bargaining and compromise. Japanese objections to including CFC-113 were finally answered at the Montreal meeting through a concession permitting countries to shift consumption among the various CFCs, so long as their total ozone depletion potential was not exceeded (Montreal Protocol). The conclusions of the Würzburg meeting enabled UNEP to persuade countries to include halons in the list of controlled substances. At the last minute, it was learned that the USSR was using a halon that no other country produced. The Soviets agreed to include it on the list of controlled chemicals; in exchange, they were allowed to include two CFC plants already under construction in the 1986 baseline.

The U.S. proposal that entry into force should require ratification by countries representing 90 percent of production, a concession to those who wanted to protect U.S. industry from unfair competition, was widely criticized (Doniger 1988:90). Agreement was reached that the treaty would enter into in force when countries representing two-thirds of 1986 consumption had ratified it.

One last stumbling block, which had lingered since the Vienna Convention, generated a surprising degree of conflict in Montreal. The problem involved how the EC was to be defined and how production was to be rationalized among its member countries. To put the complex legal matter in simple terms, the United States apparently viewed the EC as trying to be treated as one nation with twelve votes, while the EC saw the U.S. as trying to sabotage its movement toward unification. Tolba convened a meeting of the twelve major producer countries to resolve the issue, a meeting that did not adjourn until after midnight. Lee Thomas and Laurens Brinkhorst, the EC representative, met until 3:00 a.m. In the end, it was agreed that the EC would be treated as a single entity, thereby allowing industry to redistribute production among plants in different countries to guarantee maximum efficiency (interview with Lee Thomas).

The final agreement required a freeze at 1986 levels of domestic CFC consumption six months after the treaty entered into force. By July 1993, consumption was to be cut by 20 percent and, by July 1998, by a further 50 percent. Cuts in production, however, were allowed to lag by 10 percent to supply importing countries and to allow EC countries to rationalize production. Developing countries were allowed an exception: if its annual consumption of CFCs were less than 0.3 kilograms per capita (i.e., less than one-fourth the U.S. level), then a country could delay implementation of the phasedown schedule for ten years. In the interim, developing countries were free to build new CFC plants. The treaty's trade provisions prohibited imports of bulk chemicals beginning in 1990 and of products containing them in another three years, thereby removing the incentive for countries not to become party to the agreement. Periodic scientific reviews, which may lead to revision of the treaty's provisions, were to be held every four years.

The treaty, signed on September 16, 1987, by twenty-four of the sixty-two nations at Montreal, was upheld by UNEP as "unprecedented." Tolba called it "the first truly global treaty that offers protection to every single human being on this planet . . . unique because it seeks to anticipate and manage a world problem before it becomes an irreversible crisis" (UNEP 1987c). The Montreal Protocol gave material expression to the discursive shift toward a precautionary approach to the ozone layer that began with the Vienna Convention.

International decision making in the face of scientific uncertainty involves a rich and complex set of interactions among facts and values, knowledge and interests. Uncertainty can be a source of scientific legitimation for a wide array of contending interests, thereby furnishing an obstacle to political consensus. Predictably, then, scientific consensus can facilitate international cooperation, although it does not make it inevitable. In the case of the Montreal Protocol, industry and the EC emphasized the uncertainties and framed what was known in terms most favorable to their own interests in averting strict regulations. The United States, stressing both what was known and the need to mitigate the risks, also framed the science in terms of its own interests. In both cases, interests were not independent variables but were themselves a function of accepted knowledge.

Scientists were important actors in the process, but saying the issue was science-driven does not say that the scientists themselves were the driving force. First, they rarely made policy recommendations. Second, and more importantly, once the science became enmeshed in the policy debates, other contextual factors determined how it would influence policy. Foremost among these was the Antarctic ozone hole, which, although it was only in the background of the policy debates, provided a strong case for those who wished to err on the side of caution. Another major factor was the existence of an international consensus, set out in the 1986 WMO/NASA assessment and fortified by the Würzburg meeting, that uncontrolled CFC emissions might lead to devastating consequences. The position of the U.S. delegation, most articulately expressed by EPA officials, was that a long-term perspective was required and that the high stakes mandated strict controls. That position was reinforced somewhat by the predictions of the atmospheric models, and more emphatically by the discovery of the Antarctic ozone hole.

In general, uncertainty increases as the causal chain of events moves further into the future. Not only does this empower experts to advise policymakers but, when combined with the perception of great risk, it can require policymakers to employ a different kind of decision making. John Ruggie (1986:231) describes it as a " 'bias shift' . . . away from a conventional problem-solving mode, wherein doing nothing would be favored on burden-of-proof grounds, toward a risk-averting mode, wherein prudent contingency measures would be undertaken to avoid risks we would rather not face." Many of those I interviewed explicitly refer to such a "bias shift" in their accounts of the negotiations.

The kind of power exercised by the scientists and those who successfully translated their information into viable policy proposals was not a function of control and domination but rather entailed persuading delegates to reevaluate their conceptions of their nations' interests. The ability to persuade was a function both of external contextual factors and skillful employment of knowledge in support of particular positions. Perceptions were key—most importantly, perceptions of the extent of the risks and of the dependability of the scientists' knowledge. These perceptions were heavily influenced by the persuasive power of specific experts and knowledge brokers who were able to expand the time frames of most of the delegates and heighten the sense of urgency.

5 • Necessity, the Mother of Invention: New Science, New Policies

> The measures agreed here are the strongest package of global environmental law ever enacted. The question remains, however: is this enough? We are in the hands of scientists. From them we know that the answer is "No." —*Mostafa Tolba, Copenhagen, 1992*

Perhaps the greatest innovation in the Montreal Protocol is the institution of periodic treaty reviews based on new knowledge. Although the treaty was hailed as a diplomatic milestone for its precautionary approach to a global environmental problem, the nonlinear relationship between CFCs and ozone depletion indicated that far more drastic measures would be necessary. Within a matter of months after Montreal, a scientific consensus had emerged on three vital issues: that the Antarctic ozone hole was caused by CFCs, that ozone losses were occurring globally, and that the stratospheric chemistry above the Arctic was highly perturbed.

Superficially, it appears that, once CFCs were clearly identified as the culprits, the debates were no longer formulated in terms of science but reduced to the more traditional dynamics of bargaining and political compromise. To be sure, the emerging scientific consensus was mirrored in a new symmetry between the positions of the USA and the EC. In comparison to the Montreal Protocol negotiations, debates about scientific knowledge were quite scarce in the post-Montreal period. A consensus on these issues had been forged, thereby facilitating, though not necessitating, the emergence of a political consensus. The major source of contention soon became the issue of assisting developing nations to obtain CFC substitutes, chemicals that would cost three to five times as much as the ozone-depleting CFCs. Yet the developing countries did not contest the science; nor did they frame the issue in scientific terms. Rather, they expressed their concerns in terms of economic equity and national sovereignty.

While there is some merit in this interpretation of events, it fails to recognize the ways in which scientific and technical discourse continued to be a driving force behind the treaty revision process. And, in downplaying the role of knowledge, this view inevitably overlooks the extent to which policy was shaped by specific modes of framing and interpreting the available knowledge. Moreover, on at least one issue—control measures for methyl bromide—there has been substantial scientific disagreement between North and South. Throughout the amendment process, as in the earlier negotiations, science did not simply provide a set of objective and value-free facts from which a policy consensus was forged. Rather, distinctive ways of presenting and interpreting information were instrumental in shaping policy outcomes.

The interplay between science and politics has reemerged during the treaty revision process in many of the same guises discussed in the preceding chapter. One particular method of framing the available scientific knowledge, the chlorine-loading approach, dominated the treaty revision deliberation. As before, this interpretive mode gained salience from contextual factors gleaned from observational data, but it was not mandated by the data. That schematic approach to the data, elaborated after the Montreal Protocol by knowledge brokers from the EPA and NASA, shaped the revised control measures adopted in 1990 and 1992.

Further evidence of the multidimensional relationship between science and politics, one that was touched on in the last chapter, is the problem of substitute availability. Superficially, this seems to be a technical matter involving chemical research. Initially, industry raised strong objections to the 50 percent reductions in CFC emissions called for in the Montreal Protocol, claiming that substitutes would not be available to meet the control schedule. Yet, within three years, the CFC industry was largely supportive of a full phaseout within the same time frame. The astonishing speed of technological development has been, as much as the new scientific findings of increased ozone depletion, a driving force behind the treaty amendment process. The availability of substitutes enabled policymakers to adopt far more stringent controls than they otherwise might have. But that availability, I will argue, was dictated by psychological and market forces, not by chemistry or technology, and these forces were in turn guided by scientific and policy discourse.

To attribute the post-Montreal discursive shift to an epistemic community, as Peter Haas does (1992a:215–18), is to truncate the story. While knowledge brokers were important players, their central role was in framing the science rather than in promoting specific policies. The epistemic communities approach misses this fundamental dimension of interpretation. In his brief discussion of the treaty revision process, Haas actually refers to environmental nongovernmental organizations rather than to an epistemic community in accounting for words and outcomes. While a kind of ozone "club" of negotiators and experts had developed over the years, the bonding principles of that group were not so much epistemic as it was political and personal (interview with Eileen Claussen).

The post-Montreal events can be read as an extension of the precautionary discourse launched with the Vienna Convention and formalized in the Montreal Protocol. And yet, once unprecedented ozone losses were being measured and once the Antarctic ozone hole was decisively linked to human sources, the control measures were no longer truly precautionary. Action did not precede evidence of environmental degradation but instead responded to it in order to prevent things from going from bad to worse. The question really became how to save the ozone layer and, in the long run, how to repair the damage already done. Hence, it is more accurate to speak of a shift toward a dominant conservation discourse, which was articulated in London in 1990 and Copenhagen in 1992.

Immediate Responses

Even before the ink on the Montreal Protocol had dried, scientists were uncovering new data that would dispel many uncertainties. Scientists on the second Antarctic expedition, announcing their preliminary results just two weeks after the treaty was signed, concluded that CFCs had caused the hole (*Washington Post* 1987h; *Nature* 1987a). Immediately, many calls to amend the treaty were heard (*Nature* 1987a; *Washington Post* 1987i).

The Montreal Protocol was roundly praised by the press (see *Newsweek* 1987; *The Washington Post* 1987g). Yet the disturbing news from Antarctica suggested that the treaty may have done too little, too late. For the first time since the 1970s, environmentalists began to mobilize on a large scale at the grassroots level to save the ozone layer. The easiest targets were aerosols and foam packaging, for which alternatives were readily available (Shea 1988:35). In the United States, the city of Berkeley promptly banned fast-food packaging made with CFCs, and activists convinced McDonald's to abandon its use of styrofoam containers made with CFCs (*Washington Post* 1987). Soon afterward, environmental groups, working with the EPA, negotiated an agreement with U.S. styrofoam manufacturers to stop using CFC-11 and CFC-12 by the end of 1988. In Canada, a major grocery chain removed CFC-based packaging from its shelves. The European Environmental Bureau (EEB) and the European Bureau of Consumers' Unions (BEUC) formed a powerful alliance, calling for an 85 percent reduction in CFC use and demanding that industry implement voluntary reductions beyond those in the protocol or else face a major boycott (Jacht-enfuchs 1990:268). In Britain, Friends of the Earth (FOE) announced a boycott of aerosol products containing CFCs, causing ICI to pledge a halt to the use of CFCs in aerosols by 1990. Prince Charles joined the boycott, banning the products from his household (FOE 1988). Initially, environmentalists thought that the ozone problem was a clear-cut consumer issue. Yet once CFCs were eliminated in aerosols and food packaging, there was little that could be done through boycotts; consumers were unlikely to stop buying refrigerators and cars (interview with Liz Cook).

European industry, especially in Britain and France, was critical of the agreement, continuing to question the CFC–ozone depletion link (Environmental Data Services 1988). While expressing considerable ambivalence, U.S. industry was a bit more receptive. The Alliance for a Responsible CFC Policy praised the treaty as "an unprecedented step to protect the global environment" while persisting in its claim that "current use of the compounds presents no significant risks to health or the environment" (1987:I.8–9).

Despite industry's reluctance, the treaty and the ensuing calls for revisions propelled it into an unprecedented race to find chemical substitutes. Recognizing that marketability for CFC substitutes could be hastened through cooperation on toxicological and environmental testing, fifteen CFC producers from nine countries joined together in an innovative effort to expedite research on new chemicals. In December 1987, the Programme for Alternative Fluorocarbon Toxicity Testing (PAFT), based at ICI in Britain, was launched to address the toxicology of two compounds: HCFC-123 and HFC-134a, potential substitutes for CFC-11 and CFC-12, respectively. Within a year, twelve chemical producers formed the Alternative Fluorocarbons Environmental Acceptability Study (AFEAS), based in Washington, D.C., to assess the environmental risks of potential CFC substitutes (AFEAS/PAFT 1991). Since then research results have been pooled among the member companies and forwarded to the appropriate regulatory agencies to speed the approval process.

Industry's interest in CFC replacements was evident at a Substitutes and Alternatives trade fair cosponsored by the EPA and Environment Canada in January 1988. Several hundred CFC users and producers packed the workshop to the point of overflow. The Montreal Protocol had become a marketing opportunity for new products. Alternative foam-blowing agents like methylene chloride, pentane, and carbon dioxide, were discussed, as were hydrocarbon aerosol propellants, used widely in the USA since the 1978 aerosol ban. Petroferm, a small Florida-based company, unveiled a substitute solvent for CFC-113 made from chemicals found in citrus fruit rinds and tested successfully by AT&T (*New York Times* 1988b). An independent study presented at the workshop found that this new compound alone could replace as much as one-half of total projected CFC-113 use in the U.S. electronics industry. Soon after the workshop, Du Pont announced plans to build a new plant in Texas to manufacture HFC-134a, a chlorine-free refrigerant that would sell for about seven times the price of CFC-12 (*Wall Street Journal* 1988b; *Washington Post* 1988b). Du Pont and several other CFC producers began actively to promote the partially halogenated HCFC-22.[1]

Not only did the Montreal Protocol herald markets for new chemicals, it spurred the search for alternative practices and technologies that could reduce the need for CFCs. Even before 1987, new product designs, like side vent windows in cars and solar ventilation systems for indoor heating, were being promoted by some environmentalists (Miller and Mintzer 1986). The level of interest increased greatly after Montreal. Halon emissions could be reduced significantly by not discharging during testing. New refrigerator designs could use helium or ammonia refrigerants instead of CFCs (Shea 1988:30–31). Despite their objections to regulation, both CFC users and producers were determined to make the best of the situation.

Industry was not the only ambivalent actor; some developing countries were also skeptical of the treaty. A few, most notably Mexico, the first nation to ratify the protocol, as well as Egypt, Venezuela, Kenya, and Indonesia, were quite supportive. Malaysia, however, was an outspoken critic of the treaty, claiming that the "inequitable" treaty was equivalent to "trade war by environmental decree" (Jaafar 1990; cited in Benedick 1991:100). While Malaysia's actions were unlikely to damage the ozone layer substantially, its language was adopted by other developing countries. In particular, India and China, together accounting for 40 percent of the world's population, registered strong reservations to the treaty. No sooner had the Montreal Protocol been negotiated than the stage was set for a confrontation between North and South.

The EC was divided on how to implement the protocol. At a December 1987 meeting, the United Kingdom proposed that the EC as a unit, rather than individual countries, should meet the treaty's guidelines. The FRG, the Netherlands, and Denmark, adopting their familiar environmentalist stance, advocated going beyond the protocol toward an eventual CFC ban (European Commission 1987). Recognizing that the easiest way to reduce CFC emissions quickly was to cut their use in aerosols, as the United States had done a decade earlier, European companies began to phase out CFCs as propellants (Benedick 1991:107).[2] The Netherlands acted most quickly, banning CFCs in aerosols in response to a national campaign organized by environmental groups (FOE 1988).

Amid growing concern, UNEP's executive director, Mostafa Tolba, convened a meeting of representatives from governments, industry, and nongovernmental organizations (NGOs) in January 1988 to discuss implementation of the Montreal Protocol. Despite the increased level of activity in industry and environmental groups, no nation had yet ratified the treaty. In order for the treaty to enter into force by the target date of January 1, 1989, ratification was required by nations or regional economic integration organizations representing at least two-thirds of 1986 CFC consumption (article 16 of the Montreal Protocol, UNEP 1987a). The January meeting generated an implementation timetable, scheduling three important meetings for October 1988 in The Hague: a scientific symposium to review new ozone research, a meeting of legal and technical experts to set the agenda for the First Meeting of the Parties, and a technical workshop for industry on substitutes and alternative technologies. And, recognizing that the treaty revision process should progress quickly, the group also decided to move up two critical dates: the First Meeting of the Parties was rescheduled from November to May 1989 and the scientific, environmental, economic, and technological assessments were to be completed in 1989 rather than in 1990 (Benedick 1991:109).

Thus, within four months of Montreal, preparations were under way for a revised treaty. Article 6, mandating assessment and review of the control measures beginning in 1990 and at least every four years thereafter, may have been the most important element of the treaty. A combination of new scientific evidence, renewed and expanded activism on the part of environmental groups, and industry's energetic pursuit of new technologies was already creating a discursive shift in support of more decisive action to control ozone depleting chemicals.

New Science and the Discourse of Damage Limitation

On March 15, 1988, the Ozone Trends Panel, established by NASA in collaboration with UNEP, the WMO, and two other U.S. agencies to reanalyze nearly all satellite and ground-based measurements of ozone, released the executive summary of its report. The panel, formed in October 1986 and involving over a hundred scientists from ten countries, was primarily a response to Donald Heath's controversial satellite data. That data had shown annual global ozone losses of 1 percent since 1979 (interviews with Ralph Cicerone and Robert Watson). The panel concluded that actual losses were about half what Heath had measured, with greater decreases in the upper stratosphere ranging from 3 to 9 percent (NASA 1988:1–4). Most important for galvanizing political concern was the finding that significant ozone depletion had already occurred over heavily populated areas in the Northern Hemisphere, ranging from 1.7 to 3.0 percent, with far greater losses in the winter months. The modeled predictions for these latitudes were only 0.5 percent, casting even more doubt on the reliability of the computer models. The Ozone Trends Panel also reported the findings of the second Antarctic expedition. Large amounts of chlorine gas were found in the stratosphere during the formation of the ozone hole, indicating that CFCs and other anthropogenic sources of chlorine and bromine were depleting the Antarctic ozone layer. Moreover, ozone losses were not limited to the Antarctic spring, but were observed year-round (NASA 1988:19).

Many observers, both scientists and laypersons, were troubled by the fact that the full report would not be available for several months, thereby leaving the basis for the executive summary's conclusions unavailable for public scrutiny. One science writer, describing a host of complex factors involved in stratospheric chemistry and data calibration, noted that, "although many problems with the data have no doubt been addressed in some way, the science would be best served if the methods used were published, as is presumably the intent in the full report" (Trenberth 1988:26). With the future of international controls on ozone-depleting chemicals at issue, the timely release of the full report was important not only from a scientific perspective but also from environmental, political, and economic standpoints.

Yet it was nearly three years before the full report was finally published, causing some people, particularly those representing affected industries, to claim that the delay was caused by squabbling among the scientists (interview with Kevin Fay). That claim, however, was laid to rest in the minds of most observers when Allied-Signal commissioned an independent reanalysis of the data, released in August 1988, that substantiated the findings of the Ozone Trends Panel. Apparently, the tardiness of NASA's final report was actually the consequence of a series of administrative blunders. In the end, NASA's budgetary allocations for document publication having been spent, the industry consortium AFEAS contributed the funds needed to print the document (interview with Robert Watson). Although the report itself established an unprecedented consensus implicating CFCs in ozone depletion, the delay in publication furnished a handful of skeptics with further grounds for their position. To some extent, the credibility of scientific information became hostage to bureaucratic procedures.

Nonetheless, the executive summary of the Ozone Trends Panel Report, essentially performing a knowledge brokerage function, was generally accepted on the basis of the authority of the scientists involved and their sponsoring agencies. The document prompted more calls for a strengthened Montreal Protocol. Those asking for the revision noted that the treaty's emission targets still allowed atmospheric concentrations of CFCs to double from their 1986 levels (interviews with John Hoffman and David Doniger). On the basis of the new scientific findings, Sweden became the first country to ban CFCs, passing legislation in June 1988 to implement specific plans for a full phaseout. Although Sweden used only 1 percent of the world's CFCs, its bold action showed that a global phaseout was not inconceivable (Shea 1988:34).

But nowhere was the reaction swifter than at Du Pont, the world's leading CFC producer. Less than a week after the report's release, the company announced that it would halt all production of fully halogenated CFCs as soon as possible (Glas 1989:150). The announcement came as a surprise; only three weeks before, Du Pont's chief executive officer had written to three U.S. senators that "scientific evidence does not point to the need for dramatic CFC emission reductions." He claimed that reductions beyond those mandated by the Montreal Protocol would be "both unwarranted and counterproductive" (cited in Reinhardt 1989:15). Yet after hearing about the panel's findings on the evening news, Joseph Glas, director of Du Pont's Freon Division, met the next day with Environmental Manager Joseph Steed, and the division's top ozone scientist, Robert McFarland. McFarland, the only industry representative on the Ozone Trends Panel, had read the entire draft report but had been "sworn to secrecy" until the executive summary was released (interview with Robert

McFarland). At the meeting, "the business end of things was never even discussed" (interview with Joseph Steed). On the basis of McFarland's corroboration of the panel's findings, Glas recommended to Du Pont's board of directors that the company stop manufacturing all chemicals regulated by the Montreal Protocol by 1999.

The Du Pont decision, while apparently demonstrating the persuasive power of consensual scientific knowledge, was not so simple. Contending interpretations of Du Pont's actions suggest once more that scientific facts alone rarely drive policy decisions. Rather, science, framed in terms of interests and perceptions, interacts with existing discourses to produce a new discursive milieu. The timing of Du Pont's decision, just after the Ozone Trends Panel released its findings and only weeks after the firm's chairman had insisted that further CFC reductions were unnecessary, supports the view that Du Pont was motivated primarily by the new scientific findings. While Du Pont was the leading researcher on CFC substitutes, the company's supporters argue that the decision to forfeit existing markets—amounting to $600 million in revenues for 1987—for the sake of a vague future could not have been motivated solely by the quest for profits. Proponents of this interpretation also emphasize that Du Pont's corporate culture is very science-oriented, that "Du Pont's name has historically been synonymous with science" (Reinhardt 1989:9).

The most cynical explanation for Du Pont's decision comes, not surprisingly, from environmentalists, who maintain that the company was motivated primarily by the bottom line. FOE published a report in which they point out that Du Pont's CFC business was declining and that the Freon Division's operating profits were far below those of the company's other divisions.[3] The prices of CFC replacements would be several times those of existing compounds, and existing plants for manufacturing CFC-11 and CFC-12 could be retrofitted to produce HCFC-22. Du Pont also strategically renamed the partially halogenated chlorofluorocarbons, formerly called CFCs along with those regulated by the Montreal Protocol, "HCFCs" (FOE 1991d:43). Clearly, the Montreal Protocol furnished a marketing opportunity for any company that could take the lead in producing substitutes. Ironically, the account offered by U.S. environmentalists echoes the reaction of some representatives from the European CFC industry, who labeled the ozone treaty "the Du Pont Protocol" (interview with Mike Harris).

A middle position is that Du Pont's decision grew out of a combination of respect for scientific knowledge, practical concern for profitability, and corporate responsibility. Du Pont, a huge company with only 2 percent of its profits generated by CFC production, was unwilling to risk its public reputation for the sake of one family of dangerous compounds (interview with Stephen Seidel).[4] As Joe Steed declared, "Since we are two hundred years old, we tend to take a longer view. We couldn't let the whole company get a bad name just because of those chemicals. . . . I've found that the big corporations actually tend to be the most responsible, contrary to what most people to think. We have to be more concerned with our reputations" (interview). This interpretation of Du Pont's action combines the motivation of economic self-interest with a sense of corporate responsibility. It also suggests that the company's decision was inspired by considerations that went far beyond the scientific data.

Even more remarkable than Du Pont's action was the reversal in the British position. Prime Minister Margaret Thatcher was deeply distrustful of the Ozone Trends Panel report. The panel was international and included British scientists, but Thatcher was suspicious of NASA's leadership role in it. She requested that the British Stratospheric Ozone Research Group (SORG) assess the issue. SORG published a summary of its findings in June 1988 and the full report in October, corroborating the NASA report and supporting a phaseout of CFCs and halons. Scientists, including the head of Britain's environmental ministry, Crispin Tickell, appealed to Thatcher on the basis of her training as a chemist. She was also under some political pressure, the House of Lords having just passed a resolution calling for 85 percent reductions in CFCs and halons (*London Observer* 1988). At that point, Thatcher became personally committed to protecting the ozone layer, delivering a speech before the Royal Society that marked a sharp turning point in her government's policies on global environmental problems (Thatcher 1988). In her speech, she announced that she would convene a major international conference in London the following year to promote an 85 percent global reduction of CFCs.[5] Jonathan Porritt, executive director of Friends of the Earth, declared, "Blimey, the speech is impressive, a milestone for the environment" (*Washington Post* 1989b). Once the United Kingdom had endorsed decisive action, the way was paved for the EC to follow suit.

At roughly the same time, industry's independent review of the Ozone Trends Panel findings was released. Once the conclusions had been substantiated, industry as a whole followed Du Pont. In September 1988, within days of each other, the European Fluorocarbon Technical Committee (EFTC), industry's liaison with the EC and the national governments, ICI, and the U.S.-based Alliance for a Responsible CFC Policy all announced their support for a phaseout on the substances controlled in the Montreal Protocol.

The Ozone Trends Panel report inspired a substantial shift in the terms of public discourse on ozone, suggesting that more stringent international regulatory action would be required. No longer was precautionary action possible; damage was already occurring, and the question was now one of slowing the rate of future destruction. With new consensual knowledge implicating CFCs, the dominant policy discourse on ozone shifted from one rooted in the precautionary principle to one seeking damage control. But that knowledge only came to be universally accepted after the primary skeptics were persuaded by their own trusted informational sources. And the economic value of the new knowledge varied widely within the CFC industry, with Du Pont apparently having the most to gain from it.

Implementing the Discourse of Damage Limitation

In October 1988, UNEP sponsored meetings in The Hague to focus world attention on the ozone problem and the need to strengthen the Montreal Protocol. At that meeting, the following four panels that would provide the knowledge base for revising the treaty were established: scientific, environmental effects, economic, and technical.[6] The panels, involving hundreds of experts from all over the world, represented a pioneering effort in knowledge production aimed at solving a global environmental problem. Panel members had known each other, in some cases, for many years and had developed a strong, practical network for information sharing. The CFC producers were intentionally excluded from the technology panel not only because of a general distrust of them but also to encourage nonchemical alternative technologies (interviews with Stephen Anderson and Robert Watson).

The Hague meeting also called attention to the fact that ratification was proceeding slowly, particularly in the EC. Although several EC states had already decided to surpass the Montreal Protocol's requirements and phase out CFCs by 2000, the formality that all member states, plus the commission, must ratify simultaneously delayed ratification until December 1988, just in time for the treaty to take effect on January 1, 1989.

While the EPA's Lee Thomas called for a CFC phaseout in September 1988, election-year politics virtually guaranteed that official action would be delayed. The Natural Resources Defense Council (NRDC), seeking to hasten things, launched its Atmospheric Protection Initiative and filed a new lawsuit against the EPA (NRDC 1988:4). The NRDC initiative was bolstered by new findings that an ozone hole was forming over the Arctic (*New York Times* 1988d).

Despite the dramatic ozone losses, the dominant view was that ozone-depleting chemicals could only be banned if substitutes were available. Thus, the perceived availability of CFC substitutes had a strong effect on discourse about ozone. For some sectors, especially aerosols and foam blowing, alternatives to CFCs were relatively simple to find (*Christian Science Monitor* 1988; *Wall Street Journal* 1988a). While producers, especially Du Pont, were pressing ahead in the search for new compounds, some user industries were quite disturbed by the situation (Monastersky 1988:234). The refrigeration and air conditioning industries, in particular, were facing new federal energy-efficiency standards just as proposals to ban the highly efficient CFCs were being broached. Potential substitute chemicals and alternative technical designs were likely to conflict with the goal of conserving energy to curb global warming. Hydrofluorocarbons (HFCs), which pose no threat to ozone because they contain no chlorine, were possible chemical substitutes, but they are potent greenhouse gases. In the melodramatic words of one industry representative, the situation had "all the earmarks of a calamity" (Corcoran 1988:113).

Industry emphasized the cost of the transition to new chemicals—some $5.5 billion between 1990 and 2010 in the United States alone, rising to $27 billion by the year 2075 (interview with Kevin Fay). But those amounts paled in comparison to the EPA's projected cost of three million additional skin cancer deaths in the absence of the Montreal Protocol. In monetary terms, to say nothing of less tangible factors, the treaty would save U.S. citizens $6.5 trillion in medical costs by 2075 (interview with Stephen Seidel).

Amid such discussion, along with new reports of severe ozone depletion over the Arctic (*Science* 1989:1007), preparations were under way for Prime Minister Thatcher's London Conference on Saving the Ozone Layer. In February, Canada announced that it would ban CFCs and halons within ten years (*San Francisco Chronicle* 1989). On March 3, 1989, the EC's Environment Council unexpectedly voted to eliminate CFCs completely by the end of the century (*New York Times* 1989a). With the British change of heart, France, maintaining that unilateral reductions would not save the ozone layer and would only benefit non-European companies, had found itself isolated in its opposition to stringent reductions. But France relented, apparently favoring its political interests over its economic interests. President Mitterrand, taking a leadership role in efforts to prevent global climate change, was cosponsoring an international conference on the global environment in The Hague later that month.[7] Had his government blocked efforts in the EC to save the ozone layer, Mitterrand would have been in an embarrassing position at that conference (Jachtenfuchs 1990:271). The day after the EC vote, President Bush announced that the United States would also ban all production of CFCs by the end of the century and would also eliminate halons (*Washington Post* 1989a). The stage was set for a unified push by the United States and the EC, at loggerheads during the Montreal Protocol negotiations, for a total phaseout of CFCs.

Although the U.K.-sponsored conference was not part of the official treaty revision process, it was cosponsored by UNEP, and it paved the way for the First Meeting of the Parties, to be held two months later in Helsinki. One hundred twelve nations participated in the conference, the first high-level international gathering on ozone since 1987; just eighteen months earlier, only half that number of countries were represented at Montreal.[8] The London Conference laid out the main themes and potential stumbling blocks for the ensuing revision process. In sharp contrast to earlier meetings, a consensus now prevailed on the science of ozone depletion as well as on the need to eventually eliminate CFCs. The treatment of developing countries, which hitherto had been considered a minor issue, became a central concern. While Thatcher was unsuccessful in overcoming objections from the Soviet Union and developing countries to an 85 percent reduction of CFC and halon emissions, she did garner commitments from twenty additional countries to ratify the Montreal Protocol (*New York Times* 1989c).

The strongest and most ominous objections were raised by India and China, two countries that had not signed the treaty. They argued that developing countries should not have to forgo necessities like refrigeration in order to help solve a problem caused by industrialized countries. Nor should they, they argued, be forced to pay higher prices for substitutes, thereby contributing to the profits of the chemical companies that had caused the problem. China and India submitted an innovative proposal that a fund be established to finance the transfer of substitute technology to developing countries (*Christian Science Monitor* 1989). That proposal was destined to become a dominant theme during discussions of treaty amendments during the next year.

Two months after the London Conference, the First Meeting of Parties was held in Helsinki. Although the treaty could not legally be revised at that meeting, the delegates were able to agree on a nonbinding declaration and a concrete timetable for the assessment process. The EPA made a key presentation on future chlorine concentrations in the atmosphere according to various emission scenarios for CFCs and other chlorine-containing chemicals. (The scientific underpinnings of that presentation, and its implications for policy discourse, are discussed in greater length below.) On the basis of that presentation, many delegations supported the addition of methyl chloroform and carbon tetrachloride to the list of the treaty's controlled substance (*New York Times* 1989d). The Helsinki Declaration called for a phaseout of CFCs no later than the year 2000, a phaseout of halons with no specific target dates, and control and reduction of other ozone-depleting chemicals as soon as feasible (UNEP/OzL.Pro.1/5).

The other major issue at the Helsinki meeting was the contentious one of financial and technical assistance for Article 5 countries. Developing countries, backed by the Nordic countries and New Zealand, proposed that a fund be established along the lines of China and India's suggestion at the London conference, but the major donor countries rejected the proposal. In the end, a special working group was established to formulate recommendations on a funding mechanism to be considered by the Second Meeting of Parties the following year (UNEP/OzL.Pro.1/5:20).

Even as the delegates were meeting as Helsinki, the nearly five hundred scientists and technical experts on the four assessment panels were assembling their reports. Almost two thousand pages of work were completed and peer-reviewed during the summer and then consolidated into a fifty-page summary, known as the "Synthesis Report" (UNEP/OzL.Pro.WG.II[1]/4). That document, presented to the Open-Ended Working Group of the Parties at its Geneva meeting in November 1989, became the basis for the first treaty review. Perhaps out of necessity, since the bulk of the world's technical expertise relevant to the ozone problem resides in the North, the four review panels were heavily dominated by developed countries. Each panel was chaired by either an EC or a North American country, with representatives from the United States serving as either chairs or cochairs on three of the four panels. Nonetheless, despite the apparent potential for dissension, there was surprisingly little debate about the reports.

Of the four assessments, the scientific one was clearly the most critical; estimates of present and future ozone depletion were the driving force behind the treaty revision process. More of the Synthesis Report was devoted to the science assessment than to the other three assessments combined. The observational findings, including data on the Antarctic ozone hole, perturbed Arctic chemistry, and long-term ozone losses in the Northern Hemisphere, were largely drawn from the Ozone Trends Panel report. These findings revealed the defects in the gas-phase computer models used to guide the Montreal Protocol, sparking laboratory studies and model simulations of surface-induced chemical processes. One important study, mentioned in the 1989 Synthesis Report, concluded that a major volcanic eruption could spew large quantities of sulfuric acid particles into the stratosphere, thereby causing on a global scale the same sort of chemical reactions taking place on the ice clouds of Antarctica (UNEP/OzL.Pro.WG.II[1]/4:6; *New York Times* 1989e:C-4).

With the computer models cast in doubt, the chlorine-loading approach, analyzed in the previous chapter in relation to the Antarctic ozone hole, became the dominant way of framing the scientific information. As discussed earlier, that discursive strategy was based on a rather simplistic calculation of the atmospheric abundance of chlorine given various emission scenarios. The chlorine-loading approach was the basis of the statement that an immediate 85 percent reduction in CFC emissions was required simply to stabilize atmospheric concentrations of chlorine at existing levels. That statement drew attention to the long atmospheric lifetimes of CFCs, debunking the intuitively appealing notion that a simple freeze would be sufficient to stabilize chlorine concentrations at existing levels. The 85 percent figure, first cited by the EPA and environmentalists throughout the Montreal Protocol talks, was later embraced by Prime Minister Thatcher and others who wanted to strengthen the treaty.

Once the Antarctic ozone hole had been definitively linked to CFCs, especially in the absence of models accounting for the phenomenon, the chlorine-loading methodology became the most credible discursive strategy for analyzing alternative policy proposals. The observations of the hole, along with perturbed Arctic chemistry and long-term ozone decreases, led to the recognition of major gaps in the computer models used for past assessment studies (UNEP/OzL.Pro.WG.II[1]/4:5). If chlorine was the culprit, then the logical conclusion was that chlorine concentrations should be reduced to levels lower than those at which the hole appeared. The Antarctic ozone hole emerged when concentrations exceeded two parts per billion (ppb) (preindustrial levels of atmospheric chlorine were only 0.6 ppb [UNEP/OzL.Pro.WG.II(1)/4:28]).[9] Eliminating the hole, therefore, would require decreasing chlorine levels to below 2 ppb.

It should be noted that all participants seem to have assumed that Antarctica's ozone will recuperate if chlorine concentrations return to less than 2 ppb. This assumption, although a reasonable conjecture given past experience, may be erroneous; the nonlinearity of ozone depletion processes indicates that other outcomes are possible. Nonetheless, the entire treaty review process, from 1988 until 1992, was based upon this assumption.

The chlorine-loading approach was not wholly uncontroversial. The British CFC industry continued to harbor objections to a CFC phaseout, framing those objections in terms of skepticism regarding the chlorine-loading approach. First, they claimed, the predictions were scenario-dependent; the choice of different scenarios would change the predictions. Second, the chlorine-loading approach does not look at ozone depletion or increased ultraviolet radiation, which are the real concerns. Third, they argued, chlorine loading is a "remote parameter, correct only if all the earth is like Antarctica" (interview with Mike Harris). Despite these objections, for most participants, the observational data warranted the shift to the chlorine-loading approach.

John Hoffman of the EPA, one of the original proponents of this methodology, began working out proposals to revise the treaty based on the chlorine-loading approach the day after he returned from Montreal in 1987 (interview). He calculated that the chlorine abundance under the provisions of the Montreal Protocol would skyrocket to 11 ppb by the end of the next century (see figure 5.1). Even with a complete phaseout of CFCs by the year 2000, chlorine-loading values would still reach an astounding 9 ppb. Hoffman saw that lower levels could only be achieved by regulating carbon tetrachloride (CCL_4) and methyl chloroform (CH_3CCl_3, also known as 1,1,1-Trichloroethane). Even then a complete phaseout, in addition to eliminating CFCs, would only bring the peak chlorine levels down to 4 ppb; the 2 ppb target would not be achieved for over eighty years.

Recognizing that recuperation of the ozone layer would require controlling emissions of chemical substitutes for CFCs, Michael Prather and Robert Watson of NASA expanded upon Hoffman's work (interview with Robert Watson). Their work, eventually published in *Nature*, served as the scientific basis for the treaty revision process and was incorporated into the Synthesis Report (Prather and Watson 1990). Figure 5.1 was included in the Synthesis Report, along with other graphs depicting additional scenarios. According to Robert Watson, "The delegations found more useful information in those pictures than in the whole panel report" (interview). The diagrams made it obvious that, in order to bring chlorine concentrations below 2 ppb, not only CFCs but methyl chloroform and carbon tetrachloride would have to be eliminated, that HCFCs could only be used as transitional substitutes, and that full compliance would be necessary.

The Synthesis Report considered the transient use of substitutes by examining scenarios with a range of phaseout dates for hypothetical chemicals chosen to mimic actual substitutes. Compound X has a fifteen-year lifetime (like HCFC-22), a single chlorine atom, and a steady-state chlorine-loading factor of 0.10 relative to CFC-11; compound Y has a six-year lifetime (like methyl chloroform), with one chlorine atom and a steady-state chlorine-loading factor of 0.04 (UNEP/OzL.Pro.WG.II[1]/4:32). Table 5.1 presents the chlorine concentrations by date for one scenario: elimination of CFCs, methyl chloroform, and carbon tetrachloride by the year 2000 and various substitute phaseout schedules. Figure 5.2 depicts this hypothetical scenario graphically for compound X.

The Synthesis Report also looked at other approaches, including revised values for ozone depletion potentials (ODP) and global warming potentials (GWP). As discussed in chapter 4, ODPs are calculated with a chem-

Figure 5.1. Atmospheric Chlorine Concentrations with Different Chemical Control Options

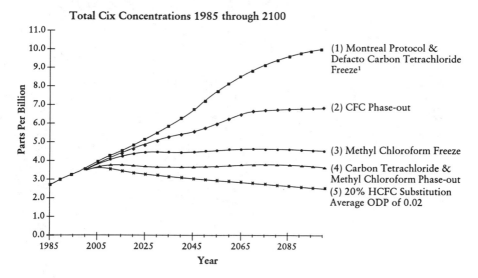

Assumptions: 2000 phaseout of fully halogenated CFCs (except curve 1); HCFCs capture 60 percent of what CFC market would have been without regulation (except curve 1), assumed annual average growth rates 1986 to 2060 (after 2060, use is assumed to be constant); average ODP of substitutes is 0.05 (except curve 5); 100 percent global participation.
* While possibilities exist for an increase in carbon tetrachloride use, such growth is unlikely given the awareness of carbon tetrachloride's potential contribution to stratospheric ozone depletion.

Source: UNEP/OzL.Pro. WG.II(1)/4:27.

ical model of the ozone layer and, in contrast to the relative chlorine-loading values, they include the effectiveness with which the gas releases its chlorine in the stratosphere. But the models that generate ODP values are limited to gas-phase chemistry and so did not predict the Antarctic ozone hole. Consequently, the simpler chlorine-loading approach was employed to a greater extent than ODP calculations in both the policy discussions and the Synthesis Report. Chlorine-loading potential (CLP) is a conservative measure of the amount of stratospheric chlorine that may be available to destroy ozone; in most cases, it is higher than ODP because it assumes that all the chlorine will be available. (See table 5.2 for a comparison of

Table 5.1. Atmospheric Chlorine Concentrations in ppb with Substitution of Compounds X and Y

year	no subst.	X 25%	X 50%	X 100%	X 50%*	Y 25%	Y 50%	Y 100%	Y 50%*
1985	2.98	2.98	2.98	2.98	2.98	2.98	2.98	2.98	2.98
1990	3.62	3.62	3.62	3.62	3.62	3.62	3.62	3.62	3.62
1995	4.24	4.24	4.24	4.24	4.24	4.24	4.24	4.24	4.24
2000	4.78	4.78	4.78	4.78	4.78	4.78	4.78	4.78	4.78
2005	4.21	4.31	4.41	4.61	4.43	4.29	4.37	4.53	4.38
2010	3.84	4.01	4.18	4.53	4.25	3.95	4.07	4.30	4.12
2015	3.57	3.79	4.02	4.47	4.16	3.70	3.83	4.09	3.93
2020	3.35	3.61	3.87	4.40	4.12	3.49	3.62	3.90	3.78
2025	3.16	3.45	3.74	4.32	4.12	3.30	3.44	3.72	3.67
2030	2.99	3.30	3.61	4.23	4.15	3.14	3.28	3.56	3.59
2035	2.84	3.07	3.29	3.73	3.67	2.91	2.97	3.09	3.10
2040	2.71	2.86	3.02	3.34	3.30	2.73	2.76	2.81	2.82
2045	2.58	2.69	2.81	3.03	3.00	2.59	2.630	2.63	2.63
2050	2.46	2.54	2.62	2.79	2.76	2.47	2.47	2.48	2.48
2055	2.35	2.41	2.47	2.53	2.57	2.35	2.35	2.36	2.36
2060	2.25	2.29	2.33	2.42	2.40	2.25	2.25	2.25	2.25
2065	2.15	2.18	2.21	2.27	2.26	2.15	2.15	2.15	2.15
2070	2.06	2.09	2.11	2.15	2.14	2.06	2.06	2.06	2.06
2075	1.98	2.00	2.01	2.04	2.04	1.98	1.98	1.98	1.98
2080	1.90	1.91	1.93	1.95	1.94	1.90	1.90	1.90	1.90
2085	1.83	1.84	1.85	1.86	1.86	1.83	1.83	1.83	1.83
2090	1.76	1.77	1.77	1.78	1.78	1.76	1.76	1.76	1.76
2095	1.70	1.70	1.71	1.71	1.71	1.70	1.70	1.70	1.70
2100	1.64	1.64	1.64	1.64	1.64	1.64	1.64	1.64	1.64

* +3%/yr growth in substitute.

Table 5.2. Halocarbon Data: Atmospheric Lifetimes, ODPs, and CLPs

Compound	Atmospheric Lifetime (years)	ODP	CLP
CFC-11	60	1	1.0
CFC-12	120	0.9–1.0	1.6
CFC-113	90	0.8–0.9	1.5
CFC-114	200	0.6–0.8	2.1
CFC-115	400	0.3–0.5	3.0
HCFC-22	15	0.04–0.06	0.15
HCFC-123	50	0.01–0.02	0.02
HCFC-124	129	0.02	0.04
HCFC-141b	76	0.07–0.11	0.15
HCFC-142b	215	0.05–0.06	0.19
CC14	50	1.0–1.2	1.02
CH3CC13	6	0.1–0.2	0.11
Halon-1211	15	3.0	
Halon-1301	110	10.0	
Methyl bromide	1.5	0.6	

Adapted from UNEP/OzL.Pro.WG.II(1)/4:18, 50, and WMO/NASA 1991:6.15.

Figure 5.2. Atmospheric Chlorine Concentrations with 100 percent Halocarbon Cuts by 2000 and Substitution with Compound X (*=growth)

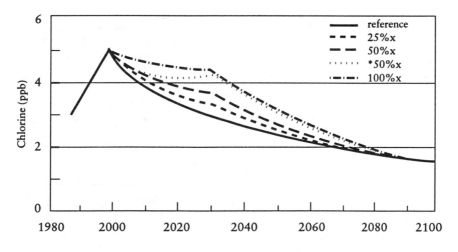

Source: UNEP/OzL.Pro.WG.II(1)/4:47.

CLPs and ODPs, along with atmospheric lifetimes, for the primary chlorinated compounds considered in the treaty revision process.)

Two parameters, both of which can be depicted either graphically or by analogy, became the focus of concern: lowering the peak atmospheric chlorine concentrations and shortening the length of time before which concentrations would return to 2 ppb. The first problem came to be known as "peak shaving"; as figure 5-3 shows, lowering the peak chlorine concentrations is analogous to slicing pieces off the top of a cake. The second problem was a matter of time and momentum, and the metaphor employed was that of the time required to stop a loaded freight train or a supertanker. The long atmospheric lifetimes of many of the halocarbons ensured that chlorine concentrations would exceed 2 ppb for many years to come; the problem was how to minimize the number of years before that would occur. Both these sets of images and analogies were used during the policy debates.

Although the chlorine-loading approach was used both before and after the Montreal Protocol, the purposes for which it was used were very different. Prior to 1987, the approach, with its emphasis on the long atmospheric

Figure 5.3. Four Scenarios for the Elimination of Halocarbons

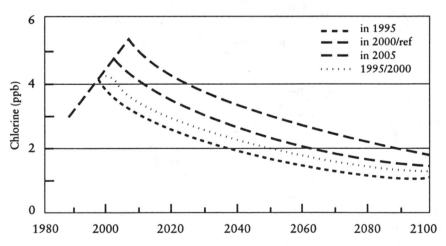

100% cut of all Halocarbons

* The reference panels took this as their yearerence year.

Source: UNEP/OzL.Pro.WG.II(1)4:46

lifetimes of CFCs, was used to inspire a long-term perspective; the problem was framed in terms of stabilizing atmospheric concentrations of chlorine. But by 1989, amid the growing recognition that the world might have to adjust to life without CFCs, the question then became one of peak shaving—i.e., figuring out how to lower the peak chlorine concentration, which would occur sometime around the year 2000, as quickly as possible. The emphasis therefore shifted from the ozone-depleting chemicals with long atmospheric lifetimes to those with short lifetimes. Compounds with the shortest lifetimes, like methyl chloroform, which lasts only six years in the atmosphere, became a major focus because the benefits would be reaped most quickly. Thus, the same approach that was used as the basis for a long-term perspective before Montreal was now used in support of measures with a more short-term advantage.[10] The knowledge brokers responsible for framing the science were quite aware that the same approach could be used for both purposes and intentionally applied that knowledge to the development of policy options (interviews with John Hoffman and Robert Watson).

Carbon tetrachloride, one of the cheapest and most toxic organic solvents, has an ODP significantly greater than any of the five regulated CFCs. With an atmospheric lifetime of fifty years, this compound is an extremely potent ozone destroyer (UNEP/OzL.Pro.WG.II[1]/4: 27). Yet it was overlooked in the Montreal Protocol; in fact, prior to 1988, there was virtually no mention of it in the context of saving the ozone layer. The reasons for its omission were essentially political. Prior to 1988, ozone depletion was tacitly defined as a problem for the industrialized countries; the principal adversaries in the Montreal Protocol negotiations were the USA and the EC. Because of its extreme toxicity, carbon tetrachloride had been banned or severely restricted in most industrialized countries, so its omission from the negotiations seems to have been unintentional. Yet the negotiators overlooked the fact that the low cost of carbon tetrachloride—only twenty-five cents per pound—made it an attractive solvent in developing countries (Makhijani, Bickel, and Makhijani 1990).

Another oversight related to bromine, a far more potent destroyer of ozone on a per molecule basis than chlorine. Halon-1301, for instance, has an astronomical ODP of 10.0. The scientific assessment Panel had stated that closing the seasonal Antarctic ozone hole would also require a phase-out of the halons. It did not, however, make any recommendations regarding methyl bromide, a less significant source of atmospheric bromine; that compound did not become a source of widespread concern until the subsequent 1991 assessment.

Thus, relying on the chlorine-loading methodology, the 1989 science review indicated that recuperation of the ozone layer would require major revisions of the Montreal Protocol, including a ban on CFCs, methyl chloroform, and carbon tetrachloride and only a transitional usage of HCFCs. Even if all anthropogenic sources of chlorine were eliminated immediately, atmospheric concentrations of chlorine would remain above 2 ppb for many decades to come; hence, even in the best of circumstances, the Antarctic ozone hole would recur for the foreseeable future. Only the chlorine-loading method of framing the science generated such conclusions, but the urgency of the situation, along with the obvious limitations of the models, gave credence to this approach over the alternatives.

With the growing sense of urgency, however, it was easy to forget that the health and environmental effects of increased ultraviolet radiation (UV-B) were the real threat—not ozone depletion per se. Yet, while funding for stratospheric science had increased sharply, funding for research on the effects had essentially remained at pre-Montreal levels (interviews with Stephen Seidel and Robert Watson). As a result, the 1989 environmental effects assessment contained little new information about the impact of increased UV-B on terrestrial plants, aquatic ecosystems, tropospheric air quality, and materials damage beyond that found in the EPA's 1987 study (EPA 1987a). In terms of human health, the emphasis continued to be on skin cancer and cataracts, despite the fact that increased UV-B radiation could have serious immunological consequences (interview with Margaret Kripke). The emphasis on skin cancer, which primarily afflicts fair-skinned people, seems particularly surprising at a time when developing countries were becoming key players in the policy debates. Yet there were few attempts to shift the emphasis, and there were virtually no challenges to the science.

This apparent anomaly can only be explained with reference to the prevailing discursive practices on ozone. Rational models of decision making would predict that, since increased UV-B radiation was the real problem, there would have been a substantial research effort into the health and environmental effects of ozone depletion. And past experience would suggest at least the possibility that developing countries would frame their objections to the treaty and the proposed revisions in scientific terms, perhaps arguing that skin cancer was not their concern. Yet neither of these possibilities occurred; in fact, there was almost no attention paid to this section of the Synthesis Report.

Instead, the scientific assessment was the driving force behind the revision process. The dominant perception was that something unprecedented

and potentially catastrophic was happening in the stratosphere and that it
was not necessary to quantify precisely the likely effects of that event. The
graphs and charts made it obvious to the participants that drastic action was
required; the discourse of damage limitation became predominant in policy discussions almost automatically.[11] In the words of one participant, the
prevailing attitude among members of the Open-Ended Working Group
and other participants was "that of the man on the street: 'Don't fool with
Mother Nature' " (interview with John Hoffman). This sentiment also
informed the precautionary discourse embodied in the Montreal Protocol,
but with the mounting evidence of impending catastrophe, it was no longer
controversial. By the time of the 1989 Synthesis Report, the discourse of
damage limitation had become universally accepted. Only the precise control measures had yet to be determined by the Second Meeting of the Parties in June 1990.

The 1989 technology assessment provided information on the technical feasibility of reducing ozone-depleting substances. Most important was
the finding that, by the year 2000, the five controlled CFCs and carbon
tetrachloride could be phased down by at least 95 percent and methyl chloroform by at least 90 percent (though this conclusion was most controversial). The panel disagreed on whether a complete phaseout of halons was
technically achievable by 2005. There was a consensus that 30 percent of
the existing CFC market would be captured by HCFCs and 10 percent by
HFCs, with the remaining 60 percent of demand satisfied by product and
process substitutes (UNEP/OzL.Pro.WG.II[1]/4:10–11).

Although the issue of technology transfer and assistance to developing
countries would later dominate the treaty revision process, the 1989 economic assessment was not particularly controversial. The panel acknowledged the need for special provisions for developing countries to obtain the
more expensive chemical substitutes but made no specific recommendations. The panel also calculated that the long-term economic benefits of
safeguarding the ozone layer, while difficult to quantify, would far out-
weigh the short-term costs of reducing CFC and halon usage. However, as
industry was prone to emphasize, a very rapid phaseout (much faster than
ten years) would be far more costly because of capital abandonment
(UNEP/OzL.Pro.WG.II[1]/4:12–13). Perhaps because of poor communication between the economics panel, largely drawn from academic circles,
and the science and technology panels, the economic review did not
explore the crucial issues of reducing methyl chloroform, carbon tetrachloride, and HCFCs.

The chemical industry reacted negatively to two implications of the Synthesis Report: that HCFCs should be used only as transitional substances and that methyl chloroform should be sharply reduced. At UNEP's Nairobi meeting in August 1989, where the Synthesis Report was first discussed, Du Pont distributed literature promoting industry's position that "potential regulation of HCFC and HFC alternatives will delay or prohibit investments and the transition away from CFCs" (Du Pont 1989:6). However, by the June 1990 Meeting of the Parties, U.S. industry backed away from this position, causing a split with its European counterparts. Recognizing that chlorine concentrations would only return to pre–ozone hole levels if HCFCs were regulated, American industry saw that definite phaseout dates were preferable to a vague threat of eventual regulation. Thus, at the London meeting, ICI continued to distribute brochures opposed to including HCFCs on the list of controlled substances, while the Alliance for a Responsible CFC Policy circulated literature advocating "prudent HCFC phaseout dates" (ICI 1990; Alliance for a Responsible CFC Policy 1990:3). U.S. industry, however, remained adamant that any phaseout schedule adopted in London should be compatible with the thirty- to forty-year lifetime of equipment using HCFCs (interview with Kevin Fay).

Industry on both sides of the Atlantic was also disconcerted by the implication that methyl chloroform, a metals and electronics solvent and a potential substitute for CFC-113, might be added to the list of controlled substances. Industry felt that the technology panel's work on methyl chloroform was weak and done too hastily, a sentiment shared by others who were not necessarily sympathetic to industry's aims (interviews with Stephen Anderson and Stephen Seidel). Yet at least some environmentalists had earlier recognized that methyl chloroform was a significant part of the ozone problem (Makhijani, Bickel, and Makhijani 1990). One obstacle to consensus was that the issue brought in a new set of players not conversant with the ozone problem. ICI, which had been active in the international negotiating process from the beginning, was a primary producer of methyl chloroform in Europe. But Dow Chemical, with no previous involvement in the issue, was the primary producer both in the United States and the world, accounting for nearly half of global production. Unlike Du Pont, which had two atmospheric scientists working only on the ozone problem, Dow Chemical had none. Had Du Pont, rather than Dow, been the top producer, perhaps events would have transpired differently (interview with Stephen Seidel). In any case, ICI and Dow Chemical joined together to lobby against strong controls on methyl chloroform.

Once again, through creative framing and the inclusion of partial information, scientific knowledge was used to promote parochial interests. Industry, with Japan's support,[12] emphasized methyl chloroform's low ozone depletion potential—only about 0.1—and its short atmospheric lifetime of approximately six years. Reminiscent of the CFC industry's statements in 1986, the methyl chloroform industry also claimed that production was declining, a claim that was later refuted (interview with Stephen Seidel). Industry itself was surprised when the 1989 production figures were announced in April 1990, just two months before the Meeting of the Parties, showing a major increase over 1988 levels (interview with Mike Harris).

At the Geneva working group meeting in November 1989, where the final draft of the Synthesis Report was considered, three industrial associations argued that the maximum technically feasible reduction of methyl chloroform was 23 percent by the year 2000. This figure was at odds with the technology assessment, which concluded that a full phaseout was achievable by the same date. The science panel responded to industry's claim, noting that even a 20 percent reduction in 1986 emissions by the year 2000 would still increase chlorine concentrations by 0.4 ppb and would delay recovery of the ozone hole by thirty years. Because of the huge quantities being produced—as much as all the CFCs combined—methyl chloroform was responsible for approximately 16 percent of the total anthropogenic chlorine loading (UNEP/OzL.Pro.WG.II[1]/7:40). In the end, the science assessment overshadowed industry's objections; in particular, the graphs included in the report provided strong evidence in favor of a phaseout (see the figures in this chapter, especially figure 5.1).

By 1990, with the Second Meeting of the Parties approaching, industry saw the inevitable and relented. The Nordics had proposed a phaseout date as early as 1995, and the U.S. Clean Air Act called for regulation of methyl chloroform domestically. Within less than a year, Dow Chemical and ICI shifted from vociferous opposition to reluctant support of a phaseout. Many observers were critical of Dow for its initial recalcitrance, particularly in contrast to Du Pont's apparently cooperative attitude. Yet Dow Chemical arrived at its position of support for the regulators in only one year, in contrast to Du Pont's ten-year journey to a comparable position (interview with Stephen Anderson).

Proposals to reduce sharply or eliminate carbon tetrachloride were not nearly so factious (UNEP/OzL.Pro.WG.II[1]/4:27). As noted earlier, most Western industrialized countries had already severely restricted its use, except as a feedstock for CFCs. But the industrialized countries were shocked to learn how widely used the compound was in the Soviet Union, Eastern Europe, and developing countries (interview with Eileen Claussen). The Soviets led the effort to salvage carbon tetrachloride, but they were unable to galvanize sufficient support among other countries.[13]

Although a broad consensus existed on the need to phase out CFCs, to reduce halons more quickly, and to add carbon tetrachloride and methyl chloroform to the list of controlled substances, the specific dates and interim reduction steps proved to be more contentious. At the Nairobi meeting where the Synthesis Report was reviewed, only the Nordic group called for concrete steps to bring chlorine levels below those at which the Antarctic ozone hole formed: a CFC and methyl chloroform phaseout by the year 2000, with 50 percent cuts before the mid-1990s; a carbon tetrachloride phaseout by the mid-1990s; and controls on all substances with ozone depletion potentials greater than 1 percent of those of the CFCs. Environmentalists lobbied their governments to adopt the Nordic position (FOE 1989b:3). Most countries supported a CFC phaseout by the year 2000 but would not commit to eliminating the other chemicals. The Open-Ended Working Group was compelled to meet on a bimonthly basis, to delegate many duties to smaller groups, and to establish a Bureau of the Parties to formulate specific recommendations for control provisions (UNEP/OzL.Pro.Bur.1/2).

As it became clear that CFCs were likely to be eliminated, developing countries became increasingly vocal, although only a handful of them were parties to the treaty. Article 5 granted them a grace period of ten years to reduce their CFC usage by 50 percent, but CFCs were likely to become scarce and expensive soon in light of the proposed treaty revisions. Developing countries did not want to increase their dependency on a family of obsolete chemicals, nor did they want to pay far higher prices to the industrialized countries' chemical companies for substitutes. Yet the science assessment had demonstrated that, even with full compliance under the Montreal Protocol, chlorine concentrations would rise to an astronomical 11 ppb, an unacceptable scenario for developing and industrialized countries alike.

As I mentioned earlier, the developing countries did not state their reservations in scientific terms, even though they were barely represented on the science and environmental panels and so could have challenged the veracity of these panels' findings on that basis alone. Other arguments were also there to be made: ozone depletion was occurring at the poles and the upper latitudes, not over the tropics, and skin cancer was not likely to become a health problem for non-Caucasian populations. The recurring Antarctic ozone hole, with its dilution effect throughout the Southern Hemisphere, certainly drew the attention of the South. But it should be remembered that only 7.5 percent of the world's population lives in the Southern Hemisphere (United Nations 1989). A few countries—namely, Argentina, Chile, Australia and New Zealand—are directly at risk because of the Antarctic hole, but the bulk of developing countries' population is concentrated in the tropical regions of the Northern Hemisphere, the area of the globe least at risk.

But developing countries neither disputed the findings of the science panel nor questioned whether their own populations would be vulnerable to the health and environmental consequences of increased ultraviolet radiation (interviews with Mohammed Ilyas and M. Margarita Prendez). Perhaps this can be explained by their relative lack of scientific infrastructure; clearly, stratospheric research is not a priority for poor countries. Or perhaps the developing countries were simply persuaded by the information contained in the Synthesis Report. But that alone does not seem sufficient to explain their almost automatic acceptance of the science. Again, it seems that the discourse of damage limitation had become so ubiquitous and had gained so much momentum that there was virtually no effort to supplant it with a alternative discourse, even from those—industry and the developing countries—with the greatest interest in promoting something different. Instead, a new wave of environmental concern was spreading, even among many of the developing countries (see FOE 1989a).

With a consensus that CFCs would be eliminated, developing countries focused their energies on the problems of financial compensation and technology transfer. During a lengthy EPA visit in 1988 to China, the sole focus of discussion was CFC substitutes and the economics of technology transfer (interview with Eileen Claussen). At the Nairobi meeting of the Open-Ended Working Group in August 1989, developing countries stated that they could only abide by the terms of the Montreal Protocol if they received technical and financial assistance. They reiterated the desirability of establishing a multilateral trust fund administered by UNEP and funded by industrialized countries over and beyond existing aid programs (the principle of "additionality"), and they sought equal access to new chemical substitutes without incurring economic penalties (the principle of "preferential and non-commercial technology transfer") (UNEP/OzL.Pro.WG.I[2]/4).

These principles were quite controversial. At least some participants from industrialized countries feared that developing countries would use environmental problems as an excuse to demand a global redistribution of wealth, and some even suspected that this was part of Mostafa Tolba's agenda (interview with Ed Shykind). Some industrialized countries, most notably the United States, the U.K., and Japan preferred to provide assistance through an existing institution like the World Bank, a proposal viewed with suspicion by developing countries, which believed they could exert more influence with UNEP. One major uncertainty was how large the fund should be, a calculation that required accurate information on present and future CFC demand, as well as on the future cost and availability of chemical substitutes. A controversial study done by a Netherlands consulting firm was cited by Mostafa Tolba at the August meeting in Nairobi. That study estimated the cost to developing countries to be $400 million annually for ten years (Tolba 1989b). Because of the tremendous uncertainties entailed in making reliable estimates, the delegates at the Nairobi meeting decided to commission feasibility studies in sample developing countries to identify their needs and the eventual cost of complying with the treaty. Developing countries, however, were disappointed, viewing the move to study the issue as an attempt by industrial nations to avoid committing actual funds (FOE 1989b:2).

The question of technology transfer and financial compensation became the focus of debate between North and South until the 1990 London Conference of the Parties. Between late 1989 and June 1990, one working group or another was meeting almost constantly, with this issue frequently dominating the agenda. India, for instance, expressed a desire that all CFC production should be stopped, but only after developing countries received alternative technology (*International Environment Reporter* [*IER*] 1990).[14] In the meantime, Tolba asked the EPA and other environmental agencies in industrialized countries to coordinate "country studies" to ascertain the cost of the transition to CFC substitutes. The sample countries included Mexico, Brazil, India, China, India, Venezuela, Kenya, and Malaysia.

At the February 1990 meeting of the Open-Ended Working Group, the results of two general studies on the costs of developing countries' compliance with the Montreal Protocol were discussed. One study was done by a British firm (Markandya 1990), and the other was done by an Indian firm (Pargal and Kumar 1990). The two research teams reviewed each other's data and methodologies and presented a joint report on their areas of agreement and disagreement. They agreed on some broad principles regarding what should be considered legitimate costs, but they disagreed on the key factor of demand growth projections. As in the Montreal Protocol negotiations, growth projections reflected the political and ecnomic interests of the parties making the projections. Predictably, the Indian report foresaw higher future demand for CFCs and their substitutes in developing countries and therefore concluded that a larger fund would be required. But because the executive summary of the Indian report was vague, containing no specific cost estimates, the British report was more authoritative. That study's executive summary proposed an initial allocation of $200 to $300 million for the first three years. The credibility of the British report was bolstered when the EPA estimated that the incremental costs to Article 5 parties would be approximately $100 million for the next three years, and $100 to $200 million more if China, India and other nonsignatory parties were to sign (UNEP/OzL.Pro.WG.II[2]/7). With this remarkable concordance between studies, the amount of $200 to $300 million over three years came to be bandied about as a plausible amount for the fund (UNEP/OzL.Pro.WG.IV/8).[15]

That figure could be little more than conjecture, however. As late as the March meeting of the Open-Ended Working Group, there was no reliable data on 1986 levels of CFC consumption in developing countries. Several delegations proposed that UNEP should hire a consultant to present a "best available estimate," but others doubted whether such information could be prepared in time for the May funding meeting (UNEP/OzL.Pro.WG.III[1]/3:7). If past levels of consumption were unknown, then clearly predictions of future levels were necessarily that much more obscure. Yet, because of the political deadline imposed by the upcoming Meeting of the Parties in June, the participants were compelled to accept the figures presented in the EPA and Markandya studies.

The discussion of preferential and noncommercial access to substitute technology raised the thorny issue of intellectual property rights. Industry was loath to invest in substitute technology only to have it donated to developing countries; yet without new technology, the goals of the Montreal Protocol, particularly an amended protocol, could not be met. The International Chamber of Commerce (ICC) felt that this bid to mandate technology transfer by treaty could set a dangerous precedent; governments, it claimed, have no authority to compel companies to share their research and technology on a noncommercial basis (ICC 1990). Moreover, as some industry representatives pointed out, chemical substitutes need not be the focus of concern; technologies and processes to reduce, conserve, and recycle were already available to reduce developing countries' demand for CFCs. Building a domestic manufacturing base for chemical substitutes, they argued, should be a low priority, especially when nobody was certain what the new compounds would be (interview with Tony Vogelsburg; ICC 1990).

The principle of additionality was not particularly controversial until the eleventh hour. Just before the special funding meeting in May, the United States announced that it would only support a special funding mechanism within the World Bank if no additional donor contributions were required. The rationale for this position was that the requirement of additional donor contributions would set a dangerous precedent, particularly as the much larger problem of greenhouse warming was gaining attention. The U.S. decision was made by John Sununu, White House Chief of Staff, and Richard Darman, budget director, over the objections of EPA administrator William Reilly (*Washington Post* 1990a). This was the first time that the United States had raised serious objections to the principle of additionality (Tolba 1989b).

Domestically, the reaction was quite negative (*Time* 1990; *Washington Post* 1990b). The reversal was characterized as cynical and irrational; the U.S. share of the CFC fund would be a paltry $8 to $25 million per year, compared to a savings of billions in medical costs. The U.S. chemical industry, which stood to gain from the fund, pointed out that the U.S. contribution would be a tiny portion of the estimated $5.7 billion that the government stood to collect in taxes on windfall profits (*New York Times* 1990b; see also DeCanio and Lee 1991). Critics also pointed out that the new policy would undermine American environmental diplomacy, casting doubt on the USA's reliability as a negotiating partner. Moreover, the decision, emanating from the Office of Management and Budget and the White House chief of staff, sent the message that the nation's top environmental experts and diplomats were to be excluded from the process (Pell 1990). Legislation was introduced in both houses of Congress to fund the U.S. contribution in case the Bush administration maintained its position (*IER* 1991f:637).

Internationally, the response was equally critical, in both industrialized and developing countries. At the May funding meeting in Geneva, the other key donor countries expressed their support for the fund, and a representative of the World Bank stated that institution would participate only if the principle of additionality were adopted. China and India declared that they would not sign the treaty without the guarantee of additional funds (UNEP/OzL.Pro.WG.III[2]/3). Members of the U.S. delegation were put in the awkward position of having to retract their support for policy recommendations that, in some instances, they themselves had authored (interview with Eileen Claussen).

This incident bears a striking resemblance to the "hats and sunglasses" episode within the Reagan administration during the Montreal Protocol negotiations. In both cases, ideologically oriented cabinet members who were not directly involved in the negotiations sought to foil the efforts of the EPA and the State Department. And both episodes resulted in significant political embarrassment for the respective administrations. Unlike the first episode, which resulted from a simplistic interpretation of scientific information, the funding proposal, while framed in terms of fairness, was based more explicitly on perceived long-term economic self-interest. It was also more clearly an instance of symbolic politics; if aid additionality were truly the issue, then the United States could simply have chosen to cut its development assistance programs by a few million dollars. Although progress was made at the May meeting of the Working Group, the U.S. position cast a pall over the deliberations.

Updating the Protocol: London 1990

The Open-Ended Working Group met during the week before the Meeting of Parties to finalize a text for the high-level meeting. With over eighty governments and thirty nongovernmental organizations dealing with a myriad of extremely complex issues, the task was unwieldy, and many issues remained unresolved at the end of the week. Two parallel working groups were created to simplify the negotiations: one for control measures and the other for assistance for developing countries.[16] The Working Group was not able to complete its work in time for the ministerial meeting, and some of the decisions reached there did not hold when the ministers arrived. When they did convene, the ninety-five ministers mostly worked in small informal groups, as they had in Montreal, with substantial help from Mostafa Tolba (Benedick 1991:169).

Going into the Second Meeting of the Parties, two sets of issues dominated the debate on control measures: the grim evidence of rapid ozone depletion and industry's progress in finding substitutes and alternatives. These two factors gave a strong impetus to the treaty revision process in London. Regarding the second, progress had been much more rapid than had been expected. Some chemical substitutes were available in all sectors, including refrigeration and air conditioning, the most difficult of all; for some sectors, including aerosols, foam packaging, and electronics solvents, CFCs were already being phased out. Singapore had already reduced its CFC consumption by 60 percent.

Of course, the new chemicals carried greater health and environmental risks than their chemically inert predecessors, as well as a greater financial burden (*New York Times* 1990c; Manzer 1990). But other avenues, such as recycling and conservation, were both cheaper and safer. Halon and methyl chloroform consumption, for instance, could be cut in half simply through conservation efforts (interview with Stephen Anderson). Overall, the perceived availability of substitutes and alternatives made it easier for delegates to consider stronger control provisions. Of course, the process was circular: the likelihood of stronger controls, prompted by the alarming scientific evidence, also drove the search for alternatives.

At the opening of the London meeting in June 1990, Ivar Isaksen distributed new scientific information to the delegates, including data on unprecedented ozone losses over New Zealand and a surprising decrease of 3 percent in equatorial regions. The Australian delegate reported a 15 percent ozone loss over MacQuarie Island, a region outside the South polar vortex extending over a range that includes one-eighth of the planet. Prime Minister Margaret Thatcher cited a statement by Joe Farman, head of the research team that had discovered the Antarctic ozone hole, that the unexpected events over Antarctica could well be replicated over the Arctic (UNEP/OzL.Pro.2/3). Not surprisingly, this prompted the countries nearest the poles (the Nordic countries, Australia, and New Zealand) to put forth the strongest proposals for controlling ozone-depleting chemicals. The United States had no official position on a CFC phaseout going into the London meeting (interview with Eileen Claussen).[17]

Even with the new evidence, most of the proposals considered at the London meetings went no further than those formulated in Helsinki one year earlier. Mostafa Tolba's proposal, modeled on the Helsinki Declaration, served as the basis for the London talks (see table 5.3 for its main elements). Yet, in the interim since Helsinki, many countries—among them, Australia, Austria, the Federal Republic of Germany, the Netherlands, New Zealand, Norway, Sweden, and Switzerland—had unilaterally adopted significantly more stringent measures. The West German cabinet, responding to pressure from environmental groups, approved a measure banning CFCs and halons by 1995, carbon tetrachloride and methyl chloroform in 1992, and certain uses of HCFC-22 by 1993 and 2000 (*IER* 1991b). In

January 1990, the European Commission proposed the elimination of CFCs by the end of 1997 (Jachtenfuchs 1990:272). Meeting just prior to the London conference, the EC Council of Ministers weakened the language by adding the phrase "or no later that 2000" (Council of the European Communities 1990), but this did not detract from the fact that several EC member states, including the FRG, Denmark, Belgium, and the Netherlands, were intent on phasing out the chemicals by 1995.[18]

Environmental groups, of course, argued that if Germany, one of the major CFC producers, could ban CFCs by 1995, then other countries could certainly do better than 2000. Environmentalists constituted a well-organized presence at the London meeting and proved themselves to be adept at employing scientific knowledge to promote their goals (see FOE 1990a; NRDC 1990). They found the chlorine-loading approach to be particularly useful. Criticizing Tolba's proposal, they argued that it did not even go as far the recommendations implicit in the 1989 Synthesis Report. Tolba's position, if implemented, would allow peak chlorine levels to reach 4.5 ppb, a 50 percent increase over 1990 levels. Worse, even with full compliance not only on the control measures but also on the nonbinding resolution, the levels would remain above 4 ppb until 2050, and the Antarc-

Table 5.3. UNEP Executive Director's Proposal for Control
Measures, London Meeting

Substance	Reduction (%)	Date
CFCs, new and old	20	1993
	85	1997
	100	2000
Halons	50	1995
	100	2000
Carbon tetrachloride	85	1995
	100	2000
Methyl chloroform	freeze	1993
	30	1995
	50	2000
Nonbinding Resolution		
Methyl chloroform	phaseout	2010
HCFCs	phaseout	2040
Other halons	20	1993
	85	1997
	100	2000

Source: UNEP/OzL.Pro.WG.IV/2/Rev./1.

tic ozone hole would not be healed until at least 2080. Environmentalists also joined with Sweden in advocating an early phaseout of methyl chloroform; based upon the scientific evidence, they argued, this was the fastest way of reducing chlorine concentrations in the atmosphere (FOE 1990b:4). They bolstered their position with information from the technology assessment, in which 90 to 95 percent reductions of methyl chloroform were deemed to be technically feasible (Benedick 1991:165).

Industry was also well represented at the London meeting, particularly because the impending treaty revisions involved a broader range of users and producers than did the original protocol. While industry favored a later phaseout date for CFCs—2000 rather than 1997—it was not particularly vocal on this issue (interview with Kevin Fay). The major CFC producers were mostly concerned that HCFCs, now considered "transitional substances," not be strictly regulated (interview with Tony Vogelsburg). Du Pont and ICI circulated literature stating that early phaseout dates would discourage commercial investment in substitutes, thereby deferring the far more critical CFC phaseout date. The German CFC industry, in contrast, was silent on the issue of HCFCs, having chosen not to invest in chemicals that would only be transitional and to rely instead on ozone-safe HFCs. On methyl chloroform, U.S. and European industry were both resigned to some reductions, but they diverged in their preferences on the amounts. Under the amended Clean Air Act mandating a methyl chloroform ban, U.S. industry was subject to very different conditions and therefore favored stricter international regulations in order to create a level playing field (FOE 1990b).

On the question of adjustments in the CFC phaseout schedule, the principal adversaries were the EC, with the support of the "strong revision coalition" (the Nordic countries, Canada, Australia, and New Zealand), favoring 1997 and, on the other side, the United States, Japan, and the Soviet Union favoring the year 2000. Developing countries were less concerned with the actual phaseout date than with preserving their ten-year grace period to comply with the protocol's provisions. Ultimately, the least-common-denominator effect, so familiar in international environmental negotiations, prevailed, and the 2000 phaseout date was adopted.

The United States was able to marshal critical information on its behalf: UNEP's own technology assessment had found that a phaseout was technically feasible by the year 2000. This employment of consensual knowledge swayed the balance in the United States' favor (interview with Stephen Seidel). The reduction schedule was changed to 20 percent of 1986 levels by

1993, 50 percent by 1995, 85 percent by 1997, and 100 percent by 2000. Developing countries maintained their ten-year grace period and will not have to reduce CFC use until 2005, when a 50 percent cut will be mandatory. The revisions also closed a potential loophole by including ten "other CFCs" not included in the original protocol because they were not being produced. Thirteen countries broke publicly with the London meeting, issuing a formal declaration pledging to end CFC production by 1997.[19] Britain, when challenged, claimed not to have been asked to sign, but informally declared its support for the 1997 phaseout date.

Environmentalists were quite disappointed with the London CFC revisions (FOE 1990b). They were not, however, so dissatisfied with the outcome on methyl chloroform. Initially, the United States, along with the EC and Japan, backed Tolba's proposal for a 50 percent cut by 2000.[20] The Soviet Union, which did not use the chemical, was joined by West Germany and "the strong revision coalition" mentioned above in pressing for 85 percent reduction by the year 2000. Again, consensual knowledge was brought to bear. The science assessment had shown that reducing methyl chloroform, with its short atmospheric lifetime, would yield the quickest results in lowering chlorine concentrations. And the technology panel had found that 90 to 95 percent reductions were feasible by the year 2000.

But political factors also turned the tide. With a domestic methyl chloroform ban legislated by the Clean Air Act, the U.S. position was not clearly in its own best interest. The Norwegian environment minister, objecting to the nonprecedential language required by the United States on the financial mechanism, consented to include it only if the USA agreed to a methyl chloroform ban. Eileen Claussen enjoyed calling John Sununu, who was far more concerned with the financial mechanism than with the control measures, and saying, "We can get this language, but we have to give up methyl chloroform for it." Sununu, who was only concerned about the financial mechanism, approved the trade immediately (interview with Eileen Claussen). The final agreement was a freeze in 1993, a cut of 30 percent in 1995, 70 percent in 2000, and 100 percent in 2005 (article 2E of the London Revisions, UNEP/OzL.Pro.2/L.6). Thus, an unusual combination of consensual knowledge, domestic U.S. politics, and adroit bargaining on the part of a small state led to action on methyl chloroform that went beyond even the strongest proposal on the table.

While environmentalists were pleased with the results on methyl chloroform, they were extremely displeased with the outcome on HCFCs. A number of governments had already taken measures to curb their usage. In the amended Clean Air Act, the U.S. Senate had set a phaseout date of 2030, and the House of Representative had set a date of 2035. In his proposal, Tolba had suggested 2040. While the CFC producers had reluctantly accepted Tolba's recommendation, their lobbying raised concerns among participants that if HCFCs were formally controlled, companies would not invest in them. Just before the congressional vote on the Clean Air Act, Du Pont announced to the press that it was delaying plans to build HCFC plants pending the outcome of proposed regulations. In the end, however, the EC blocked consensus, and no restrictions on HCFCs were adopted. Instead, a nonbinding resolution was accepted urging efforts to limit the use of HCFCs and setting a voluntary phaseout date of 2040 (annex VII of the London Revisions, UNEP/OzL.Pro.2/L.6). Environmentalists pointed out that the science assessment had demonstrated that controls on transitional substances would be necessary to close the Antarctic hole within the next century. They pledged to bring HCFCs formally into the protocol at the next review meeting, in 1992 (FOE 1990b:8).

There was no organized opposition to Tolba's proposal to eliminate carbon tetrachloride by the year 2000, which was based firmly on the technology assessment's conclusions. The parties could not agree on interim reductions beyond the 85 percent cut in 1995. Some minor differences arose on the baseline date for the new substances, carbon tetrachloride and methyl chloroform; in the end, 1989 was chosen over 1986, the base year for the Montreal Protocol, because the more recent production data was more reliable (interview with Eileen Claussen). Annex II, the protocol amendment covering all new substances, took effect in January 1992.

Given the prominence of the chlorine-loading approach in the debates, it is not surprising that this was the touchstone against which the agreement was measured. The same evidence, however, was used to support different judgments of the control measures adopted at London. Figure 5.4 reproduces an EPA graph that compares the predicted chlorine levels for the Montreal Protocol and the London Revisions. Citing the dramatic difference between the two, Richard Benedick applauds the control measures adopted in London (Benedick 1991:176). Environmentalists, however, pointed out that, under the London Revisions, chlorine levels will reach 4 ppb, twice the amount at which the ozone hole appeared, and will not return to prehole levels until 2080. On this basis, they decried the "dangerously slow timetables" adopted at London (FOE 1990d). The scenarios in the science assessment had given governments "powerful tools," one environmentalist stated at the London meeting, "and they will be judged to have acted knowingly" (FOE 1990b:10).

For the most part, developing countries were not deeply involved in the debates on control measures. They were, however, quite concerned about the procedure for voting on adjustments. The original procedure adopted in Montreal, requiring that amendments be approved by two-thirds of the parties representing at least 50 percent of consumption, made sense when the primary participants were industrialized countries. However, by the time of the London meeting, it was widely perceived as unfair to developing countries. The new voting procedure required that adjustments be approved by two-thirds of all parties, and simple majorities of developing and industrialized countries (article 2H of the London Revisions, UNEP/OzL.Pro.2/L.6). Article 2, paragraph 4, was changed to grant the additional production allowance only to developing countries to meet their basic domestic needs. Article 4 on trade restrictions was revised in two important ways. Paragraph 2 banning the export of controlled substances

Figure 5.4. Montreal Protocol Versus London Revisions

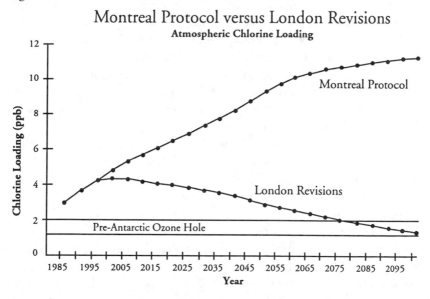

Note: Although the London revisions do not control HCFCs, the graph assumes that HCFCs, with an atmospheric lifetime of eight years, replace 30 percent of the CFC market and that HCFC production is frozen in 2020 and phased out in 2040.

Source: U.S. EPA.

to nonparties would now apply to all parties, not just developing countries. And the industrial rationalization clause was adjusted to facilitate the EC's needs (article 4).

In spite of the complexity of the control measures adopted at London, it was the funding mechanism that dominated the meeting. Just prior to the meeting, the United States withdrew its objections to the principle of additionality. But it continued to insist upon several conditions: the addition of language about the fund's nonprecedential nature, a preliminary statement that the ozone problem had been scientifically verified, a permanent seat on the fund's managing committee, and a provision that the majority of seats be held by donor countries (*Los Angeles Times* 1990b). The second condition implicitly referred to the fact that global climate change had not yet been measured, nor was it likely to be conclusively documented for many years (Intergovernmental Panel on Climate Change 1990). Developing countries, however, opposed the conditions (*Los Angeles Times* 1990c).

Despite the objections, the first three conditions were met, although the final language, "without prejudice to any future arrangements," was a slightly weaker version of the original U.S. condition (article 10, paragraph 10). As mentioned above, Norway withheld approval of this clause until the United States agreed to a methyl chloroform ban. The USA was granted a permanent seat by the rather awkward method of constituting it as a separate region unto itself out of the seven established among industrialized countries. Developing countries, however, were also divided into seven regions and were thus given voting power on the Executive Committee equal to that of the donor countries.

India and China, neither of whom had yet signed the Montreal Protocol, indicated that they would only sign if they were satisfied with the details of the funding mechanism. India insisted that developing countries should receive not only funding but also the knowledge and patents necessary to produce the new technologies on their own. Du Pont responded with a position paper emphasizing the importance of patent protection in ensuring industry's willingness to invest in a new generation of chemicals (FOE 1990a:11). Malaysia also complained that developing countries were not able to obtain adequate supplies of the increasingly scarce and overpriced CFCs. The developing countries believed that they should not be obligated to abide by the treaty if they were not satisfied with the workings of the financial mechanism. In the final revision, they were not freed from their treaty obligations, but a statement was inserted indicating that their ability to abide by the treaty would depend on the effective workings of the financial mechanism and technology transfer (article 5, paragraph 8).

Because a permanent funding mechanism could not, according to the treaty's terms, operate until 1992, an "Interim Multilateral Trust Fund" (hereafter called the Multilateral Fund) was set up to operate for three years beginning January 1, 1991. The amount of the fund, determined by the results of the country studies, was set at $160 million for the first three years, plus another $80 million should China and India become parties. The fund covers a range of expenses, including projects to retrofit existing CFC-using equipment, to convert CFC plants to substitute production, to import higher-priced substitutes, and to establish recycling programs (UNEP/OzL.Pro.2/L.6). Contributions are to be made according to the U.S. assessment scale. The principle of additionality was putatively adopted, although it is not enforceable. Under certain circumstances, bilateral assistance can count as a contribution to the Multilateral Fund if it provides additional resources (article 10, paragraph 6). Three agencies—UNEP, the World Bank, and the United Nations Development Programme—were designated the implementing agencies of the fund, with the World Bank given the key functions of administration and management (annex IV, appendix 4).[21]

China, followed by India, announced that it was satisfied with the results and would sign the treaty. With the important exception of the United States, most delegates applauded the fund. "The U.S. is the only government that doesn't want to admit that the ozone fund is a ground-breaking precedent," said one observer. "It will help gain developing country cooperation on other pressing environmental problems" (FOE 1990d:7).

Ironically, the immediate beneficiaries of the London Revisions would be the world's largest chemical companies (*Wall Street Journal* 1990). The phasing-out of CFCs meant a guaranteed market for substitutes, a market that favored the chemical giants with their large research budgets and laboratories. But the London Revisions, even if they were considered too weak by environmentalists, went far beyond the Montreal Protocol in limiting global ozone depletion. They continued the movement, launched with the Vienna Convention, toward precautionary action and concretized the discourse of damage limitation based on the chlorine-loading methodology. Moreover, because of the new mechanisms for funding and technology transfer, the treaty was now truly global. Yet, sensing that the revisions might not be sufficient, the participants at the London meeting decided to move up the next scientific and technical review in order to pave the way for additional revisions in 1992.

Further Revisions: Copenhagen 1992

The international effort to save the ozone layer was, more than anything else, driven by information. As one of UNEP's assessment panels observed, "It is information on the extent of ozone damage and the contingent damage costs that motivates the ODS substitution process, and it is information on alternative technologies and processes that makes substitution possible. Furthermore, the effectiveness of the Interim Multilateral Ozone Fund will be built on efficient information flows" (UNEP 1991c:15).

The two primary factors that drove the treaty revisions, the scientific observations of unprecedented ozone losses and the rapid progress in generating alternative technologies, continued to dominate policy discussions in the aftermath of the London meeting. Scientific discourse, framed in terms of the link between atmospheric chlorine concentrations and ozone losses, pointed to the necessity of further controls on ozone-depleting substances. And technological developments highlighted the possibility of implementing such controls. Together, science and technology suggested policies that would concretize the discourse of damage limitation. Reminiscent of events in the immediate aftermath of the Montreal Protocol, by the time of the Third Meeting of the Parties, held in Nairobi in June 1991, new developments suggested that the London Revisions had not gone far enough.

Since the London meeting, only one year before, the situation had become much more critical. The Antarctic ozone hole, which had hitherto evinced a biennial oscillation with weaker holes in even-numbered years, was as bad in 1990 as in 1987 and 1989 (*Science* 1990). New observations made since the 1989 scientific assessment indicated major ozone losses near the Arctic—as much as 43 percent over Scandinavia (*IER* 1991a). Just two months before the Nairobi meeting, NASA announced that total column ozone over North America was being depleted twice as fast as had been previously thought. Scientists were uncertain about whether it was sulfate aerosols or polar stratospheric clouds that provided the mechanism for CFCs to deplete ozone in the Northern Hemisphere, but they were certain about the observations (*IER* 1991b). Sherwood Rowland, coauthor of the original CFC–ozone depletion theory, declared that NASA's data, which used 1978 as a base year, had underestimated the ozone losses. In response, Albert Gore led thirty other senators in urging President Bush to follow the lead of the EC, which had approved in March 1991 a phaseout of CFCs by 1997 (*IER* 1991c).22 Environmentalists, calling the new data "frightening," urged their governments to adopt Germany's 1995 CFC and halon ban (*IER* 1991b).

New technologies, including both new chemicals and new processes, continued to be developed for the approximately thirty-five hundred specific applications using CFCs (interview with Tony Vogelsburg). Every year since the signing of the Montreal Protocol, thousands of users had attended the Substitutes and Alternatives Conference jointly sponsored by UNEP and the EPA. And every year, several important new technologies were announced at the conference (interview with Stephen Anderson). With a guaranteed market for CFC substitutes, industrial firms such as Atochem, ICI, and Du Pont were actively commercializing HCFC-141b, -142b, -134a, and -123 and HFC-134a. Chemical substitutes were even found for halons, previously thought to be the most difficult to replace. Great Lakes Chemical Corporation of Indiana, for instance, reported that FM-100 has the same fire suppression ability as halons but with an ozone depletion potential of only 1.1 compared to 10 to 13 for halons (*Wall Street Journal* 1991a).[23]

In many cases, new processes were more important than new chemicals. New recycling methods were developed for the refrigeration and air conditioning industry. The international fire protection community, with its long-standing concern for human health and safety, became very active in finding ways to recycle and redeploy halons. In some cases, the politics of ozone protection made for strange bedfellows. At a conference sponsored by NATO, the U.S. Air Force, and the EPA, participants agreed that essential military and civilian uses of halon were small and could be served by existing stocks if "halon banks" could be established (U.S. Air Force, EPA, and NATO 1991).[24]

Progress on substitutes and alternatives, however, was determined more by innovative arrangements for information-sharing than by major technological breakthroughs. Two industry research consortia, PAFT and AFEAS, have already been discussed. With the help of the EPA, the Industry Cooperative for Ozone Layer Protection (ICOLP) was also established to make available nonproprietary, CFC-alternative information through technology-transfer workshops, an electronic database, and guidebooks. The ICOLP database, OZONET, has been linked to UNEP's International Cleaner Production Information Clearinghouse (ICPIC) in Paris. UNEP also established the OzonAction Information Clearinghouse (OAIC), with an electronic mail capability for users to exchange information, as well as data bases on alternative technologies, equipment, and product suppliers; expert contacts; country programs; corporate initiatives; and literature abstracts (*OzonAction Newsletter* 1991).

Some companies rose to new heights of corporate responsibility in sharing information and technology. Northern Telecom, for instance, developed a no-clean process that costs far less than and eliminates the need for CFC-113 in electronics. Digital Corporation produced an aqueous cleaning technology to replace CFC-113. In the only two instances of this sort in environmental protection, both these companies have licensed their patented technologies worldwide without a fee (interview with Stephen Anderson).

Innovative partnerships involving industry and government agencies from both developing and industrialized countries sprang up to speed the elimination of ozone-depleting substances in developing countries. The Mexican government, in partnership with the EPA, the ICOLP, and Northern Telecom, announced plans to eliminate CFCs on the same schedule as industrialized countries under the Montreal Protocol. CFC consumption in Thailand, a signatory to the Montreal Protocol, rose exponentially from 1986 to 1990; in the first four months of 1991, Thailand used 45 percent more CFCs than it did during all of 1990. Solvents constituted nearly half of this CFC use, and 97 percent of that was by Japanese and U.S. companies and joint ventures (*IER* 1991d). In response, several Japanese and American industry associations, along with the Thai government, the EPA and the Japanese Ministry of International Trade and Industry (MITI), announced plans to phase out solvents controlled by the protocol. In other industrialized countries as well, multinational corporations pressured their foreign subsidiaries and their host governments to reduce CFC consumption.

Meeting for the first time in September 1990, the executive committee of the Multilateral Fund designated UNEP as the fund's treasurer and established the fund's secretariat in Montreal. The most difficult task was to work out the fund's complex operational details. Unlike other programs addressing global environmental problems, the fund allocated resources before determining a process for allocation, and it placed administrative and managerial responsibility in the hands of three agencies. Establishing equitable and consistent project eligibility criteria proved to be a great challenge. The decision to fund on a concessionary basis raised thorny issues: the availability of grants and low-interest loans, for instance, could lead some countries and companies to shelve investments they had already planned to make. The fund's most straightforward task was the development of country studies to ascertain the needs and costs of individual developing countries. Within the first year, new studies were launched for seven countries (*IER* 1991f).

Environmentalists were critical of the fund's executive committee for being preoccupied with procedural and administrative issues during its first year of operation. The three implementing agencies seemed more concerned with their own bureaucratic interests than with coordinating their work plans to make the fund operational. As of the April 1991 meeting of the executive committee, only $2 million in contributions had been received for the 1991 budget of $50 million, and the fund had distributed no ozone-friendly technology to developing countries. Environmental NGOs and industry were disappointed when their request for observer status at executive committee meetings was denied; only those groups specifically invited would be permitted to attend (FOE 1991b:2).

Despite the early problems with the fund, the financing of technology transfers to developing countries seemed to be an easier task than had been originally envisioned. The first country studies suggested that as many as half of the initial projects would offer a positive financial return to the implementing country (*IER* 1991f:638). This surprising finding was a direct result of the fact that CFC substitutes and alternatives were turning out to be far cheaper and more readily available than anyone had imagined a few years earlier. Many of the industrial modifications involved cost-effective recycling or process changes that could have been implemented prior to the Montreal Protocol. Once the need, dictated by the interplay of science and policy, was clear, the cognitive impediments to change fell away, and new technologies quickly became available.

With the Third Meeting of the Parties approaching, the combination of scientific urgency and technological progress ensured that new treaty revisions would be on the agenda. Atmospheric scientists, reluctant to make any policy recommendations prior to Montreal, were now quite willing to advocate specific policies. In April, two months before the Nairobi meeting, Robert Watson told the U.S. Senate that four actions were necessary: an accelerated phaseout of controlled chemicals; worldwide compliance with the treaty; chemical recycling; and the development of not-in-kind substitutes for CFCs. In particular, Watson warned against a dependency on long-lived HCFCs and HFCs. This warning was reinforced by research by the National Oceanic and Atmospheric Administration showing that HCFC-141b has an ODP 50 percent greater than was initially estimated, making it as harmful to ozone as methyl chloroform (U.S. Senate 1991).

Unlike the First Meeting of the Parties, which generated the Helsinki Declaration prior to the London revisions, the Third Meeting of the Parties in Nairobi in June endorsed no new treaty revisions, despite the new scientific evidence. Instead, delegates at Nairobi requested other bodies to develop recommendations for adjustments and amendments to be taken up in 1992 at the fourth meeting. The parties directed a special working group to make recommendations regarding a more detailed noncompliance procedure (UNEP/OzL.Pro.3/11:15) and instructed the assessment panels to look at "the possibilities and difficulties of an earlier phaseout of the controlled substances, for example, a 1997 phaseout" (UNEP/OzL.Pro.3/11:18). They also asked the panels to suggest a possible phaseout date for HCFCs. Seven European governments, dissatisfied with the call for further study, reaffirmed their commitment to a 1997 phaseout for CFCs, halons, and carbon tetrachloride, and a 2000 phaseout for methyl chloroform.

Following the general pattern of events, scientific data soon indicated a worsening of the ozone problem, sparking new calls for stronger policies. In October 1991, the Antarctic ozone hole hit a record low (*Science* 1991). Shortly afterward, NASA scientists announced that ozone was thinning throughout the year, even during the summer, and everywhere except over the tropics (*Science News* 1991:278). Du Pont responded by announcing plans to hasten its phaseout of CFCs and halons: 1996 for CFCs and 1994 for halons (*Los Angeles Times* 1991).

The NASA study also cast doubt on the presumed role of CFCs in global warming, suggesting that the loss of ozone, also a greenhouse gas, could counterbalance the warming effect of CFCs, with the result that eliminating CFCs would have little or no effect on the climate (interview with Robert Watson). True to the principle that knowledge can be employed on behalf of a range of interests, this information was used by some to praise and by others to criticize U.S. policy on global warming. Those who supported the Bush administration's wait-and-see approach to the climate problem argued that the scientific uncertainty regarding the role of CFCs in global warming vindicated the administration's policy (*New York Times* 1991). The critics, however, presented a more complex argument. The Bush administration's "Comprehensive Strategy" lumped together all greenhouse gases and called for a freeze on emissions at 1987 levels by the year 2000. Those countries who were major producers of CFCs, with their enormous global warming potentials, could achieve their targets through the Montreal Protocol provisions and could meanwhile continue to increase their emissions of carbon dioxide, the principal greenhouse gas. The GWP of CFC-11 relative to carbon dioxide, for instance, is 4,500; for CFC-12, it is 7100 (U.S. Task Force on the Comprehensive Approach to Climate Change 1991).[25] Thus, critics declared that the new NASA study "poked a gaping hole in the administration's strategy for dealing with global warming" (*Wall Street Journal* 1991b). Ultimately, this argument was persuasive, and the administration was compelled to abandon its "comprehensive approach" in the negotiations on climate change.

The discovery that ozone depletion may have offset a portion of the greenhouse warming during the previous decade was only one of five major findings announced in the *Scientific Assessment of Ozone Depletion*, published in December 1991. There was also evidence for the first time that significant ozone losses occur in spring and summer in both the Northern and Southern Hemispheres at middle and high latitudes. In addition, the biennial modulation of the Antarctic ozone hole seemed to be giving way to a severe hole annually, accompanied by large increases in ultraviolet radiation, and losses over the Arctic, while not so enormous, had the potential to affect populated areas. Other new evidence supported the conclusion that chlorine and bromine were responsible for the ozone losses over both poles. Finally, while most of the newly calculated ODPs were similar to those in previous assessments, the new GWP results indicated that many of the GWPs reported in the Intergovernmental Panel on Climate Change (1990), especially that of methane, were likely to be incorrect (WMO/NASA 1991:xi–xiii).

Although these were the major findings outlined in the executive summary, others also had implications for policy. For instance, the new models incorporating heterogeneous processes on sulfate aerosols predicted as much as two to three times as much ozone depletion compared to models containing only gas-phase processes (WMO/NASA 1991:xiii). This finding that a major volcanic eruption could have devastating implications for the ozone layer reinforced the drive toward precautionary action. In addition, the science panel also reported that the new ODPs were larger for substances with long stratospheric lifetimes, such as the HCFCs, than for those with shorter stratospheric lifetimes, like methyl chloroform and carbon tetrachloride (ch. 6, p. 7). This finding strengthened the case for controlling HCFCs. Finally, while the science panel found that methyl bromide was the principal source of stratospheric bromine, a far more potent destroyer of ozone than chlorine, its anthropogenic sources were uncertain. Nonetheless, the assessment noted that each 10 percent reduction in methyl bromide emissions would be comparable to a three-year acceleration of the CFC phaseout schedule (xvii). The methyl bromide issue would turn out to be one of the major controversies of the 1992 treaty review process.

While they did not make specific policy recommendations, scientists in 1991 were willing to offer general advice. As in the 1989 assessment, that advice was framed in terms of limiting atmospheric chlorine loading. Even with full compliance under the amended protocol, the 1991 abundance of chlorine (3.3 to 3.5 ppb) was expected to rise to 4.1 ppb by the end of the century, thereby greatly increasing the risk of ozone loss over the middle and high latitudes. Reducing that risk, the assessment concluded, "requires further limitations on the emissions of chlorine- and bromine-containing compounds" (WMO/NASA 1991:xvii). Like the 1989 Synthesis Report, the 1991 assessment provided scenarios for limiting chlorine concentrations, although in a table rather than the more visually appealing graphs (see table

Table 5.4. Scenarios for Reducing Chlorine Emissions (1991)

Scenario	Peak CI (ppbv)	Years at 3 ppv	Years at 2 ppv	Integral (CI>3 ppbv)
1	4.1	2027	2060	22.7
2	-0.18	-10	-7	-7.6
3	-0.03	0	0	-1.3
4	-0.10	0	0	-2.9
5	0.00	-7	-3	-2.0*
6	-0.03*	-10	-3	-4.4*
7	+0.01	0	0	+0.8
8	+0.02	+1	0	+1.5
9	+0.01	+5	+2	+4.2
10 = (2 + 4)	-0.21	-11	-7	-10.4

*These values should be reduced by a factor of about 2 to 3 when evaluating ozone loss rather than chlorine loading.

1. Montreal Protocol: A ten-year lag of 10 percent of CFCs plus CCl_4; no lag for CH_3CCl_3 and halons; HCFC-22 increases at 3 percent per year from 1991 to 2020, ramps to 0 by 2040; no substitution of CFCs with HCFCs.

2. No substitutions of CFCs with HCFCs. Three-year acceleration of the schedules for CFCs and CCl_4.

3. No substitutions of CFCs with HCFCs. Three-year acceleration of the schedules for CH_3CCl_3.

4. No substitutions of CFCs with HCFCs. CH_3CCl_3 on the accelerated CFC phase-out schedule.

5. No substitutions of CFCs with HCFCs. HCFC-22 ramp to zero between 2000 and 2020.

6. No substitutions of CFCs with HCFCs. HCFC-22 on the accelerated CFC phase-out schedule.

7. Twenty percent initial substitution of HCFC-A in 1995, with no growth in 2000 and then growth of 3 percent per year to 2020 and growth of ramp to zero by 2030. HCFC-A has a two-year lifetime, one chlorine molecule, and an ODP of 0.013.

8. Schedule as above, but with 40 percent initial substitution of HCFC-A.

9. Schedule as above, but with 20 percent initial substitution of HCFC-B. HCFC-B has a two-year lifetime, one chlorine molecule, and an ODP of 0.13.

Source: Adapted from WMO/NASA 1991:xiv.

5.4). The scenarios included a three-year acceleration of the phaseout of existing controlled substances and limitations on HCFC substitution.

In many ways, as they did in 1989, the scenarios set the agenda for the policy debates. But in 1991, the range of scenarios presented was more limited. In particular, the only phaseout date considered for CFCs and carbon tetrachloride was 1997. Environmentalists criticized the assessment for failing to consider earlier dates, particularly in light of the fact that some governments had already adopted stricter timetables (interview with Liz Cook).

As in 1989, the environmental effects panel report was far less comprehensive than the scientific assessment. In fact, there was so little new information in 1991 that the panel only published an update, which included summaries for each of the 1989 chapters, rather than a full assessment. Introducing the update, the panel chairs admitted that progress had been "disappointing" and pointed to the fact that funding for research on the consequences of increased ultraviolet radiation was meager, "typically less than 1 percent of what is made available for atmospheric research in relation to ozone depletion" (UNEP 1991a:i).

Still, some new information was reported. Perhaps most important was the conclusive link between immunosuppression in humans and UV-B radiation, among dark-skinned as well as light-skinned populations (UNEP 1991a:iii). Moreover, in addition to skin cancer, exposure to sunlight was also associated with cancer of the salivary gland, suggesting the possibility of a systemic effect of UV-B in humans since the salivary gland is rarely exposed (15). Research on aquatic ecosystems focused on the effects of UV-B on phytoplankton, particularly in the waters under the Antarctic ozone hole. Phytoplankton are essential to the productivity of marine biomass, the source of more than 30 percent of the animal protein consumed by humans. New research found that targets other than DNA in photoplankton, including intrinsic proteins of the photoreceptor and photosynthetic apparatus, absorb UV-B radiation. Most importantly, a decrease in phytoplankton populations could alter cloud patterns and, concomitantly, the global climate. A hypothetical loss of 10 percent of phytoplankton would reduce the annual oceanic uptake of carbon dioxide by about 5 gigatons, an amount equal to the annual emissions of carbon dioxide from fossil fuel consumption. Thus, like the science assessment, the environmental assessment was compelled to consider climate change issues.

Despite these important new findings on phytoplankton and the human immune system, the environmental assessment was rarely cited during the ensuing policy discussions. As had been the case historically, atmospheric research set the terms of policy discourse—even though ultra-violet radiation, not ozone depletion per se, is the real threat to life on the planet. Perhaps this choice of emphasis reflects the tacit knowledge (Polanyi 1958) embedded in precautionary discourse: "Don't fool with Mother Nature." Perhaps it was enough to know that major ozone losses were occurring, whatever might be the effects. Or perhaps the lack of attention to, as well as funding for, health and environmental effects reflects the wider society's hierarchy of the sciences, under which those scientific disciplines furthest removed from everyday human life, especially physics, are frequently considered the most prestigious and are therefore the best-funded. Either way, the dynamics underlying both the production and the reception of the environmental assessment were very much a product of social factors.

Predictably, technology continued to be a driving force of the treaty revision process, second only to atmospheric science. The 1991 technology and economics assessment, involving 240 experts on six committees, included a great deal of new information uncovered since in the 1989 assessment.[26] Since 1989, technological advances had made early reductions possible, largely because industry and consumers were reducing their dependence on ozone-depleting substances more quickly than had been anticipated at the London meeting. So impressive was the progress that, by 1992, CFC consumption would be reduced to 50 percent of 1986 levels— a three-year advance on the requirements of the Amended Protocol (UNEP 1991b:ES-2). Many of the ingredients of this rapid progress, such as new processes, partnerships involving industries and governments, information-sharing arrangements, and the halon bank, have been outlined above and are acknowledged in the 1991 assessment. Thus, the Economic Options Committee found that "technological optimism" was justified because "problems which were regarded as big and difficult not so long ago have been successfully dealt with much more quickly and a lower cost than expected" (UNEP 1991c:13).

The 1991 technology assessment concluded that it was technically feasible to eliminate virtually all consumption[27] of CFCs, halons, and carbon tetrachloride between 1995 and 1997 and of methyl chloroform between 1995 and 2000. These technically feasible phaseouts are depicted in figures 5.5 and 5.6. The refrigeration and air conditioning sector was the most problematic, mostly because the early retirement of equipment would cost several billion dollars (see figure 5.7 for the assessment's projections for a CFC phaseout for refrigeration in industrialized countries). While a 1997

Figure 5.5. Technically Feasible Production Phaseout for CFCs and
Methyl Chloroform (1991)

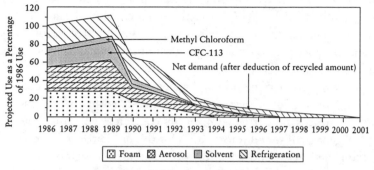

Technically Feasible Production Phaseout of CFC and 1,1,1-Trichloroethane

Note 1: The amounts of CFC used in sterilants and miscellaneous uses are small and cannot be depicted in the scale used. Some of the technical options committees agreed on a range of phase-out dates. This chart presents the technically optimistic case.

Note 2: The use of controlled substances is presented on an ODP=weighted basis.

Adapted from UNEP 1991b:ES-11.

Figure 5.6. Production Phaseout Projection for Halons (ODP weighted)

Production Phaseout Projection for Halons (ODP weighted)

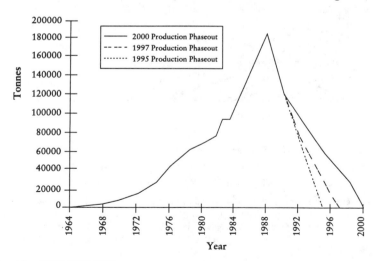

Adapted from UNEP 1991b:ES-13.

phaseout was technically feasible, it would cost $6.2 billion more than a phaseout in the year 2000 (UNEP 1991b:7–23). The added expense constituted a particular problem for developing countries, where refrigeration accounted for 63 percent of the total CFC use, compared to 25 percent globally (UNEP 1991b:7–17). Nonetheless, because of the speed of technological progress, the Economic Options Committee recommended reducing the grace period for developing countries under the Montreal Protocol by two to five years (UNEP 1991c:17).

Knowledge production and employment were key to all aspects of the technology assessment. To a greater extent than the other panels, this panel attracted enthusiastic participation in its committees because the expert networks generated useful information for the participants themselves. In fact, the panel's research helped to speed technical progress by fostering information exchange and ongoing relationships among industry representatives. The panel also emphasized the primacy of information-sharing arrangements in advancing the phaseout dates for ozone-depleting substances, such as industry consortia for researching new substitute com-

Figure 5.7. CFC phaseout for Refrigeration in Industrialized Countries

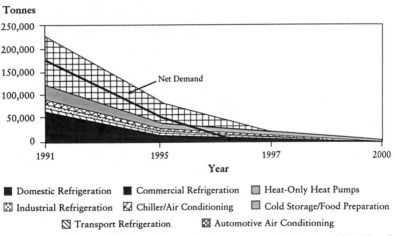

CFC for Refrigeration in Developed Countries

Note: Net demand to equal to the total demand minus the recycled CFCs available. Therefore, the net demand is the amount of new CFCs that must be produced. Accelerated retrofit begins in mid-1996, reflecting the inadequate supply of recycled CFC when production of virgin CFCs is halted in 1997. After 1997, the equipment that cannot be serviced with recycled CFCs is retrofitted or retired.

Adapted from UNEP 1991b:ES-12.

pounds, information sources like UNEP's clearinghouse and trade association data banks, and ad hoc partnerships among industries and government agencies. Because public awareness of the ozone issue was also important, the panel promoted the establishment of new "knowledge centers" especially in developing countries (UNEP 1991b:6–11).

Thus, the drive toward stronger precautionary action that began in the aftermath of the Montreal Protocol continued with the 1991 assessments. Both the science and the technology reports adopted 1997 as the hypothetical phaseout date for CFCs and carbon tetrachloride, and this date initially seemed likely to be incorporated into the amended treaty. The combination of urgent scientific findings and technological optimism assured that new treaty amendments would be adopted in 1992. But whether those revisions would suffice to keep pace with the rapidly deteriorating ozone layer was not at all clear.

In the United States, environmentalists were skeptical. In December 1991, the NRDC and other groups filed a petition to compel the U.S. government to honor its commitments under the amended Clean Air Act and speed the phaseout of ozone-depleting substances. The NRDC petition cited the German phaseout date of 1995 and also demanded that the EPA phase out methyl bromide. Under the U.S. law, chemicals with an ODP over 0.2 are required to be listed as Class I substances and must be eliminated; methyl bromide has an ODP of 0.7 (FOE et al. 1992:26). While seemingly confrontational, the NRDC petition was actually negotiated with the EPA; in the aftermath of the Montreal Protocol, the agency and environmentalist organizations had developed a cooperative relationship (interview with Eileen Claussen). As in 1986, domestic processes involving the Clean Air Act had foreign policy implications; in both cases, an NRDC petition spurred the United States to adopt a more far-reaching ozone policy internationally.

The environmentalist position was bolstered by new scientific findings during the winter and spring of 1992. In February scientists, reporting levels of chlorine monoxide over New England and Canada higher than those found during flights into the Antarctic ozone hole, announced that an ozone hole was likely to form over populated regions of the northern hemisphere. The scientists attributed the high levels of chlorine monoxide to sulfur particles from industrial pollution and the Mount Pinatubo eruption (*Science News* 1992a). Although NASA's early release of preliminary results of satellite measurements was criticized by some scientists and media sources for "setting science policy via press releases," (*Wall Street*

Journal 1992), it prompted a quick policy response. President Bush announced that the United States would phase out production of CFCs, halons, methyl chloroform, and carbon tetrachloride, except for "essential uses," by December 31, 1995. The USA would also reexamine the phaseout schedule for HCFCs, to be banned in 2030 under the Clean Air Act, and explore a phaseout of methyl bromide (The White House 1992). Shortly afterward, legislation was introduced in the EC, and later approved, to reduce CFC production by 85 percent in 1993 and altogether by the end of 1995. In addition, Denmark, Germany, and the Netherlands were considering a phaseout date as early as 1993 (*European Report* 1992).[28]

Environmentalists' demand for stricter controls on HCFCs was reinforced by new scientific research indicating that the chemicals release their chlorine much faster than had been thought, thereby posing a greater threat to the ozone layer. During the period when chlorine concentrations will be at their highest levels, HCFCs will be three to five times more destructive than previously foreseen. HCFC-22, a common refrigerant whose production had increased by 9 percent annually since 1986, was revealed to be 75 percent less depleting than CFCs, not 95 percent as originally estimated (*Washington Post* 1992).

At the April 1992 meeting of the Open-Ended Working Group, the conclusions of the assessment panels were reviewed, and proposals were developed for further treaty amendments and adjustments. These proposals included an advance in the phaseout schedule of controlled substances from the year 2000 to 1995 or 1996 and the listing of HCFCs and methyl bromide as controlled substances. Some developing countries proposed that they should only assume further obligations under the protocol after a review in 1995 (UNEP/OzL.Pro.WG.1/6/3). Greenpeace and Friends of the Earth presented a joint statement to the gathering, stating that "unlike the situation on many difficult policy questions, you are in the fortunate position to have all the science you need to take effective decisions." The statement outlined the major scientific findings and framed the parties' responsibility in terms of their legal commitment in the Vienna Convention to take precautionary action (Hohnen 1992).

For the first time since 1987, a major scientific controversy became the focus of a policy debate. One of the greatest uncertainties in the 1991 science assessment was the extent to which methyl bromide posed a threat to the ozone layer. The chemical is used as a preplanting, postharvesting, and structural fumigant. While the panel found methyl bromide to be the principal source of stratospheric bromine, each molecule of which is 30 to 120 times more effective at destroying ozone than is chlorine, it made no recommendations on methyl bromide because the reasons for the chemical's destructiveness were not well understood (WMO/NASA 1991:xii). Because very little of it reaches the stratosphere and its atmospheric lifetime is less than two years, it had been ignored previously. Environmentalists, however, insisted that the compound should no longer be overlooked.

At the April 1992 meeting, the Open-Ended Working Group, hoping to agree on a set of proposed treaty amendments to be presented at the Fourth Meeting of the Parties in the fall, could not agree on methyl bromide controls. The United States, under domestic pressure to enforce the Clean Air Act, proposed a phaseout by the year 2000; other industrialized countries favored only a freeze. Mostafa Tolba proposed a 20 percent reduction by the year 2000. Israel, however, with support from some developing countries, called for further study. Mexico went beyond most developing countries, calling for a freeze in 1995 (interview with Paul Horowitz). The working group requested a special study on methyl bromide, which was published in June and incorporated new findings presented at the international Methyl Bromide Science Workshop.

The special assessment was hastily put together; within a matter of months, the methyl bromide issue had emerged from obscurity to become perhaps the most controversial dimension of the ozone issue. There were enough uncertainties about methyl bromide to allow parties to frame the available knowledge according to their perceived interests. Yet, although the study found uncertainties, it indicated that methyl bromide could account for one-sixth of the predicted ozone loss by the year 2000 if emissions continued to grow at nearly 6 percent per year. The primary implication for policy formulation, the report concluded, was that elimination of anthropogenic methyl bromide could contribute as much to restore the ozone layer as would a three-year advance in the CFC and carbon tetrachloride phaseout schedule (UNEP 1992a:3).

Methyl bromide, the most widely used nonpetroleum pesticide after petroleum, is produced in eight countries, with industrialized countries consuming 80 percent of all production. The United States, which requires fumigation for many purposes, is the largest user, consuming 43 percent of global production. In the USA, methyl bromide is manufactured by Great Lakes Chemical Corporation and Ethyl Corporation; combined, their output is half of all global production (FOE 1992c:3). Yet, because of the Clear Air Act and domestic pressure, the world's top producing country was placed in the anomalous position of being the strongest supporter of strict controls. As in the Montreal Protocol negotiations, the United States wanted a "level playing field" (interview with Paul Horowitz). By contrast, the EC, despite its progressive CFC legislation, proved to be the strongest opponent of methyl bromide controls. Israel, the world's second largest producer and agricultural user, garnered support for its position from developing countries receiving aid, even though these countries used very little of the compound.

For the first time since Montreal, developing countries framed their political position in terms of scientific knowledge. They were joined by Israel and the Mediterranean countries within the EC. Drawing upon the uncertainties in the special assessment, critics of methyl bromide controls constructed three arguments. First, most methyl bromide is from natural sources—as much as 75 percent (UNEP 1992a:6); therefore the relatively small amount emitted from anthropogenic sources militated against controls. This argument is the weakest since only human sources of methyl bromide can be controlled. Second, an unknown quantity of methyl bromide is removed by soils and vegetation. This argument, too, is weak because the special assessment, seeking to make a conservative estimate, assumed that a large amount was deposited on soils and vegetation (7). As little as 3 to 5 percent of methyl bromide actually makes its way up to the stratosphere (FOE et al. 1992:5). The argument with the greatest credibility was that the oceans could provide a major sink for methyl bromide emissions (7). Yet the scientists also took this consideration into account and concluded that there was still cause for concern. Nonetheless, even though more was known about methyl bromide in 1992 than about halons in 1987, the scientific uncertainties were great enough to supply ammunition to those who opposed controls on methyl bromide (interview with Stephen Seidel).

The methyl bromide issue bears some similarity to the question of methyl chloroform during the first treaty review. Both problems were studied hastily, and both brought a new set of actors into the debates. Many methyl bromide producers had some experience with the ozone issue since they also produced halons, the other bromated ozone-depleting substance. But never before had the agricultural sector been involved. That involvement entailed a host of new considerations, and although there was much resistance to controls, there were also incentives for users to reduce their dependence on methyl bromide. Farmers, for instance, are at a higher risk than the rest of the population from the consequences of increased UV-B radiation. Not only are they more susceptible to skin cancer because they work outside, their crops are also vulnerable. Perhaps the strongest incentive, however, is methyl bromide's extreme toxicity; the EPA has classified it as a Category I acute toxin, the most deadly category of substances (EPA 1986c).

Environmentalists active on the ozone issue were able to coalesce with those involved in toxics, pesticides, and rural issues. In November 1992, in time for the Fourth Meeting of the Parties in Copenhagen, a coalition of seven environmental groups published a study of methyl bromide. They also launched a campaign to persuade users and producers to phase out consumption and production within the next five years. The study framed its conclusions in terms of the scientific rationale and the technological feasibility of regulative action. Emphasizing methyl bromide's high ODP and short atmospheric lifetime, the report framed the available knowledge in a powerful manner: "Over the next 20 years," it stated, "every kilogram of methyl bromide that is released into the atmosphere will contribute far more to ozone depletion than a kilogram of a better known ozone destroyer such as CFC-11" (FOE et al. 1992:1). Recognizing that action would not result from scientific information alone, the report also stressed technical information suggesting the feasibility of a phaseout. Six case studies were included: the Netherlands ban, two phaseouts in agriculture, two in grain storage, and one in residential fumigation. Citing the history of controls on ozone-depleting substances, the report argued that substitutes were constantly being found for chemicals that industry had claimed only a few year earlier were irreplaceable (16–23).

Controlling methyl bromide was one of the three major issues facing the delegates as they met in Copenhagen in November 1992, the other two being control measures for HCFCs and the structure of the Montreal Multilateral Fund. By the time of the preparatory meeting for the Fourth Meeting of the Parties, representatives had a history of working together and a certain clubbish atmosphere prevailed. No major battles were anticipated (interview with Eileen Claussen).

Agreement on the phaseout schedules for controlled substances was relatively easy. Representatives from sixty-five countries at the preparatory meeting agreed to eliminate CFCs, carbon tetrachloride, and methyl chloroform by 1996 and halons by 1994. As usual, Mostafa Tolba circulated his own personal proposal on the most contentious issues, suggesting a freeze of methyl bromide production and consumption in 1995 at 1991 levels, a 25 percent cut by 2000, and a scientific study of the chemical to determine future control measures. Tolba also proposed a freeze on HCFC consumption by the end of 1995, a cut of 25 percent by 2000, of 50 percent by 2010, and a full phaseout by 2020. Last, Tolba suggested that the Interim Multilateral Fund be transformed into the Montreal Multilateral Fund, as called for at the London Conference two years before, and that $500 million be allocated for the years 1994 through 1996 (UNEP 1992a). All three proposals were accepted at the preparatory meeting and presented to the ministerial meeting the following week (UNEP/ OzL.Pro.4/Prep/2).

Meeting from November 21 through 23, the ministers and high-level officials from seventy-four countries and the EC agreed to Tolba's proposed phaseout schedules for CFCs, carbon tetrachloride, methyl chloroform and halons. They also agreed to phase out all but essential uses of HCFCs by 2020, with interim reductions beginning in 2004. Perceiving a need for extended HCFC use in air conditioners for large buildings, the United States argued successfully for a total phaseout in 2030. On the contentious issue of methyl bromide, Israel and the Mediterranean countries in the EC blocked agreement on reductions, despite support for such measures from all other industrial countries. Instead, the parties agreed to freeze production and consumption at 1991 levels by 1995 for Article 2 countries, with no restrictions on use by Article 5 countries. The decision was accompanied by a nonbinding resolution calling for an evaluation of methyl bromide within two years, with a possible phaseout by the year 2000.[29] For a summary of the Copenhagen revisions, see table 5.5.

Table 5.5. Summary of 1992 Adjustments and Amendments

Substance	Reduction	Date*
CFCs	75.0 percent	1994
	100.0 percent	1996
Halons	100.0 percent	1994
Methyl chloroform	50.0 percent	1994
	100.0 percent	1996
Carbon tetrachloride	85.0 percent	1995
	100.0 percent	1996
HBFCs	100.0 percent	1996
HCFCs	freeze	1996
	35.0 percent	2004
	65.0 percent	2010
	90.0 percent	2015
	99.5 percent	2020
	100.0 percent	2030
Methyl bromide	freeze	1995

*All dates are January 1.

Source: UNEP/OzL.Pro.4/15.

The Copenhagen meeting also addressed the financial mechanism. Contributions to the fund for 1991 and 1992 had come late from many contributors; some parties, including Eastern European countries, had financial difficulties, and others, such as France and the U.K., had the wherewithal but did not meet their obligations. Moreover, developing countries, frustrated with the attempt by some parties to alter the structure of the Multilateral Fund, had walked out of a meeting of the Open-Ended Working Group in July 1992 (UNEP/OzL.Pro.4/15:2). Yet, on the positive side, developing countries that doubted in 1989 whether they could achieve 50 percent reductions in CFC use by 2010 were now planning to eliminate the chemicals entirely by the year 2000. This transformation was made possible by information sharing and the Interim Multilateral Fund (Tolba 1992:3). Contrary to the expectations of many and despite the financial shortfalls, representatives from industrialized and developing countries on the fund's executive committee were working together harmoniously and efficiently and had adopted all decisions by consensus (UNEP/OzL.Pro.4/15:6).

The Copenhagen meeting agreed to establish the Multilateral Fund on a permanent basis, to operate in 1993 with a $113 million budget for that year and $340 to $500 million for 1994 through 1996. The Open-Ended Working Group was requested to advise the Fifth Meeting of the Parties at the end of 1993 about the exact size of the fund from 1994 through 1996. It was also decided that the executive committee should operate under the procedures and guidelines formulated for the Interim Multilateral Fund. The temporary difficulties of Hungary, Bulgaria, and Poland in making their contributions in convertible currency were noted, and those parties were urged to explore in-kind contributions (UNEP/OzL.Pro.4/15:22).

Although article 8 of the Montreal Protocol states that the parties shall establish procedures and institutional mechanisms for determining noncompliance, the London revisions had skirted the issue. Consequently, the parties at the Copenhagen meeting adopted a noncompliance procedure and created an implementation committee consisting of ten parties that are to meet twice a year. Reservations regarding a party's implementation of its treaty obligations are to be submitted to the secretariat, which gathers information about the matter and may refer it to the implementation committee, which in turn seeks an amicable solution and may refer the matter to the Meeting of the Parties. According to the situation, the noncomplying party may be given appropriate assistance to facilitate compliance, or it may receive a warning, or it may be suspended from its rights and privileges under the protocol (annexes IV and V, UNEP/OzL./Pro.4/15:46–47).

The Copenhagen Revisions received a mixed response. UNEP's own press release, while lauding the amendment process as "an environmental success story," suggested that the new control measures were not sufficiently stringent. On the one hand, the measures represent "the strongest package of global environmental law ever enacted." On the other hand, according to Mostafa Tolba, "the question remains, however: is this enough? We are in the hands of scientists. From them—and we have sought advice from the best in the world—we know that the answer is 'No.' This package is not enough. We have made progress, but we have far to go" (UNEP 1992b).

Thus, even UNEP, with a clear bureaucratic interest in reveling in its own success, had to admit that the agreement was based more on political and economic considerations than on the scientific requirements for saving the ozone layer.

Environmental organizations were even more forthright in expressing their misgivings about the Fourth Meeting of the Parties. They were especially critical of the parties for failing to reduce methyl bromide emissions, pointing out that the parties' own scientific advisory panel had concluded that methyl bromide reductions would bring substantial near-term benefits to the ozone layer. Environmentalists also complained that the agreement: (1) sanctioned a further thirty-eight years of HCFC use, despite the widespread availability of safer CFC substitutes; (2) aligned the phaseout dates for CFCs and halons nearer to the schedules of the chemical industry than the requirements of the ozone layer; and (3) allowed essential-use exemptions for most chemicals, creating a loophole that could allow continued production indefinitely. Citing a pattern of events that had begun in Montreal, environmentalists recalled that each agreement had been rapidly outstripped by accelerating ozone destruction. The Copenhagen accord, they predicted, would be no exception (FOE 1992b).

Clearly, the Copenhagen Revisions served further to institutionalize the discourse of precautionary action on ozone, first articulated by the international community in 1985 with the Vienna Convention and continued with the Montreal Protocol and the London Revisions. Yet, rather than committing themselves to a full ounce of prevention, which might have been worth a pound of cure, the Montreal Protocol parties, in Copenhagen just as in London two years before, opted for only half an ounce of prevention. Consequently, while the new control measures represented progress, they did not represent a solution to the problem.

Within five years of the signing of the Montreal Protocol, the treaty had already been revised twice as policymakers attempted to keep pace with scientific and technological developments. Clearly, from the 1974 discovery of the CFC-ozone link to the 1992 treaty revisions, ozone policy was knowledge-driven. Yet science and technology did not provide a set of objective facts from which policy could be deduced. Rather, specific modes of framing and interpreting the available knowledge were incorporated into policy discourses. Even after Montreal, when the range of scientific uncertainty had greatly narrowed, rhetorical and discursive strategies continued to be integral elements of the policy milieu. With the emergence of greater scientific certainty and the discovery of indisputable evidence of CFC-induced ozone depletion, policy action could no longer properly be considered precautionary. The new goal, therefore, was to stem the tide of environmental deterioration and to limit damage to the ozone layer rather than to prevent any harm whatsoever from occurring. But the rapidly deteriorating ozone layer—over Antarctica, over the Arctic, and globally—suggests that precautionary action was implemented inadequately and belatedly.

Many of the discursive strategies employed during the Montreal Protocol negotiations were also prevalent during the treaty revision process. First, the chlorine-loading approach, which was implicit in the original treaty negotiations, became the predominant mode of framing scientific information after Montreal. Other approaches, including computer-generated models and ozone depletion potentials, were also employed, but policy goals were always framed in terms of reducing atmospheric chlorine concentrations. Moreover, as had been the case historically, ozone discourse continued to be dominated by the atmospheric sciences, and the health and environmental consequences of ultraviolet radiation received almost no attention.

Second, even during the Montreal Protocol negotiations, the perceived availability of chemical substitutes and alternatives was more a matter of political and economic factors than of science and technology. After Montreal, those political and economic factors generated a major psychological shift among both producer and user industries, resulting in an astonishing rate of technological progress. The rapid developments engendered a sense of optimism in policy circles: not only *must* ozone-depleting chemicals be strictly controlled, they *could* be. Thus, scientific and technological discourse combined to effect swift and decisive action.

Third, developing countries became key participants after Montreal. Although many developing countries had strong misgivings about the treaty, they never voiced their reservations in scientific terms. While they framed their concerns in terms of equity and sovereignty, their compliance with the treaty was determined largely by the availability of technical information. The controversial question of the financial mechanism was ultimately a matter of redistributing knowledge from the information-rich North to the information-poor South. Both sides had much to gain from the arrangement. The North was most vulnerable to the effects of ozone depletion and could not expect the South to sacrifice its economic welfare to rectify a problem caused by its own consumption habits. The South also embraced the discourse of damage limitation and had a perceived interest in saving the ozone layer, especially if it could do so without hurting itself economically. Despite the nonprecedential language demanded by the United States, the Multilateral Fund, which is at root an information-sharing mechanism, does indeed establish a precedent for future environmental agreements.

One may view the Montreal Protocol and its revisions in either a positive or a negative light. On the one hand, the revised treaty represented "the strongest package of environmental law ever enacted." In 1987, the parties reluctantly agreed to a 50 percent reduction of CFCs by the year 2000; in 1992, with little debate, they decided to eliminate the chemical by 1996. Other aspects of the treaty were equally progressive. On the other hand, environmentalists were correct in claiming that the revisions did not go far enough. Part of the problem is that, because of the accumulation of the long-lived CFCs in the atmosphere, little could be done at such a late date to bring peak chlorine concentrations below 4 ppb. Yet environmentalists rightly claim that the parties did not do everything possible to protect the earth's ozone layer. While future levels of damage were limited, the precautionary principle was not applied rigorously.

6 · Implications for Theories of World Politics

In our modern societies, most of the really fresh power comes from science—no matter which—and not from the classical political process.

—Bruno Latour, *The Pasteurization of France*

In chapter 1, I presented a deductive argument in support of a reflectivist approach to international environmental politics. In essence, I argued that the dominant approaches, neorealism and neoliberal institutionalism, fail to grasp the nonmaterial nature of knowledge-based power; nor do they dig beneath the surface to explore the process of interest formation. In this chapter, I reexamine this question in light of the case study, asking whether existing theories of regime formation can account for the development of the international regime for ozone protection. The central importance of knowledge in international environmental negotiations as both a political resource and an arena for struggle suggests that conventional theories are inadequate, at least for this issue area. This chapter examines the dominant theoretical approaches to international regime building as a mode of entry into the larger question of knowledge and political power. All of these, from structural realism to bureaucratic politics to interest group approaches, neglect the role of intersubjective understandings as the basis for international cooperation.

As if in reaction to past materialist excesses, a good deal of attention has recently been given to ideas and information as sources of foreign policy and international collaboration.[1] While much of that literature focuses on political and economic ideologies, some of it looks at scientific knowledge as a foundation for international cooperation. The Montreal Protocol, characterized by a high level of involvement by atmospheric scientists, seems at first glance to be an ideal case for applying the epistemic communities approach. Building upon the theoretical arguments advanced in chapter 2, however, I show in this chapter why the global ozone regime was not the work of an epistemic community.

Instead, I argue for a discursive practices approach that sees knowledge and power as mutually interactive. The power of competing knowledges—likely to be decisive under conditions of scientific uncertainty—was the critical factor. An emphasis on discursive practices, rather than on states, bureaucracies, or individuals, would interpret international regimes as loci of struggle among various networks of power/knowledge. In contradistinction to the epistemic communities approach, issues of framing, interpretation, and contingency are central to this approach.

If those scholars who discern a trend toward a postindustrial or informational world order are correct, then this argument has important implications not just for environmental issues but more generally for the nature of power in the emergent global system. One trend may be the diffusion of the sovereign power of nation-states to nonstate actors and the proliferation of disciplinary micropowers. Consistent with this diffusion would be the displacement of power toward those actors most proficient at controlling and manipulating informational resources. As is already evident in the global warming debates, the implications of this trend for relations between information-rich and information-poor nations are both intriguing and unsettling. In any case, it is not clear that politics in a postindustrial world is likely to be any less conflictual than in the past.

Alternative Approaches to Regime Formation

Neorealism has relatively little to say about regime creation in general and even less about global environmental regimes in specific. According to Kenneth Waltz (1979), the structure of the international system shapes both the most significant aspects of nations' interests and the outcomes of their interactions. The distribution of capabilities—in particular, military capabilities—is the key element of structure. Yet military force seems quite irrelevant to environmental preservation. The structure of the international system, until recently a bipolar one, tells us little about national interests or bargaining outcomes for environmental problems. The collapse of the Soviet Union and the end of bipolarity had no apparent effect, except perhaps in a few details, on the evolution of the ozone regime.

Those structural theories that posit a unipolar rather than a bipolar system fare no better. Neither of the two versions of hegemonic theory offers a satisfying account of the ozone regimes. The first attributes regimes to a hegemonic power acting altruistically to supply a public good, while the second sees them as imposed upon weaker states by a dominant power.[2] Both versions associate regime creation with the existence of one dominant nation. Yet the recent period of intensive environmental regime building, beginning in the early 1970s, coincides with what most observers regard as a period of dwindling U.S. hegemony and a diffusion of power (Kennedy 1987; Rosecrance 1986; Keohane 1984). Admittedly, the theory does not maintain that great powers are *sufficient* for international collaboration, yet the timing of the recent increase in environmental regime formation suggests that they are not even necessary.

Keohane and Nye have proposed a more disaggregated "issue-structural" model of hegemonic stability theory that applies under conditions of "complex interdependence" (1977:50–52). For certain issue, they argue, military force is beside the point, power is not fungible, the line between international and domestic politics is blurred, and transnational actors may be as important as nation-states. The distribution of capabilities for a specific issue, or the structure of the subsystem, may differ from the overall structure of the international system. For instance, although Brazil and Malaysia are not global powers, they are dominant actors for the issue of tropical deforestation.

Because international environmental problems are characterized by complex interdependence, it makes sense to apply Keohane and Nye's model. Yet one is immediately confronted with a mix of theoretical and empirical obstacles. Even for a narrow issue area, there is no straightforward method for gauging the distribution of power. Taking the case of the Montreal Protocol, one could argue that, since the USA and the EC each accounted for about 30 percent of the CFC market, there was no single dominant power. With a rough balance of power between two adversaries, hegemonic stability theory might incorrectly predict that no meaningful agreement would be reached.

A different tack would be to argue that because most research on stratospheric ozone was generated in the United States, there was indeed a scientific hegemony in the technical debates. Clearly, without the United States pushing for a virtual phaseout of CFCs, there would have been no reason to move beyond the freeze or the cap on production capacity initially favored by the EC, Japan, and the Soviet Union. Yet this argument cannot explain the ends to which the United States applied its superior access to scientific knowledge. Why, for instance, did it not employ scientific discourse in support of a weak treaty? Nor can it explain why the U.S. negotiating position was so compelling, even for those with strong material interests to the contrary. Nor does it explain the leadership role of other countries during the treaty revision process. An adequate account must move beyond structure to an examination of the dynamics of discursive power and the strategies of specific agents.

At the core of these difficulties lies the failure of structural approaches to examine the nature and constitution of state interests. Once a state's interests are determined, it will, of course, use its resources, technical and otherwise, to further those interests. The truly engaging question, however, is how those interests are constituted—a question about which structural theories are essentially mute. As Stephen Haggard and Beth Simmons observe, "structural theories must continually revert in an ad hoc way to domestic political variables" (1987:501). And since information and ideas generally enter into the policy-making process via domestic politics, this means that structural theories tend to neglect these factors as well.

The failure of structural approaches to consider the nature and origins of national interests is rooted in their ties to the "choice-theoretic" tradition (Oye 1986). Once the state is accepted as a rational, unitary actor, many of the most significant political questions are swept under the carpet. While a choice-theoretic approach permits an abstract analysis of the potential for cooperation in strategic situations, it provides little insight into the determinants of those situations and therefore into the question of how often or under what conditions nations will cooperate (Wendt and Duvall 1989:56). The ozone case demonstrates that actors' interests, and thus the structure of the games they play, are shaped by the knowledge they accept. Because of the flaws in their underlying assumptions, choice-theoretic approaches routinely disregard the impact of knowledge on behavior. The assumption of stable preferences that can be neatly ordered conflicts with the many cases where interests and preferences are at issue. And the persistence of uncertainty subverts the assumption of perfect information. Not only can uncertainty confound efforts to assign probabilities to alternative ends and means, it can even hinder agreement on what the proper ends and means should be.

The fact that the state seldom acts as a unitary actor further complicates matters. William Zimmerman claims that only two types of issues are amenable to a structural approach that treats the state as a rational unitary actor: those that threaten vital national interests and those that have little impact on domestic interest groups and bureaucracies. After Theodore Lowi, he calls these "the poles of power and indifference" (Zimmerman 1973; Lowi 1967). As it turns out, however, relatively few issues fall into either of these categories.

International environmental problems are among the vast majority of issues lying somewhere between the poles of power and indifference. They are the cumulative result of many local actions by domestic actors, and international agreements addressing them entail new regulations by national governments. Thus, any analysis in this area must incorporate domestic-level processes. As Harold and Margaret Sprout argued at the dawn of the environmental movement, a key ramification of environmental problems is the "progressive convergence of domestic and external politics" (1971:10).

The two traditional ways of looking at the impact of domestic actors on foreign policy are through bureaucratic politics and through interest groups, the first being state-centered and the second being society-centered. Clearly, both have something to contribute to an understanding of international environmental politics in general and the ozone regime in specific. Among the primary actors in the ozone negotiations were national agencies, various industries, and environmental pressure groups.

The bureaucratic politics model claims that actors' policy stances are largely determined by their organizational post—as the truism goes, "where you stand depends upon where you sit" (Allison 1971:176). Rather than being the result of rational analysis by a unitary governmental actor, national decisions are the outcome of internal wrangling among competing agencies with conflicting interests. In the United States, for instance, intense struggles over ozone policy found their way up to the cabinet level, with many of the competing agencies taking fairly predictable positions. The EPA advocated strong control measures, both before and after Montreal, that would have enhanced its own power as a regulatory agency. The State Department's Bureau of Oceans and International Environmental and Scientific Affairs took a similar position, which can be interpreted as an attempt to raise its status from an obscure outpost to a potent diplomatic force. As the world's preeminent research agency for ozone science, NASA certainly had much to gain from the heightened sense of public concern that accompanied the international negotiations. Because regulations may be costly, at least in the short run, the Office of Management and Budget's resistance to them was consistent with its role as guardian of the government's purse strings. The Department of Energy initially opposed stringent CFC reductions because insulating foams made with CFCs had become an important component of the agency's energy conservation program since the mid-1970s. Until 1987, the Pentagon opposed regulation of the halons because they were necessary for a certain type of fire-extinguishing equipment. As the primary governmental advocate for U.S. industry, the Commerce Department predictably opposed a stringent Montreal Protocol.

The same pattern is observable in other countries and among international organizations. As a bureaucratic politics approach would anticipate, the principal ministries advocating a stringent ozone regime were environmental agencies, while those associated with industrial interests tended to resist strong measures. In those countries where industry-related agencies were most influential, namely Britain, France, and Japan, the governments were slowest to back stringent controls on CFC emissions. The global status of UNEP, not to mention its budget, would be enhanced by a strong Montreal Protocol, so there is nothing surprising in UNEP's role as principal catalyst for the ozone regime.

While the overt power of an agency, a function of its budget and other material resources, is an important indicator of its influence in the policy process, another source of influence is its access to information. The bureaucratic politics model suggests that agencies can shape foreign policy by virtue of their ability to select the information that is given to top political leaders (Art 1973:467). Indeed, this was an important dynamic in the ozone negotiations, where a group of knowledge brokers was able to control, frame, and interpret much of the information disseminated to both domestic and foreign decision makers.

But the bureaucratic politics approach leaves some important questions unanswered, each of which points to the distinctive role of knowledge and beliefs in formulating policy. It cannot explain why the influence of particular agencies waxes and wanes over time. Why, for instance, was the EPA, a relatively small U.S. agency, able to dominate the ozone policy process, while its voice was barely heard for several years in discussions on greenhouse gases? Moreover, as an exercise in comparative statics, the bureaucratic politics model has little to say about why the positions adopted by a particular agency vary over time. It cannot account for the dramatic shift in the EPA's stance on CFC reductions between the early Reagan years and 1986, a shift that occurred primarily because of the different attitudes toward risk-taking of EPA administrators Anne Gorsuch and Lee Thomas. Likewise, the bureaucratic politics model alone cannot explain the different positions taken by the various national environmental ministries.

Psychological attitudes and philosophical orientations are at least as important as bureaucratic position in determining actors' policy stances. The differences between Gorsuch and Thomas, for instance, cannot be reduced to bureaucratic position. Along the same lines, in many cases the preferences of certain officials could not be determined by their positions. Why should Donald Hodel, secretary of the interior, have been so vehemently opposed to regulating CFCs? Nor is there any obvious bureaucratic explanation for why French environmental officials differed so widely from their Scandinavian counterparts. To answer these questions, one must consider cognitive factors.

The bureaucratic politics model ignores the distinctive role of knowledge; persuasive ability is not determined by institutional position but by the power of alternative discursive practices. The EPA's ability to prevail during the domestic interagency review process was undeniably due more to its discursive competence than to any conventional measure of bureaucratic prowess. When scientists did propose specific policy recommendations, their influence was due to their persuasive ability and their status as authoritative experts rather than to their bureaucratic position.

An interest group approach suffers from the same shortcomings. While interest groups were important actors, the global ozone regime was not primarily the result of bargaining among or pressure from those groups. Rather, expert knowledge and specific modes of framing that knowledge were critical mediators of the ultimate outcomes. The main antagonists were industry and environmental pressure groups, with industry being the more overtly powerful of the two. Throughout the regime-building process, many of the proposed control measures were actively opposed by industry, especially before substitutes became available.

The influence of environmental NGOs was substantially related to their ability to frame and manipulate information. During the Montreal Protocol bargaining process, environmentalists in the NRDC employed the chlorine-loading methodology to promote an 85 percent reduction of CFCs. Later, they publicly ridiculed Donald Hodel's personal protection plan by pointing out the pitfalls of framing the issue narrowly in terms of skin cancer. After Montreal, environmental groups became more influential, and they learned that influence flowed from the ability to define the issues. In the aftermath of Montreal, they became quite savvy in the employment of scientific discourse. Friends of the Earth and other groups always framed their positions and criticisms in terms of the scientific assessments. Recognizing the universal appeal of scientific discourse, these groups rested their claims to legitimacy on the persuasiveness of their arguments, rather than on the appeal of their ideals or their ability to mobilize human and material resources. Thus, without taking into account the political implications of scientific discourse, an interest group approach alone does not contribute much to an understanding of the evolution of the ozone regime.

The argument that discourse may be an integral factor in the policy process is related to the broader claim that ideas and other cognitive factors are important determinants of social processes. After several generations of emphasis on the material causes of action and events, international relations scholars are expressing a renewed interest in nonmaterial factors. Yet because the recent research stresses "the political influence of the content of ideas, not cognitive processes" (Goldstein 1988:182), the origins of ideas are often ignored. The discursive approach taken here suggests that ideas should not be taken as independent variables in explaining policy outcomes. If knowledge and interests can merge even in the natural sciences, how much more pronounced is this entanglement likely to be for trans-scientific issues?

Any attempt to treat scientific knowledge and political power in the ozone case as either a purely independent or a purely dependent variable would ultimately generate a false picture of the events that transpired. Both theoretical argumentation and empirical research indicate that knowledge and power should be understood as interactive and that science and politics function together in a multidimensional way. There is nothing novel in these observations; they are consistent with a long tradition in the social sciences that explains events in terms of the interaction of material interests and ideas. Max Weber, for instance, wrote that: "Not ideas, but material and ideal interests, directly govern men's conduct. Yet very frequently the 'world images' that have been created by ideas, have, like switchmen, determine the tracks along which action has been pushed by the dynamic of interest" (1958:280).

Inasmuch as institutions "reflect a set of dominant ideas translated through legal mechanisms into formal governmental organizations" (Goldstein 1988:181), the literature on ideas as an impetus for foreign policy echoes the work of neoliberal institutionalists. Consistent with the study of the ozone regime, "critical junctures" are "unanticipated and exogenous events that drive institution-building" (Ikenberry 1988:233). The most commonly studied crises in world politics are economic depression and war, which tend to become "watershed events in states' institutional development" (Skowronek 1982:10) by challenging the capacity of the old institutions to cope with the new situation. But environmental crises like the discovery of the Antarctic ozone hole also frequently spur new national and international institution building.

By challenging old institutions, and hence old patterns of thinking, crises clear a space for the consideration of new ideas on how to explain and solve problems. A moment's reflection on the history of environmental problems reveals that disasters are frequently the prelude to new regimes. The 1986 Chernobyl disaster and the ensuing negotiations to update the nuclear accident regime under the International Atomic Energy Agency are a case in point (Young 1989a). Similarly, two giant oil spills in the late 1960s, one from the grounded Torrey Canyon off the British coast and the other from an oil well run amok near Santa Barbara, California, led to a complete revision of the international regimes governing marine pollution (M'Gonigle and Zacher 1979:17). The massive forest death in West Germany in the early 1980s caused that country to change its acid rain policy radically, precipitating similar moves across the Europe, even though the forest death had not been conclusively linked to acid rain (Wetstone 1987). The importance of crises for catalyzing environmental regime formation bodes poorly for problems that develop more gradually, such as loss of biodiversity, tropical deforestation, and global climate change, even if the resulting damage may be huge and irreversible.

Ideas about environmental problems are rooted in two categories of beliefs that are at least analytically distinct: causal and normative beliefs. The former would include the belief that CFCs deplete the ozone layer, whereas the latter would include the belief that, in the face of scientific uncertainty, one should err on the side of caution.[3] Scientific knowledge about environmental problems is concerned with testable beliefs about causal relations, and the authority of scientists derives from their presumed expertise about causal relations in a specialized area of study. Epistemic communities are networks of experts who share knowledge about causal relations as well as a common set of normative beliefs about preferred policies. Under conditions of uncertainty, it is argued, and especially during crises, epistemic communities become the catalysts for international regime formation. What distinguishes epistemic communities from inter-est groups is their shared commitment to causal in addition to normative beliefs.

The literature on epistemic communities makes an important contri-bution to a reflectivist understanding of world politics by focusing on social agents who are united by virtue of their shared intersubjective under-standings. In problematizing interests, this literature moves beyond the constraints of structural and choice- theoretic approaches. Reflective approaches do not necessarily supersede other theoretical orientations—certain institutional preconditions may be conducive to the emergence of epistemic communities or particular discursive practices—yet by high-lighting knowledge and beliefs, reflective approaches open up new research vistas beyond the study of bureaucracies and interest groups.

Nonetheless, as argued in chapter 2, the epistemic communities approach tends toward the modernist belief that science transcends poli-tics, that knowledge is divorced from political power. While proponents of this approach are more careful than their functionalist predecessors to qualify their conclusions about the ability of science to make politics more rational and less conflict-ridden, ultimately they seem to share an underly-ing commitment to the rationality project.[4] Epistemic community approaches underestimate the extent to which scientific information sim-ply rationalizes or reinforces existing political conflicts. Just as interesting as epistemic cooperation, and perhaps even the norm under the conditions of uncertainty that characterize environmental decision making, may be epistemic dissension.

While epistemic community approaches make an extremely important contribution in their attempt to elucidate the process of interest formula-tion in light of prevailing knowledge claims, they offer only a partial pic-ture of the policy process. As the ozone study demonstrates, actors may revise their conceptions of their interests when presented with new infor-mation, but their receptivity to information is itself a function of their per-ceived interests. Knowledge and interests are mutually interactive, a possi-bility that epistemic community approaches downplay.

The power of epistemic communities allegedly rests on their privileged access to consensual knowledge, but both the nature and the role of con-sensual knowledge are ambiguous. It seems almost tautological to argue that a group of policymakers who agree on the facts is more likely to agree on policies than a group that does not. More interesting—because they are unexpected—are those instances when consensual knowledge disintegrates under political pressure (Miles 1987:37), or when ignorance, not knowledge, increases the chances of cooperation (Rothstein 1984:750). The process of negotiating the international ozone regime raises some of these counterintuitive possibilities. A body of consensual scientific knowledge may exist, yet the wide range of possible interpretations of that knowledge may limit its influence.

The two prevailing accounts of the ozone regime rightly focus on the pivotal role of scientific knowledge in shaping the outcome, but they accept science and scientists as unproblematic catalysts in the process (Haas 1992b; Benedick 1991). According to Benedick, "First and foremost was the indispensable *role of science* in the ozone negotiations. . . . Scientists were drawn out of their laboratories and into the negotiation process" (5; emphasis in original). But interpretation and contingent events determined the knowledge that was accepted by the various actors. In emphasizing the involvement of scientists, both accounts clash with the fact that virtually no atmospheric scientists, especially prior to Montreal, were willing to make specific policy recommendations. Beyond putting the issue on the agenda initially and framing the problem in terms of chlorine loading during the treaty revision process, scientists were not directly responsible for the ozone regime. The "power of problem definition" almost never remains with the scientists throughout the policy process (Weingart 1982:80).

Scientific knowledge, rather than the scientists themselves, was crucial, but its ability to facilitate international cooperation was mediated by two crucial factors. First, the science was framed and interpreted by a group of ecologically minded knowledge brokers associated with the EPA, NASA, and UNEP. Second, the context of the negotiations, defined in large part by the discovery of the Antarctic ozone hole, determined the political acceptability of specific modes of framing the scientific knowledge. Both Benedick and Haas wrongly downplay the impact of the hole on the Montreal Protocol negotiations. No body of consensual knowledge, either from the computer models or from empirical observations, indicated that major cuts in CFC emissions were necessary in 1987. Only one specific mode of framing the available knowledge supported such a conclusion, and that mode gained its plausibility from the heightened sense of risk that accompanied the discoveries over Antarctica. The importance of the chlorine-loading methodology is underscored by the fact that it became the universally accepted scientific discourse once the Antarctic ozone hole was conclusively linked to industrial sources. Discursive strategies were also prominent in the discussions of the environmental effects of UV-B radiation and substitute availability.

The critique of the epistemic communities approach suggests that the relationship between science (and scientists) and policy (and policymakers) is multidimensional. Scientists may join together in an epistemic community to influence the course of policy, but their power is circumscribed by a host of contextual factors. Policymakers may co-opt or manipulate the scientists, or they may simply ignore what the scientists have to say. Whether or not the voices of scientists are audible may depend upon seemingly extraneous contingencies beyond the control of either scientists or policymakers. Furthermore, the scientists may deliberately refrain from addressing the policy implications of their research.

Once produced, knowledge becomes available to a host of political actors. Knowledge brokers exploit the discursive nature of science and politics, framing the available knowledge in ways that promote certain policies. To a greater extent than the notion of epistemic communities, the concept of knowledge brokers connotes the competitive and conflictual dimensions of knowledge claims in the policy arena. Knowledge brokers may work for government agencies, industry, international organizations, or nongovernmental organizations; in the ozone case, they were found within all of these. If they come from domestic agencies, as did those associated with the EPA and NASA during the ozone negotiations, the distinction between the domestic and international levels becomes blurred. Knowledge brokers are influential political actors not because they possess superior material resources but because of their discursive competence. In the evolution of the international ozone regime, political power often emanated from the ability to set the terms of discourse.

Discursive competence depends on many factors besides the skill of the individual knowledge brokers, including the nature of the audience and context. It is not supremely consequential who these individuals are; their authority is often more a function of their ability to manipulate information than of their professional or bureaucratic credentials. More important than the specific identities of the agents of discourse is the content of discourse. As determinants of what can and cannot be thought, discourses delimit the range of policy options, thereby functioning as precursors to policy outcomes.

Consider, for instance, how the dominant antiregulatory discourse on ozone was supplanted by a discourse of precautionary action. This discursive shift occurred both domestically within the United States and internationally during the Montreal Protocol negotiations. The 1986 WMO/NASA report defined the scientific parameters of discourse, yet the heteroglot nature of that document is evident in the wide range of policy stances derived from it. One of the key properties of discourses is their capacity to define how issues are connected within an issue area (Keeley 1990:94). During the ozone talks, the politically messy climate issue was essentially excluded from policy discourse, even though it was a central concern of scientific research. Skin cancer was highlighted in the early years but downplayed later as it became necessary to attract the support of countries not concerned about skin cancer. Even the discourse of cost-benefit analysis, institutionalized in order to bolster an antiregulatory approach in the United States, was used by the proregulatory forces to strengthen their own position. As an emerging counterdiscourse came to dominate the field, the definition of permissible issue linkages shifted.

There is no easy method of correlating bureaucratic or professional identity with policy stance. Rather, what was important in the ozone negotiations was the structure and content of discursive practices, a subject that is easily ignored when the roles of specific agents is overemphasized. The particular identities of the knowledge brokers associated with the chlorine-loading methodology, for instance, may be noteworthy, but they tell us little about how that mode of framing the science gained its authoritative status. By contrast, an approach that takes discursive practices as central can say something meaningful about the legitimation process.

Most importantly, discourses define the menu of possible policy options. Chapter 4 maintains that the rise of discourse of precautionary action was primarily shaped by the discovery of the Antarctic ozone hole—despite the negotiators' explicit agreement to ignore it. By presenting the real possibility of unprecedented catastrophe, the hole shifted the terms of the debate in favor of those who preferred to err on the side of caution. Indeed, the hole changed the meaning of *caution* altogether; the vulnerability of ecosystems suddenly became more salient than the vulnerability of CFC industries. Thus, a discursive practices approach runs counter to any analysis of the Montreal Protocol process that downplays the discovery of the Antarctic ozone hole on the grounds that the negotiators had agreed not to consider it. This is precisely the sort of decontextualized analysis offered by Benedick and, to a lesser extent, Haas. Even a cursory glance at the press coverage during that period confirms that the Antarctic hole was at the forefront of public consciousness. And a more in-depth investigation into the perceptions of key scientists and officials indicates that the hole was very much on their minds. Under such conditions, the hole's discovery naturally had a strong influence on the dominant discursive practices.

Initially, it might seem as if the argument that crises empower counterdiscourses is little different from the neoliberal institutionalist observation that crises generate new ideas and, hence, institutional change. The key difference, though, is that the discursive approach goes beyond the institutional expressions of ideas, moves into their deeper structure and content, and explores how these are conditioned by context. This approach puts the focus on discursive practices, rather than on individuals or organizations. Unlike institutionalism, which tends to accept ideas and power as separate independent variables, it understands power as being embedded in discourse. Discursive practices are not free-floating entities; they are embodied in technical processes, institutions, and pedagogical forms that both impose and maintain them (Foucault 1977:200).

A discursive practices approach offers insights into political process that go beyond those generated by a purely materialistic approach. Environmental crises, for instance, are not just physical phenomena; they are informational phenomena as well. New information is incorporated into previously existing discursive practices, or else it is employed by knowledge brokers to empower counterdiscourses.

A poststructuralist perspective on international regimes yields very different sorts of insights and research questions from those emanating from liberal and realist approaches, both of which treat interests and rationality unproblematically. Putting the spotlight on discourse enriches these key concepts, just as it yields a more complex picture of power and social order. Realists tend to define power narrowly in terms of material resources; they explain regime formation in terms of the interests of the preponderant power. Regime analysis rooted in more liberal assumptions about the international system tend to assume that regimes are communitarian, benevolent, voluntary, and cooperative. The conventional notion of regimes as "principles, norms, rules, and decision-making procedures around which actors' expectations converge" connotes ideas of freely shared judgments, freely converging to a consensus (Keeley 1990:83–85). A discursive approach to regimes, however, offers a more variegated conception of power than that of the realists, and it assumes a more skeptical stance to the problem of community and order than that of liberal institutionalists.

A discursive practices approach regards international regimes as localized power/knowledges, with each regime providing an arena for contestation among contending discourses. Arguing on behalf of such an approach,

James Keeley states, "Adding knowledge to power and treating a regime as an implementation of both, this analysis goes *inside the regime* rather than treating it as a mere dependent variable. It is, therefore, better able to ask how regimes work and what they do and to incorporate cognitive issues into both its questions and its answers" (1990:100; emphasis added). Such an approach is particularly germane to the study of regimes in which the framing of information is decisive, as is often the case in environmental regimes. It also anticipates that regimes tend to become arenas for debate among competing power/knowledges, as the Montreal Protocol has been during the treaty revision process.

After stating the advantages of a discursive approach, it is only fair to acknowledge its methodological shortcomings. A discursive approach is helpful in answering "how" and "what" questions, but it does not fare as well in providing parsimonious explanations. (Recall, however, that approaches purporting to offer more parsimonious explanations have already been called into question earlier in this chapter.) Moreover, because of the central role it gives contingency and context, a discursive approach cannot make sweeping generalizations or offer precise predictions.

What, then, is it good for besides telling a story well? First, many would see inherent value in a well-told story, particularly if the topic were related to planetary sustainability. But I would also argue that a well-told story can offer important insights into the policy process in general and perhaps into future events as well. It can alert the analyst to certain misconceptions that might arise, and it can also alert the practitioner to the importance of alternative discursive strategies.

Implications for Global Environmental Politics and the World System

Because the global ozone regime has been lauded as a prototype for a future climate change regime, it is worthwhile to draw some comparisons between the two issues. (The comparisons are elaborated in table 6.1.) To an even greater extent than the ozone case, the problem of human-induced climate change dramatically poses the dilemma of formulating policy under conditions of scientific uncertainty when the stakes are very high. The social and environmental damage from global climate change is likely to be far more catastrophic than that caused by ozone depletion, and the perceived costs of regulation are very high. For both issues, the twin problems of accumulation and irreversibility suggest the need for precautionary action before environmental damage is conclusively measured; greenhouse gases, however, are unlikely to precipitate an environmental crisis like the Antarctic ozone hole whose causes can be definitively identified. All of these qualities suggest what experience has borne out: construction of a viable global climate regime will be a formidable task.

The political differences between the two problems are also striking. First, in contrast to the ozone issue, the United States under the Bush administration blocked all efforts to regulate fossil fuel emissions, the primary source of greenhouse gases. The fact that U.S. scientists pioneered discoveries in both fields of research demonstrates that scientific proficiency does not correlate with political leadership. In fact, once a policy decision is made to resist environmental controls, a country's access to abundant scientific information can help bolster that decision. Under the Bush administration, U.S. policy was driven not by the EPA but by the Department of Energy (DOE), the budget office, and the chief of staff. Knowledge brokers from the DOE capitalized on the supposedly enormous global warming potentials (GWP) of CFCs to promote a "comprehensive approach" to climate change. Their strategy was to substitute the CFC reductions already mandated by the Montreal Protocol for controls on fossil fuel emissions (U.S. Task Force on the Comprehensive Approach to Climate Change 1991). Scientific discourse served once more as a political tool, but this time not in the service of the global environment.

In contrast to the ozone issue, developing countries have been major players in the climate change debates from the beginning. Because the stakes are so much higher, the entrance of developing countries into the global ecology debates highlights a crucial question regarding the role of science in international politics: if scientific knowledge is an important political tool, how can an equitable policy consensus be reached between North and South when the distribution of informational resources is so radically skewed? To a greater degree than in the ozone debates, developing countries have framed their positions in terms of scientific knowledge. Thus, the development of an international scientific consensus on such issues as emissions data, rates of tropical deforestation, chemical properties of greenhouse gases, and climatological changes has become a major priority (Intergovernmental Panel on Climate Change 1990; U.S. Committee on Earth and Environmental Sciences 1992).

The level of political involvement by scientists in the climate change issue is unprecedented in international environmental politics.[5] Since

1985, scientists have been calling for action to stabilize the climate system, which would require as much as a 50 percent equivalent reduction in carbon dioxide emissions (Usher 1989:26). Such sweeping recommendations stand in marked contrast to the virtual silence of scientists on CFC reductions prior to 1987 and their relatively low profile since the Montreal Protocol. If the issue is truly shrouded in scientific uncertainty, as it is popularly believed to be, then the prominence of scientists on the political scene is rather puzzling. This puzzle can be partially clarified by considering that most of the scientific uncertainties revolve around the timing and the degree of anticipated climate change, not around whether major changes occur. A broad consensus exists among scientists that it is a "very, very real problem" and that humanity is "moving the climate into uncharted territory" (Intergovernmental Panel on Climate Change 1990). Consequently, it is not surprising that large numbers of scientists oppose behavior that will induce unprecedented conditions on a global scale.

At least some scientists were encouraged by the Montreal Protocol experience to become more outspoken on policy issues. Because ozone and climatology are both atmospheric problems, there is some overlap in the scientific communities that address them. By the late 1980s, many of the relevant scientists were accustomed to being in the political limelight. After the Montreal Protocol, both environmentalists and scientists focused their attention on the climate problem (*Nature* 1987a).

Despite the apparent existence of a powerful epistemic community of scientists, environmentalists, and political leaders in favor of regulatory measures, such measures have yet to be adopted. Because of strong objec-

Table 6.1. Comparison of Two Global Atmospheric Environmental Problems

Characteristic	Ozone*	Climate
Scientific uncertainty	High	High
Predicted damages	High	Very high
Distribution of costs and benefits	Fairly even	Uneven
Cost of controls	Moderate	Very high
Sources of pollution	Few	Very many
Major actors	North	North and South
Visible crisis	Yes	No
Human health issue	Yes	Yes

*For the sake of this comparison, the characteristics listed for the ozone issue are from before the Montreal Protocol. This makes sense because this was the period of the greatest scientific uncertainty and so is most comparable to the current situation with respect to the climate change problem.

tions by the United States, the 1992 United Nations Conference on Environment and Development (UNCED) adopted a Climate Change Convention that contains no specific control measures. Nonetheless, the treaty's stated objective is "to prevent dangerous anthropogenic interference with the climate system" (UNCED 1992). This convention, negotiated in Rio, may serve the same function for climate as the 1985 Vienna Convention did for the ozone issue: it may establish a discursive norm in favor of precautionary action that may eventually be implemented.

All of this is indicative of the limits of discursive practices. The very term *discourse* is derived from a Latin word meaning "a running to and fro." Discourses do not solve environmental problems—they merely offer alternative interpretive lenses through which problems can be viewed, lenses that lend themselves to certain policy solutions. The climate change problem demonstrates that consensual knowledge does not guarantee concerted international action. Strong opposition from one key state can lead to a perpetual "running to and fro," even if all the running is rationalized on scientific grounds.

Discursive power, particularly that associated with scientific knowledge, is likely to be increasingly important in the future. And, as environmental problems become more serious and more globalized, science can be expected to play an expanded role in institution building. Other developments in the international system are likely to reproduce and reinforce this pattern. National security, traditionally viewed in terms of military power, has become more complicated as the nature of the threats has shifted toward economic and environmental dangers (Nye 1990:179).[6] The simultaneous decrease in the utility of military power as an instrument of foreign policy and the new prominence of nonstate actors has cleared a space for knowledge-based power.[7] In the same way, the declining utility of force and the informational nature of many contemporary international problems promotes greater involvement by nonstate actors, since knowledge, once produced, is accessible to many people. The proliferation of information that has accompanied the postindustrial revolutions in computers and communications technology has been instrumental in this regard.

Many indicators, including the number of scientists and other professionals employed in the service economy, document the shift to an informational as opposed to a resource-based mode of production in the affluent countries. This shift represents a major transformation of the social structure, one that places knowledge at center stage. The new social genre has been referred to variously as "cybernetic" (Bell 1973), "technocratic"

(Brzezinski 1968), "programmed" (Touraine 1972), "post-industrial" (Touraine 1972; Bell 1973), "knowledgeable" (Lane 1966), "active" (Etzioni 1968), and "post-modern" (Kavolis 1970, 1972; Bell 1973). Despite their differences, all these thinkers emphasize the centrality of knowledge in the new social order, and most are optimistic about this development. In general, the theorists of postindustrialism devote little analysis to the key theoretical categories of information and knowledge, treating them as monolithic and uncontroversial. Thus, much of that literature is consistent with the aims of the rationality project (Stone 19888).

Nonetheless, there are real signs of a shift toward a postindustrial society, a shift that has important implications for our understandings of power.[8] Undoubtedly, a society's generally accepted view of power is determined by an entire social context. A civilization that reduces the world to a mechanical aggregate of material objects to be exploited for individual gratification is bound to reduce power to its physical dimensions (Skolimowski 1983). Perhaps a postindustrial society, based on modes of information rather than modes of production, would be more likely to grasp power in its cognitive and subjective dimensions. This reconceptualization, implicit in the recent turn toward reflective approaches to world politics, may betoken a more general trend toward the subjectivization of the study and practice of world politics.

James Rosenau offers the first comprehensive effort to explicate a theory of world politics for a postindustrial age. He suggests that "post-international politics" is increasingly bifurcated, with traditional state actors on the one side and a proliferation of nonstate actors, including businesses, social movements, experts, and international organizations, on the other (1990). Not only the actors are changing; so is the nature of power. Rosenau believes that, because "scientific proof" is becoming elevated as a major political tool, "the tendency to contest issues with alternative proofs seems likely to grow as a central feature of world politics" (203). Power in post-international politics, then, would be primarily discursive.

Other analysts concur with Rosenau's observations that postindustrial world politics are distinguished by a "diffusion of power" away from state actors to nonstate actors (Nye 1990:20). The diffusion of power coincides with a shift away from traditional notions of "hard" power to "softer" forms of "co-optive" power. The former entails influencing other states' behavior through either inducements or threats, whereas the latter rests on the attractiveness of one's ideas or on the ability to set the political agenda

(31–32). Co-optive power ranges from cultural and ideological factors to scientific information.

The prevalence of scientific discourse should not delude us into the common misconception that politics will therefore become more rational and less conflict-ridden, whether through functional cooperation, epistemic communities, or postindustrial technocracy. The modernist faith in science dies hard, however, even for those who foresee turbulence as the dominant mode of the future. Rosenau observes, for instance, that the enormous increase in the supply of information has accentuated the practice of seeking knowledge before making decisions. From this he concludes optimistically that "the 'science of muddling through' may well give way to the science of modeling through" (1990:324). Rosenau discerns within the rise of scientific proof in international politics a nascent "global culture" (421–22). The experience in negotiating the ozone regime suggests, however, that inasmuch as scientific discourse permeates political debates, as often as not it serves to articulate or rationalize existing interests and conflicts.

A discursive approach is particularly germane to a social field pervaded by the "mode of information" rather than the "mode of production" (Poster 1984). The commodification of consciousness through representation and "hyperreal simulation," for instance, provides a provocative description of postindustrial dynamics, ranging from advertising to computer modeling (Baudrillard 1975, 1981, 1983). Environmental politics can offer some key nodes for the study of disciplinary power and surveillance. The nations of the earth have fixed their collective disciplinary gaze on the earth itself, resulting in a multitude of new discursive practices.

A discursive approach suggests that the profusion of information may lead to greater confusion as the world becomes a ubiquitous market for discourses. Frederic Jameson's observation may well be correct: "No society has ever been quite so mystified as our own, saturated as it is with messages and information" (1981:60—61; quoted in Terdiman 1985:46). The gigantic volume of environmental data generated in the past two decades by a host of monitoring and research programs may at times hinder rather than facilitate the process of environmental management. The process of delegitimation is fueled by the demand for legitimation.

And, as the global warming debates have revealed so starkly, the distribution of knowledge is far from even. The proliferation of information characteristic of postindustrial society is occurring far more rapidly in the North than in the South. About 95 percent of the world's production of chemical knowledge in 1980 was available in only six languages, and two of these, English and Russian, accounted for over 82 percent (Laponce 1987:198; quoted in Rosenau 1990:427—28). As one analyst of trends in environmental information argues, "The information-rich will become richer, and the information-poor will not even suspect what they have missed" (Davis 1974:27).

The equation, however, is not so simple: the information-poor are suspicious, and they may compensate for their deficiencies in surprising ways. Most obviously, while scientific knowledge can be an important political resource, it is quite different from standard material resources. Access to knowledge does not necessarily bestow political influence; persuasion is an essential ingredient in the process. Knowledge is only a useful tool when others are convinced of its validity or, more precisely, of the validity of the proponent's interpretations of it. Such cognitive processes are not easily predictable and are shaped by seemingly serendipitous events like the weather or the Antarctic ozone hole. All of this suggests a distinctive power-of-the-weak phenomenon; those without access to informational resources may simply refuse to be persuaded.

A core issue, then, is whether the apparent "scientization of politics" observed by analysts of epistemic communities and advocates of postindustrialism is not really the "politicization of science" (Weingart 1982:73). While "the language of science is becoming a worldview that penetrates politics everywhere" (Haas 1990:46), old cleavages may simply be recloaked in new scientific garb. Epistemic dissension may be as likely an outcome as epistemic cooperation.

In this sense, there are both hopeful signs and causes for concern. Scientific discourse can be employed skillfully to persuade states to adopt precautionary policies jointly. Yet the celebratory mood that has surrounded the Montreal Protocol and its revisions must be tempered with the recognition that it took thirteen years for this "sudden global emergency" (Roan 1989) to be addressed with concrete action. The ozone protocol was too late to prevent the Antarctic ozone hole and probably would not have contained the provisions that it did without the hole. The most recent revisions, adopted in Copenhagen, are likely to be rapidly outstripped by accelerating ozone depletion. Even in this "most likely case" of the global ozone regime, there was no clear path leading from consensual knowledge to international cooperation.

This raises the larger question of the role that scientific knowledge can be expected to play in formulating environmentally responsible policies.

Conventional wisdom among environmentalists has been that scientific knowledge communicated to people and political leaders will lead to ecologically sustainable societies: education engenders action. The faith in the power of science, as I have argued, runs deep. There are, however, two arguments—based on two different views of science—against this position. The first is that, because science deals with the world of facts, not values, and because values are ultimately what inform our actions, we cannot expect science to save us. Rather, what is required is a reorientation of fundamental values regarding human relationships with the biosphere, whether through political, ethical, or religious movements (Caldwell 1985). The second argument rejects the premise that science and politics, facts and values, are wholly divorced from one another. In this view, science can promote sustainable policies when it is used as a political tool and framed in ways that enhance environmental preservation, as was the case when a group of knowledge brokers deftly defined the terms of the ozone debates. Paradoxically, the more skeptical view of science acknowledges its real power; the key questions in this view then become how knowledge is framed, by whom, and on behalf of what interests.

On a deeper level, these arguments are not fundamentally inconsistent with one another. In both cases, values are the key to developing environmentally responsible policies. As I argued in the study of the ozone regime, the discourse of precautionary action was not mandated by scientific knowledge but grew out of a particular interpretation of that knowledge. Yet, so long as science serves as a universal legitimator, values alone will not be sufficient to forge international regimes to protect the global environment; the skillful employment of scientific discourse is essential. The political impact of scientific knowledge is determined far more by its incorporation into larger discursive practices than by either its validity or the degree to which it is accepted by scientists. Science, then, is not likely to save us from environmental ruin, persistent political action informed by carefully chosen discursive strategies might.

Appendix: Montreal Protocol
Participants Interviewed

Stephen O. Anderson, director of Technology Transfer and Industry Programs, EPA Global Change Division; cochair of technology and economic assessment panel for the 1991 assessment of the Montreal Protocol; interviewed August 26, 1992

Ambassador Richard Benedick, chief U.S. negotiator for the Vienna Convention and the Montreal Protocol, deputy assistant secretary of state for environment, health, and natural resources; interviewed March 16, 1990.

Dr. Guy Brasseur, atmospheric modeler, National Center for Atmospheric Research; scientific adviser for the EC delegation to the Montreal Protocol negotiations; past member of the Belgian parliament; interviewed November 5, 1990

Dr. Ralph Cicerone, atmospheric physicist; professor of geosciences, University of California at Irvine; member of 1981 and 1986 WMO/NASA ozone assessment panels; interviewed September 10, 1990

Eileen Claussen, director of the EPA's Atmospheric and Indoor Air Programs; chair of U.S. delegation to the Second Meeting of the Parties (1990); interviewed September 7, 1992

Liz Cook, director of Friends of the Earth–USA Atmosphere Office; interviewed August 19, 1992

David Doniger, senior attorney, Natural Resources Defense Council; interviewed December 4, 1989.

Kevin Fay, executive director of the Alliance for a Responsible CFC Policy; interviewed December 4, 1989

Michael J. Gibbs, policy analyst with ICF; contractor to the EPA for economic and risk assessment studies; interviewed November 22, 1989

David Gibbons, Office of Management and Budget; convened interagency meetings to assess U.S. negotiating position for Montreal Protocol; interviewed December 6, 1989

Dr. Joseph P. Glas, manager of Du Pont's Freon Products Division; interviewed December 7, 1989

Dr. James Hammitt, senior economist at the Rand Corporation; coauthor of economic assessment studies for the EPA; interviewed November 13, 1989

Mike Harris, Regulatory Affairs Manager, Imperial Chemical Industries (United Kingdom); interviwed September 12, 1991

John Hoffman, chair of the EPA's Ozone Protection Task Force (1985–1988); interviewed September 8, 1992

Paul Horowitz, policy analyst for UNEP's Ozone Secretariat (1989–1990); international adviser, EPA Global Change Division (1990–1993); interviewed August 24, 1992

Dr. Mohammad Ilyas, chair of the Astronomy and Atmospheric Research Unit, University of Science Malaysia; member of environmental effects and science assessment panels; interviewed December 21, 1992

Dr. Ivar Isaksen, atmospheric modeler with the University of Oslo and National Center for Atmospheric Research (Boulder, Colorado); member of UNEP's Coordinating Committee on the Ozone Layer (CCOL); interviewed October 2, 1990

Michael P. Kelly, deputy assistant secretary for trade development, Department of Commerce; interviewed September 14, 1990

Dr. Margaret Kripke, immunologist and skin cancer specialist; chair of the EPA's scientific advisory board to review the 1987 risk assessment; interviewed October 3, 1990

James Losey, senior staff officer with the EPA's International Activities Office (1980–1987); interviewed September 17, 1990

Mack McFarland, atmospheric scientist, Du Pont Freon Division; interviewed October 22, 1989.

Gary MacNeil, director of the EPA's Office of Technology Transfer and Industry Projects; interviewed August 25, 1992

Alan S. Miller, executive director of the Center for Global Change, University of Maryland (1989–1993); attorney for the Natural Resources Defense Council (1979–1984); interviewed December 5, 1989

Rafe Pomerance, policy analyst, World Resources Institute; interviewed December 4, 1989

Dr. M. Margarita Prendez, professor of Chemical and Pharmaceutical Sciences, University of Chile; interviewed December 16, 1992

Stephen Seidel, senior analyst, EPA Air Office; interviewed December 5, 1989, and August 24, 1992

Dr. Ed Shykind, science advisor, Trade Development and International Trade Administration, Department of Commerce; interviewed December 8, 1989

Dr. Joseph Steed, environmental manager, Du Pont Freon Products Division (1986–1990); interviewed October 22, 1989.

Dr. Richard Stolarski, atmospheric physicist at NASA's Goddard Flight Center; interviewed December 11, 1989

Dr. Nien Dak Sze, atmospheric modeler; director of Atmospheric Environmental Research, a private firm; interviewed September 26, 1990

Lee Thomas, EPA administrator (1985–1989); interviewed November 20, 1989

Dr. Peter Usher, coordinator of UNEP's Atmosphere Office of the Global Environmental Monitoring System (GEMS); interviewed December 10, 1990

Dr. Tony Vogelsburg, environmental manager, Du Pont Freon Products Division (1988–1993); interviewed September 11, 1991

Dr. Robert Watson, director of NASA's Global Habitability Program; chair of the 1986 WMO/NASA ozone assessment; chair of UNEP's methyl bromide task force; interviewed December 13, 1989, and August 28, 1992

Notes

1. Science in World Politics: The Need for a Discursive Approach

1. While recognizing the ambiguities of this term, I use it for want of a better one. In my view, "postindustrialism" does not entail the end of industrial society; indeed, the two exist side by side and in various proportions around the globe. Rather, the term refers to a postwar shift in the economic structures of advanced industrialized countries toward a greater prominence of informational, as opposed to industrial, modes of exchange. My own stance on the political implications of this shift is spelled out in the last chapter.

2. Traditional analyses based on military and economic power are of limited value for another reason. In environmental matters, including ozone depletion, states with little military capability and small economies can nullify agreements simply by refusing to or being unable to implement them. Their power is a function of their large and growing populations, their territorial control of internationally valued ecological resources, or their lack of state capacity to enforce agreements. Global environmental politics lends itself to the peculiar phenomenon of the "power of the weak."

3. Knowledge brokers are like epistemic communities in that both are knowledge-based social groups. But I use the former term to emphasize the discursive dimensions of knowledge that are disregarded in the epistemic communities literature. The term also connotes the inherently conflictual nature of knowledge in the policy arena.

4. Trans-scientific problems straddle the line between science and policy; their solutions require input from science, but science alone is not sufficient to resolve them (Weinberg 1972).

2. Power and Scientific Discourse

1. This dynamic, of course, is not specific to knowledge-based power. Gene Sharp (1973) demonstrates that the power of social leaders derives not from their personal attributes but from their location within powerful social structures.

2. In a sense, the dichotomy between knowledge-based power and other forms of power is artificial. If power is understood as the production of intended effects, then agents must know how to produce those effects. Even producing unintended effects usually entails knowledge of social conventions. Nonetheless, some forms of power are based less on material factors and rely more heavily on manipulating information. The view of power as the production of effects by autonomous agents is eroded with the recognition that identity and interests are themselves generated through discursive practices, particularly in an information society.

3. The behaviorists' belief that interest can be discerned from behavior has been roundly criticized for both its mechanistic conception of causality and its neglect of intentionality. See Ball (1975, 1976, 1978), Clegg (1989), and Isaac (1987).

4. Some major works in the debate include Bachrach and Baratz (1970), Lukes (1974), Gaventa (1980), Stone (1989), and Waste (1989).

I do not mean to imply a dichotomy between malevolent power based upon force versus the benevolent power of persuasion. The belief that force can be used positively for self-defense or liberation underpins the just war tradition. Likewise, one can be persuaded deceitfully and perniciously to revise one's conception of one's interests, as was Othello by Iago. Yet one can also be edified about the nature of one's interests. A comprehensive conception of power should encompass all these situations.

5. Some realists, such as Henry Kissinger and Raymond Aron, argue that the international system is influenced by the presence or absence of insurrectionist powers that violate the system's norms of legitimacy. But this is a minor element of realist theory and does not regard knowledge as a source of legitimacy.

6. Foucault was greatly influenced by Friedrich Nietzsche, who saw behind the scientific "will to truth" a broader "will to power." Explicitly linking power and knowledge, Nietzsche argued that "we gain knowledge about the power and effects [of nature] so as to . . . make us masters and proprietors of nature" (1979:135).

7. Later in this chapter, I show that the glossing over of epistemological issues in many analyses of science in politics leads to exactly this conflation of different forms of authority.

8. Ludwig Fleck's *Genesis and Development of a Scientific Fact* (1979), raising almost identical issues, was first published twenty-seven years earlier but was ignored by the intellectual community.

9. Hagstrom's discussion of scientists' search for recognition provides an interesting example of disciplinary power. A scientist who openly admits to seeking recognition is considered deviant, yet such desires are nonetheless prevalent. Thus scientists's behavior is disciplined by professional norms.

10. The ubiquity of science as disciplinary power has profound environmental implications, for the natural world itself has become to a great extent the product of artifice. The unprecedented unleashing of pollutants that accompanied the Industrial Revolution and has continued with postindustrial technology has effectively transformed the planet into a huge laboratory, complete with the observational gaze of computer modeling and satellite surveillance.

11. Research on science in politics published in the aftermath of World War II dealt almost exclusively with military matters. See, for instance, Cox (1964), Lapp (1965), and Wiesner (1965).

12. Some experts misconceive their own power, mistakenly viewing it in more conventional terms as a finite resource. Hence they resist giving advice, preferring to withhold their limited influence for more important issues in the future. Some of the atmospheric scientists I interviewed expressed this view.

13. Some scientists believe that this propensity varies according to discipline, with physicists being the most prone to it and hence the most confident in the policy arena (Oppenheimer and Boyle 1990).

14. See Hiskes and Hiskes (1986), Shrader-Frechette (1985), and Fischhoff et al. (1981).

15. Some observers have carried this perspective to an extreme, reducing all environmental concern to social and psychological drives (Douglas and Wildavsky 1982). My own view is that scientific facts are rooted in both intransitive natural structures and transitive social processes; reductionism in either direction leads to distortions.

16. In the decade following 1972, the number of national environmental agencies rose dramatically. These bureaucracies are largely staffed with scientists and technically trained laypersons.

17. Morgenthau suggests an alternative breed of functionalism, one that recognizes the ubiquity of power (Morgenthau and Thompson 1985:513–25). Like Mitrany, he believes that human survival may require a functionalist world order. Unlike Mitrany, however, he believes that functional agencies can only change the context in which power operates, not power itself. Unfortunately, Morgenthau's position is not spelled out, there is no discussion of the role of knowledge, and his conception of power is uncompromisingly negative.

18. For a detailed criticism of the sociological theory of functionalism on these grounds, see Giddens (1984:293–97).

19. Durkheim, however, believes that gemeinschaft is a prerequisite for gesellschaft. Like Weber, he argues that the latter may occur at the expense of the former, such that a highly specialized elite community may be a disintegrative force rather than an integrative one. This line of thinking is consistent with critiques of technocracy as antidemocratic (Konig 1968).

20. In his most recent work, Ernst Haas examines epistemic communities in the World Bank and the International Monetary Fund (1990). Peter Cowhey (1990) looks at the economic theories of the dominant epistemic community of the international telecommunications regime. See also Ikenberry 1992; Hopkins 1992; and Adler 1992.

3. Historical and Scientific Background on Human Causes of Stratospheric Ozone Depletion.

1. For a more detailed history of CFCs and refrigeration, see Linden and Didion 1987 and Cowan 1964.

2. Du Pont devised the shorthand notation for CFCs. The digit on far right is the number of fluorine atoms; the second digit from the right is the number of hydrogen atoms plus one; the third digit from the right is the number of carbon atoms minus one. $CFCl_3$, which contains one fluorine atom, zero hydrogen atoms, and one carbon atom, becomes CFC-011 and then CFC-11, and CF_2Cl_2, which has two fluorine atoms, no hydrogen atoms, and one carbon atom, becomes CFC-012 and then CFC-12 (interview with Joseph P. Glas).

3. For the purposes of table 3.1, communist countries include the Soviet Union, the nations of Eastern Europe, China, and the other communist Asian nations. Most of these only began to make their production data available in 1986, during a series of workshops sponsored by UNEP and the EPA.

4. In an important sense, the politics drove the science on this issue by defining the salient areas of research. While climate change was perceived as a distant threat, skin cancer from ozone depletion was perceived by the public as an immediate, direct, and universal danger (see Ohi 1985).

5. Public reaction was so fervent in the USA that Congress received more letters on the issue than on any other since the Vietnam War (Brodeur 1986:71).

6. These arguments are examined in Dotto and Schiff (1978:208–14.

7. For a summary of the EPA's regulatory authority under the Clean Air Act, see "Protection of Stratospheric Ozone: Proposed Rule" (1987b).

8. Of all the producers, Du Pont had the only major research program for CFC substitutes.

9. Those countries that had already legislated regulations—the USA, Canada, Sweden, and the Netherlands—had high levels of environmental consciousness. The strongest opponents of CFC controls, including Britain, France, and Japan, lagged behind on issues like toxic substances, leaded gasoline, and nuclear prolif-

eration (Stoel 1983:68–69). Thus national CFC policies can be seen as reflecting the strength of environmentalist discourse in each country.

4. The Employment of Knowledge in the Montreal Protocol Negotiations

1. The group included, but was not limited to, the following: John Hoffman, head of the EPA's Stratospheric Ozone Task Force; Stephen Seidel, policy analyst with the EPA's Air and Radiation Office; James Losey, staff officer with the EPA's International Activities Office; Stephen Anderson, an economist with the EPA; Michael J. Gibbs, policy analyst with ICF Incorporated; James Hammitt, statistical analyst with Rand; and Frank Camm, a Rand economist.

2. The sponsors of the 1986 report were NASA, the World Meteorological Organization (WMO), the Federal Aviation Administration, the National Oceanic and Atmospheric Administration (NOAA), UNEP, the Commission of the European Communities, and the West German Federal Ministry for Research and Technology.

3. A good example are the reports written by the Stratospheric Ozone Review Group for the British government. See U.K. Department of the Environment (1976, 1979). Five years after Rowland and Molina linked CFCs to ozone depletion, the British Meteorological Office speculated that ozone losses could be counterbalanced by carbon dioxide emissions (Allaby 1979:356).

4. The 1986 WMO/NASA report was so important that some participants in the recent international talks on global climate change believe that it was the main inspiration for the Montreal Protocol. They seem to think that "all we need is three blue books for the IPCC" (Intergovernmental Panel on Climate Change). They invited Robert Watson to head a panel because "he was the one who worked the magic before" (interview with Ralph Cicerone).

5. Halocarbons include not only CFCs but methyl chloroform, carbon tetrachloride, and the bromated compounds called halons. For a classification of the chemicals, see the third section of chapter Three. Only CFCs and halons, however, were at issue during the negotiations leading up to the protocol. The other halocarbons were targeted in the subsequent review process established by the treaty.

6. Rand and ICF both contracted with the EPA to do detailed analyses of market and production trends. These studies were presented and discussed in detail at the second session of the international economic workshop (Hammitt et al. 1986; UNEP/WG.151/Background 2:paper 1).

7. The lawsuit is discussed toward the end of the fourth section of chapter 3.

8. Markus Jachtenfuchs describes the ozone talks as "quasi-bilateral negotiations between the EC and the USA, the EC getting support from Japan and the USA being the leader of a group with Canada, Norway, and Sweden participating" (1990:264).

9. Many of the scientific conclusions from the UNEP/EPA conference were presented in chapter 3 as background information.

10. Many of the EPA's arguments for stringent CFC controls were couched in terms of cost effectiveness. This was not merely a ploy to convince industry but was mandated by President Reagan's Executive Order 12291, signed shortly after he took office. This order, stipulating that all major new regulations must undergo benefit-cost analysis, was part of the administration's overall policy of "regulatory relief." The order specifies that economic efficiency should be the basis for evaluating regulations (Smith 1984:4). As a result, the EPA studied such seemingly peripheral matters as the price of replacing plastics damaged by increased ultraviolet radiation (Titus 1986:7).

11. Every person I interviewed concurs with this assessment, but this evaluation benefits from hindsight. There may have been some who, at the time, viewed the issue primarily in economic and political terms.

12. The U.S. position was still being developed. While there was a mounting consensus to move beyond the aerosol ban proposed by the Toronto Group before the Vienna Convention, the U.S. bargaining stance was not finalized until November 1986. A proposal put on the table by the Natural Resources Defense Council (NRDC) at Leesburg called for a full phaseout of CFCs over ten years (paper 6, UNEP/WG.148/3). This proposal is remarkably similar to the U.S. position that was eventually adopted, but EPA officials involved in developing the U.S. position deny any influence (interviews with Lee Thomas, James Losey, and Stephen Seidel).

13. Given industry's reluctance in 1986 to admit that growth was likely, it is noteworthy that, in an 1989 interview, Joseph Glas asserted on several occasions that it was industry that alerted the negotiators to the likelihood of increased CFC growth rates.

14. According to Joseph Glas, the real issue was fluorospar's potential lack of availability for political reasons. Du Pont had been granted an exception to U.S. trade restrictions in order to import South Africa's substantial fluorospar deposits, but South Africa was a risky trading partner. Glas admits, however, that any fluorospar scarcity would have engendered only "short-term limits to the rate of growth" (interview). If industry's predictions of a de facto freeze in CFC growth were valid, then there should have been no shortage. The suspicion arises, then, that those who deemed the fluorospar issue a red herring were correct (interview with Michael Gibbs).

15. Because the depletion was never total, the term "ozone hole" is metaphorical. Some industry representatives saw the psychological connotations inherent in the term and objected to it, preferring to speak more euphemistically of "temporary ozone losses" (interview with Kevin Fay). Names that include repeated sounds, like the three *o*'s in "ozone hole," have "an advantage in the marketplace of ideas" (*Los Angeles Times* 1986). Since the term has gained widespread acceptance, even in the scientific journals, I will use it.

16. *Crisis* here refers to a different sort of phenomenon than is typically considered in the international relations literature. There, crises entail "the perception of a dangerously high probability of war" (Snyder and Diesing 1977:6), and the perceived danger is caused by the actions of nation-states or their agents, rather than by external or natural events.

17. A Japanese team made similar observations, but their 1984 paper was published in an obscure journal (Pukelsheim 1990:540).

18. This reluctance to accept Farman's work supports my argument in chapter 2 about the social construction of knowledge. Science is deeply involved in such matters as reputation and recognition.

19. The initial reaction of all the scientists I interviewed, even those who published papers supporting other explanations, was that the hole was caused by CFCs.

20. Other, more offbeat hypotheses were advanced. Two NASA scientists proposed that meteoric particles could be trapped in the winter polar vortex and break apart later to destroy ozone (*Washington Post* 1987a). A British biochemist argued that wood-rotting fungi emit even greater quantities of halocarbons than modern industry does and that widespread deforestation was responsible for saving the ozone layer (*New Scientist* 1987:27). The plethora of theories strengthened the case of those who hoped to block strong CFC controls by emphasizing the uncertainties.

21. Heterogeneous reactions occur between chemicals in different states, e.g., between a liquid and a gas. The models used during the Montreal Protocol negotiations considered only homogeneous reactions among atmospheric gases. F. S. Rowland had already done some laboratory research on heterogeneous reactions. When his data were included in the computer model used for the 1984 National Academy of Sciences report, the predicted total ozone loss skyrocketed from the 2 to 4 percent range to 20 to 30 percent (interview with Ralph Cicerone). This information was available at the time of the 1986 WMO/NASA assessment but received little attention.

22. A team of scientists affiliated with industry published a paper in the special supplement of *Geophysical Research Letters* that favored a chlorine chemistry explanation (Rodriguez, Ko, and Sze 1986). Robert Watson, a key person in both the scientific and political circles, believes that the ozone hole was responsible for industry's "philosophical reorientation" (interview).

23. Framing the issue in terms of chlorine loading, as Hoffman did, rather than in terms of ozone depletion potential (ODP), as did the atmospheric models, is somewhat misleading because it implies that all forms of chlorine are equally menacing to ozone. But, as the discovery in Antarctica demonstrated, the models were also misleading. As one scientist puts it in 1990: "Chlorine doesn't affect us; ozone does. ODP is more sophisticated, more complicated. Two years ago, I would have said chlorine loading was a good measure; now I think we should use the state-of-

the-art models. At the time the models couldn't account for the Antarctic hole, and now they can" (interview with Nien Dak Sze).

24. The issue of whether or not other agencies were allowed sufficient input into the initial process later became hotly debated. Officials from the Commerce, Interior, and Energy Departments claim that they were excluded from the meetings (interviews with Ed Shykind and Michael P. Kelly). EPA and State Department officials contend that these departments simply disregarded the issue because they didn't realize its political and economic significance (interviews with Richard Benedick, Stephen Seidel, and James Losey). The fact that all the above departments signed the original position paper through the Circular 175 Process lends support to the second interpretation.

25. Consumption was defined as production, minus exports, plus imports, minus the amount destroyed (U.S. Department of State 1986). This issue was controversial during the negotiations because the exporting countries, primarily in the EC, objected to having CFC consumption and production equated.

26. No specific numbers were mentioned either in the suit or in the Clean Air Act under which the suit was filed. David Doniger, the NRDC's lead attorney on the ozone issue, was "pleasantly surprised" by the U.S. position (Roan 1989:195), which was much more comprehensive than the proposals of some environmental organizations. World Resources Institute, for instance, backed cuts in specific uses ranging from 25 percent for refrigeration and air conditioning to 90 percent for aerosol uses, averaging roughly 50 percent overall (Miller and Mintzer 1986:19).

27. Some knowledgeable observers believe that Thomas hoped to negotiate a major international accord and, having learned from the failures of his predecessor, William Ruckelshaus, on the acid rain issue, decided to take on the ozone issue (interview with Alan S. Miller).

28. David Gibbons claims that the OMB served as a "neutral moderator" of the meetings and that neither he nor the agency took a policy stand (interview). Others contradict this, saying that every agency, including the OMB, took a position (interviews with Richard Benedick, Michael P. Kelly, and James Losey).

29. Senator Max Baucus, chairman of the Senate Subcommittee on Environment and Public Works, charged that "secret instructions from OMB" caused the U.S. negotiating position to be watered down (*Atlanta Constitution* 1987).

30. David Gibbons of the OMB suggested at one interagency meeting that skin cancer is "a self-inflicted disease" and that the federal government should not be in the business of regulating what people do to themselves. Dr. Kripke, who oversees a cancer clinic, responded with "a scathing memo." She pointed out that farmers and oil workers have the highest incidence of skin cancers, and that doctors don't ask people how they contracted their cancer before they treat it (interview). This exchange was recalled by many of the participants I interviewed.

31. Although it is difficult to judge the impact of the proposed U.S. legislation, one participant I interviewed was in Japan during the negotiations and observed

that the issue received extensive press coverage. He believes that the Ministry of International Trade and Industry (MITI), widely viewed as the most powerful Japanese ministry, feared that its products, especially in the electronics sector, would be rendered incompatible with world trade (interview with Alan S. Miller).

5. Necessity, the Mother of Invention: New Science, New Policies

1. Partially halogenated halocarbons contain hydrogen, which causes them to break down more rapidly in the lower atmosphere. Their ozone depletion potentials are consequently much smaller than those of the fully halogenated compounds regulated by the Montreal Protocol. While HCFCs still pose some risk because they contain toxic chlorine, HFCs (hydrofluorocarbons) contain no chlorine and so do not affect the ozone layer. HCFCs and HFCs, like CFCs, are also greenhouse gases.

2. In the long run, althoughU.S. industry complained profusely about it, the U.S. aerosol ban helped it CFC producers by inducing them to develop substitute compounds and technologies. Because the United States had already eliminated aerosol uses, it had greater difficulties meeting the Montreal Protocol requirements and was forced to take the lead in developing CFC substitutes for other uses.

3. Interestingly, the FOE publication bases its conclusions on the economic data found in Forest Reinhardt's Harvard Business School case study, cited above, to make its case. Again, information can be interpreted according to subjective orientations, and the same data can lead to very different conclusions.

4. Note that, 2 percent of profits represents the same amount as the $600 million cited in the Harvard Business School case study, although the two numbers make very different impressions.

5. It is noteworthy that an 85 percent cutback, which was necessary to stabilize CFC concentrations, was originally proposed by John Hoffman of the EPA back in 1986. Once the Antarctic ozone hole had been conclusively linked to CFCs by the Ozone Trends Panel, the goal of stabilizing concentrations took on new urgency.

6. The four assessment panels effectively replaced UNEP's Coordinating Committee on the Ozone Layer (CCOL), which had been providing scientific information to participants since the Vienna Convention negotiations.

7. France's leadership role on the global climate change issue, which contrasts sharply with its sluggishness on the ozone problem, may be related to its heavy dependence on nuclear power for its energy needs. With less reliance on fossil fuels, France may be said to enjoy a comparative advantage in international efforts to combat greenhouse gas emissions.

8. One reason for the large attendance may have been that ICI, anticipating further domestic controls on CFCs, realized that they could only export to developing countries if those countries were parties to the agreement. In an ironic effort

to promote widespread ratification of the treaty it had opposed, ICI paid the travel expenses for some delegates from developing countries to attend the London conference (interview with Mike Harris).

9. The main natural source of atmospheric chlorine is methyl chloride (CH_3Cl) from the oceans (interview with Robert Watson).

10. The same rationale has been used in the global climate change debates to support controls on methane emissions. With its atmospheric lifetime of 10 years, as compared to 120 for carbon dioxide, the benefits of methane controls could be felt relatively soon (UNEP/OzL.Pro.WG.II(1)/4:18).

11. There was still the occasional skeptic, but these were iconoclasts and generally driven by an ideological motivation (see, for instance, *Wall Street Journal* 1989).

12. Japan's primary objection to controlling methyl chloroform was that its fire laws did not allow it to use alcohol-based solvents. Eventually, Japan's fire laws were rewritten (interview with Stephen O. Anderson).

13. The isolation of the Soviet Union's chemical industry was also evident in the fact that it did not produce methyl chloroform. Thus, the Soviet Union was placed in the anomalous position of promoting a ban on methyl chloroform while leading the fight to save carbon tetrachloride.

14. India, along with China, had not yet signed the Montreal Protocol at the time of this statement.

15. The results of the British, Indian, and U.S. studies, along with those of another British report, were reviewed and synthesized in a report that concurred with these estimates, which was presented at the May 1990 funding meeting in Geneva (Markandya and Pargal 1990).

16. Most countries sent different delegates to the two groups, which caused problems because delegates in one group did not know what was happening on the other (interview with Eileen Claussen).

17. Although EPA administrator Lee Thomas had pledged as early as September 1988 to eliminate CFCs, that election-year statement was never adopted as an official policy.

18. Note that these are the same EC countries that promoted a strong Montreal Protocol during negotiations four year earlier.

19. The thirteen governments were Australia, Austria, Belgium, Canada, Denmark, the Federal Republic of Germany, Finland, Lichtenstein, the Netherlands, New Zealand, Norway, Sweden, and Switzerland. The declaration was appended to the treaty revisions as a separate statement.

20. For some U.S. participants, the EC's support for a later phaseout of methyl chloroform cast some doubt on its commitment to strong action on CFCs (interview with Stephen Seidel).

21. Environmentalists, already distrustful of the funding mechanism because of the central role of the World Bank, grew even more skeptical when the execu-

tive committee barred nongovernmental observers from its meetings (interview with Liz Cook).

22. For halons, the new EC regulation called for a 50 percent cut by 1995 and a complete phaseout by the year 2000. For carbon tetrachloride, the regulation called for a 50 percent reduction by 1992, 85 percent by 1995, and a phaseout by 1998. As in the London Revisions, methyl chloroform would be banned by 2005.

23. Other companies expressed skepticism about the long-term commercial viability of any substitute compounds containing bromine. Du Pont, for instance, would not invest in bromated chemicals, believing that they were likely to be phased out in the next round of treaty revisions.

24. In November 1991, however, the U.S. Government Accounting Office published a report saying that, although the Pentagon had taken important steps to phase out the CFCs, the work was proceeding slowly. The GAO investigators found that the Navy was continuing to purchase products that used CFCs and halons (*New York Times* 1992a).

25. In essence, the plan, formulated by knowledge brokers associated with the Department of Energy, merely renamed the reductions mandated by the Montreal Protocol as a climate stabilization strategy. Ironically, the Department of Energy was one of the U.S. agencies that challenged the strong position put forth by the State Department and EPA during the Montreal Protocol negotiations.

26. In response to complaints and mishaps resulting from the chemical industry's virtual exclusion from the 1989 technology assessment panel, more representatives from producer industries were included in 1991.

27. Recall that consumption is defined by the Montreal Protocol as production plus imports minus exports.

28. Japan, under pressure from the EC and the USA, also announced that it would ban production of CFCs, halons, and carbon tetrachloride by the end of 1995 (Kyodo News Service 1992).

29. Two months after the Copenhagen meeting, William K. Reilly, in one of his final acts before leaving his position as administrator of the EPA, ordered a ban on production and importation of methyl bromide by the year 2000 (*Washington Post* 1993).

6. Implications for Theories of World Politics

1. This revival hearkens back to the recurring debate in the social sciences between materialism and idealism. It appears as if the pendulum of international relations theory may now be swinging, after several generations, in the direction of the latter.

2. Economist Charles Kindleberger, a chief proponent of the first viewpoint, ties hegemonic status to an ethical responsibility to lead (1973, 1986). The second version eschews Kindleberger's latent liberalism and is more widely accepted

among international relations theorists, particularly those seeking to explain the formation of economic regimes in the postwar period (Krasner 1976; Keohane 1980; Gilpin 1981).

3. I specify that these two categories of beliefs are only separate analytically because, as was argued in chapter 2, in practice they tend to merge. Much of the critical literature on risk analysis develops from this observation.

4. It is ironic that the field of international relations, in which conflict figures so centrally, would take such a sanguine view of the role of science. One possible explanation is the intellectual legacy that sees science as a salvation from politics or at least as providing an objective, value-free basis for political consensus. Or perhaps liberal theorists, wishing to flee the contentious nature of world politics, seek some basis for consensus, some common language. Science, as a universal legitimator, seems to provide that common ground.

5. Over sixteen hundred scientists, including the majority of the living Nobel laureates in the sciences, have signed the "Global Warning," calling upon the world's leaders to cut greenhouse gas emissions and to move away from fossil fuel dependence (*Nucleus* 1992–93).

6. On some of the pitfalls involved in applying the language of national security to environmental problems, see Deudney (1990).

7. On the declining utility of military force, see Rosecrance (1986); Baldwin (1985), and Nye (1990). While the most recent literature draws its cogency from the end of the Cold War, it also extends a school of thought that was influential during the 1970s (see Keohane and Nye 1977). Recent events such as Tien An Men Square and the Persian Gulf War seem to cast doubt on the "declining utility of force" thesis. Yet a deeper analysis reveals the striking extent to which these events, principally because of their direct coverage by the electronic media, were about ideas, persuasion, and the ability to sway world opinion.

8. Whether the shift toward postindustrialism might also entail a shift toward a postmaterialist value structure, as some have argued (Inglehart 1977), remains to be seen.

Bibliography

Adler, Emanuel. 1992. "The Emergence of Cooperation: National Epistemic Communities and the International Evolution of the Idea of Nuclear Arms Control." *International Organization* 46, no. 1 (Winter): 101–46.

Aggarwal, Vinod K. 1985. *Liberal Protectionism: The International Politics of Organized Textile Trade*. Berkeley: University of California Press.

Ahuja, Dilip R. 1990. "Views from Other Nations: India." *EPA Journal* 16, no. 2 (March/April): 40.

Alliance for a Responsible CFC Policy. 1987. *Montreal Protocol: A Briefing Book*. Rosslyn, Va.: Alliance for a Responsible CFC Policy.

———. 1990. "Realistic Policies on HCFC's Needed in Order to Meet Global Ozone Protection Goals." Washington, D.C.: Alliance for a Responsible CFC Policy.

Allison, Graham T. 1971. *The Essence of Decision: Explaining the Cuban Missile Crisis*. Boston: Little, Brown.

Almond, Gabriel and Stephen Genco. 1977. "Clouds, Clocks, and the Study of Politics." *World Politics* 29 (July): 489–522.

Alternative Fluorocarbons Environmental Acceptability Study/Programme for Alternative Fluorocarbon Toxicity Testing (AFEAS/PAFT). 1991. "Alternative Fluorocarbons Environmental Acceptability Study." December. Washington, D.C.: AFEAS.

Anderson, Walter Truett. 1987. *To Govern Evolution: Future Adventures of the Political Animal.* Boston: Harcourt Brace Jovanovich.

——. 1990. *Reality Isn't What It Used to Be.* San Francisco: Harper and Row.

Arendt, Hannah. 1970. *On Violence.* London: Allen Lane.

Aronowitz, Stanley. 1988. *Science as Power: Discourse and Ideology in Modern Society.* Minneapolis: University of Minnesota.

Art, Robert J. 1973. "Bureaucratic Politics and American Foreign Policy." *Policy Sciences* 4: 467–90.

Atlanta Constitution. 1987. "White House Budget Office Weakened U.S. Stance on Ozone, Senator Charges," May 15, 14-A.

Babai, Don. "Epistemic Communities and Development Policy." Unpublished manuscript.

Bachrach, Peter and Morton Baratz. 1970. *Power and Poverty.* New York: Oxford University Press.

Bacon, Francis. 1889. *Novum Organum.* Edited by Thomas Fowler. Oxford: Clarendon.

——. 1974. *The Advancement of Learning and New Atlantis.* Edited by A. Johnston. Oxford: Clarendon.

Bakhtin, Mikhail. 1981. *The Dialogic Imagination: Four Essays.* Translated by C. Emerson and M. Holquist. Austin: University of Texas Press.

Baldwin, David A. 1985. *Economic Statecraft.* Princeton: Princeton University Press.

Ball, Terence. 1975. "Models of Power: Past and Present." *Journal of the History of the Behavioral Sciences* (July): 211–22.

——. 1976. "Power, Causation, and Explanation." *Polity* (Winter): 189–214.

——. 1978. "Two Concepts of Coercion." *Theory and Society* (Winter): 97–112.

Barbalet, J. 1987. "Power, Structural Resources, and Agency." *Perspectives in Social Theory* (Winter): 1–24.

Barnes, Barry and David Edge. 1982. *Science in Context.* Cambridge, Mass.: MIT Press.

Barzun, Jacques. 1964. *Science: The Glorious Entertainment.* New York: Harper and Row.

Bastian, Carroll. 1972. "The Formulation of Federal Policy." In Frank Bower and Richard Ward, eds., *Stratospheric Ozone and Man*, vol. 2. Boca Raton, Fla.: CRC.

Baudrillard, Jean. 1975. *The Mirror of Production.* Translated by Mark Poster. St. Louis: Telos.

——. 1981. *For a Critique of the Political Economy of the Sign.* Translated by Charles Levin. St. Louis: Telos.

——. 1983. *Simulations.* Translated by Paul Floss, Paul Patton, and Philip Beitchman. New York: Semiotext.

Bell, Daniel. 1962. *The End of Ideology: On the Exhaustion of Political Ideas in the Fifties.* New York: Collier.

———. 1973. *The Coming of Post-Industrial Society: A Venture in Social Forecasting.* New York: Basic.

———. 1987. "The Post-industrial Society: A Conceptual Schema." in A. E. Cawkell, ed., *Evolution of an Information Society.* London: Aslib.

Ben-David, Joseph. 1971. *The Scientist's Role in Society: A Comparative Study.* Englewood Cliffs, N.J.: Prentice-Hall.

Benedick, Richard. 1987. "International Efforts to Protect the Stratospheric Ozone Layer." *Department of State Current Policy*, no. 931 (February 23): 1.

———. 1989. "Ozone Diplomacy." *Issues in Science and Technology* 6, no. 1 (Fall): 43–49.

———. 1990. "Lessons from 'the Ozone Hole.' " *EPA Journal* 16, no. 2 (March/April): 41–43.

———. 1991. *Ozone Diplomacy: New Directions in Safeguarding the Planet.* Cambridge: Harvard University Press.

Benveniste, Guy. 1977. *The Politics of Expertise.* San Francisco: Boyd and Fraser.

Berger, Peter and Thomas Luckmann. 1967. *The Social Construction of Reality.* New York: Doubleday/Anchor.

Bernstein, Richard J. 1985. *Beyond Objectivism and Relativism: Science, Hermeneutics, and Praxis.* Philadelphia: University of Pennsylvania Press.

Bhaskar, Roy. 1979. *The Possibility of Naturalism.* Brighton, U.K.: Harvester.

———. 1986. *Scientific Realism and Human Emancipation.* New York: Verso.

———. 1989. *Reclaiming Reality: A Critical Introduction to Contemporary Philosophy.* New York: Verso.

Bodansky, Daniel. 1991. "Scientific Uncertainty and the Precautionary Principle." *Environment* (September): 4–5.

Boulding, Kenneth. 1983. "National Defense Through Stable Peace." *Opinions: Journal of the International Institute for Applied Systems Analysis* 3.

Bourdieu, Pierre. 1977. *Outline of a Theory of Practice.* Cambridge: Cambridge University Press.

Brasseur, Guy. 1987. "Endangered Ozone Layer." *Environment* 29, no. 1 (January/February): 7–39.

Brickman, R., S. Jasanoff, and T. Ilgen. 1985. *Controlling Chemicals: The Politics of Regulation in Europe and the United States.* Ithaca: Cornell University Press.

Brodeur, Paul. 1986. "Annals of Chemistry: In the Face of Doubt." *The New Yorker*, June 9, 71–87.

Brooks, Harvey. 1964. "The Scientific Adviser." In Robert Gilpin and C. Wright, eds., *Scientists and National Policy-making*, pp. 73–96. New York: Columbia University Press.

———. 1987. "The Role of International Research Institutions." in H. Brooks and C. Cooper, eds., *Science for Public Policy.* New York: Pergamon.

Brown, Lester and Christopher Flavin. 1988. "The Earth's Vital Signs." In Lester Brown, Edward Wolf, and Linda Starke, eds., *State of the World 1988*, pp. 1–22. New York: Norton.

Brown, Seyom, N. Cornell, L. Fabian, and E. Weiss. 1977. *Regimes for the Ocean, Outer Space, and Weather.* Washington, D.C.: The Brookings Institution.

Brzezinski, Zbigniew. 1968. "America in the Technotronic Age." *Encounter* (January): 16–23.

Bucholtz, Barbara. 1990. "Coase and the Control of Transboundary Pollution: The Sale of Hydroelectricity Under the U.S.-Canada Free Trade Agreement of 1988." *Boston College Environmental Affairs Law Review* 18, no. 2 (Spring): 279–318.

Bull, Hedley. 1977. *The Anarchical Society: A Study of Order in World Politics.* New York: Columbia University Press.

Bush, Vannevar. 1945. *Science: The Endless Frontier.* Washington, D.C.: U.S. Government Printing Office.

Caldwell, Lynton Keith. 1985. "Science Will Not Save the Biosphere But Politics Might." *Environmental Conservation* 12, no. 3 (Autumn): 195–97.

———. 1990. *Between Two Worlds: Science, the Environmental Movement, and Policy Choice.* Cambridge: Cambridge University Press.

Callis, L. B. and M. Natarajan. 1986. "The Antarctic Ozone Minimum: Relationship to Odd Nitrogen, Odd Chlorine, the Final Warming, and the Eleven-Year Solar Cycle." *Journal of Geophysical Research* 91 (November): 10771–96.

Carr, E. H. 1964. *The Twenty Years' Crisis: 1919–1939.* New York: Harper and Row.

Cassirer, Ernst. 1955. *The Philosophy of the Enlightenment.* Boston: Beacon.

Chemical and Engineering News. 1977. "Phaseout Set for Fluorocarbon Aerosols," May 16, p. 4.

———. 1988. "Search Intensifies for Alternatives to Ozone Depleting Halocarbons," February 8, p. 16.

Chemical Manufacturers Association. 1987. "Production, Sales, and Calculated Release of CFC-11 and CFC-12 Through 1986." Washington, D.C.: Chemical Manufacturers Association.

Christian Science Monitor. 1986. "Scientists Say Ozone Data May Be Tainted by Volcanic Activity," December 10, p. 5.

———. 1987. "Trend-setting Berkeley Takes Action on Behalf of Earth's Ozone Layer," October 7, p. 4..

———. 1988. "Industry Scrambles to Find Ozone-Safe CFC Substitutes," August 12, p. 11.

———. 1989. "Why China Says Ozone Must Take Back Seat in Drive to Prosperity." March 23, p. 1.

Cicerone, R. and R. Dickinson. 1986. "Future Global Warming from Atmospheric Trace Gases." *Nature* 319 (January): 109–15.

Clark, W. C., ed. 1990. *Usable Knowledge for Managing Global Climate Change.* Stockholm: Stockholm Environment Institute.

Clegg, Stewart R. 1989. *Frameworks of Power.* London: Sage.

Climatic Impact Assessment Program (CIAP). 1973. *Impact of High- Flying Aircraft on the Stratosphere.* Washington, D.C.: Department of Transportation.

Cogan, Douglas. 1988. *Stones in a Glass House: CFC's and Ozone Depletion.* Washington, D.C.: Investor Responsibility Research Center.

Comte, Auguste. 1986. *The Positive Philosophy of Auguste Comte.* Translated by H. Martineau. London: George Bell and Sons.

Condorcet, Marquis de. 1976 *Condorcet: Selected Writings.* Translated and edited by Keith Michael Baker. Indianapolis: Bobbs-Merrill.

Connolly, William E. 1983. "Discipline, Politics, and Ambiguity." *Political Theory* 11, no. 3 (Fall): 325–41.

Cooper, Richard, B. Eichengreen, G. Hotham, R. Putnam, and C. Henning. 1989. *Can Nations Agree?* Washington, D.C.: The Brookings Institution.

Corcoran, E. 1988. "Keeping Cool: Industries Struggle to Prepare for the Upcoming CFC Crunch." *Scientific American* 259 (July): 113–14.

Cotgrove, Stephen. 1982. *Catastrophe or Cornucopia: The Environment, Politics, and the Future.* New York: Wiley.

Council of the European Communities. 1990. "Meeting Document." CONS/ENV/90/7. Luxembourg, June 7.

Cowan, Ruth Schwartz. 1964. *The Social Shaping of Technology: How the Refrigerator Got Its Hum.* Philadelphia: Open University Press.

Cowhey, Peter. 1990. "The International Telecommunications Regime." *International Organization* 44, no. 2 (Spring): 169–200.

Cox, Donald. 1964. *America's New Policy Makers: The Scientists' Rise to Power.* New York: The Chilton Company.

Cox, Robert. 1987. *Production, Power, and World Order: Social Forces and the Making of History.* New York: Columbia University Press.

Crane, Diana. 1972. *Invisible Colleges: Diffusion of Knowledge in Scientific Communities.* Chicago: University of Chicago Press.

Crutzen, Paul. 1970. "The Influence of Nitrogen Oxides on the Atmospheric Ozone Content." *Quarterly Journal of the Royal Meteorological Society* 97: 320–25.

Cumberland, J. H., J. R. Hibbs, and I. Hoch. 1982. *The Economics of Managing Chlorofluorocarbons: Stratospheric Ozone and Climate Issues* Washington, D.C.: Resources for the Future.

Dahl, Robert A. 1957. "The Concept of Power." *Behavioral Science* 2 (July): 201–15.

———. 1961. *Who Governs? Democracy and Power in an American City.* New Haven: Yale University Press.

Dahlberg, Kenneth. 1983. "Contextual Analysis: Taking Space, Time, and Place Seriously." *International Studies Quarterly* 27 (Spring): 257–66.

Davis, M. 1974. *Environmental Information: Some Problems and Solutions.* Melbourne: Center for Environmental Studies at Melbourne University.

DeCanio, Stephen J. and Kai N. Lee. 1991. "Doing Well by Doing Good: Technology Transfer to Protect the Ozone." *Policy Studies Journal* 19, no. 2 (Spring): 140–51.

Der Derian, James. 1989. *International/Intertextual Relations: Postmodern Readings of World Politics.* Lexington, Mass.: Lexington.

Descombes, Vincent. 1980. *Modern French Philosophy.* Translated by L. Scott-Fox and J. M. Harding. Cambridge: Cambridge University Press.

Dessler, David. 1989. "What Is at Stake in the Agent-Structure Problem?" *International Organization* 43, no. 3 (Summer): 441–74.

Deudney, Dan. 1990. "The Case Against Linking Environmental Degradation and National Security." *Millennium: Journal of International Studies* 19, no. 3 (Winter): 461–76.

Dickson, David. 1984. *The New Politics of Science.* New York: Pantheon.

Dietz, Thomas and Robert Rycroft. 1987. *The Risk Professionals.* New York: Russell Sage.

Doniger, David. 1988. "Politics of the Ozone Layer." *Issues in Science and Technology* (Spring): 86–92.

Dotto, Lydia and Harold Schiff. 1978. *The Ozone War.* New York: Doubleday.

Douglas, M. and A. Wildavsky. 1982. *Risk and Culture.* Berkeley: University of California Press.

Downs, Anthony. 1957. *An Economic Theory of Democracy.* New York: Harper and Row.

Dryzek, John. "Ecological Rationality." *International Journal of Environmental Studies* 21 (Winter): 5–10.

Du Pont. 1980. "Fluorocarbon/Ozone Update." June. Wilmington, Del.: Du Pont.

———. 1986. "Position Statement on the Chlorofluorocarbon/Ozone/Greenhouse Issue." September. Wilmington, Del.: Du Pont.

———. 1989. "Fluorocarbon/Ozone Update." August. Wilmington, Del.: Du Pont.

Eckstein, Harry. 1975. "Case Study and Theory in Political Science." In Fred I. Greenstein and Nelson W. Polsby, eds., *Handbook of Political Science.* Reading, Mass.: Addison-Wesley.

Elster, Jon. 1979. *Ulysses and the Sirens: Studies in Rationality and Irrationality.* London: Cambridge University Press.

Emmett, Edward. 1986. "Health Effects of Ultraviolet Radiation." In James Titus, ed., *Effects of Changes in Stratospheric Ozone and Global Climate*, pp. 129–46. Washington, D.C.: Environmental Protection Agency.

Environment Canada. 1988. *The Changing Atmosphere: Implications for Global Security.* Toronto: Environment Canada.

Environmental Data Services. 1988. *ENDS Report 157.* February. London: Environmental Data Services.

Environmental Forum. 1984. "Risk Assessment/Risk Management: A *Forum* Roundtable Discussion." *Environmental Forum* (September): 17–24.

———. 1985. "Profile: EPA Administrator Designate Lee M. Thomas." *Environmental Forum* (January): 23–26.

Environmental Protection Agency (EPA). 1980. "Ozone-Depleting Chlorofluorocarbons: Proposed Production Restriction." *Federal Register* 45 (October 7): 66726–34.

———. 1986a. *Regulatory Impact Analysis: Protection of Stratospheric Ozone.* Washington, D.C.: Environmental Protection Agency.

———. 1986b. "Stratospheric Ozone Protection Plan." *Federal Register* 51 (January 10): 1257.

———. 1986c. "Pesticide Fact Sheet: Methyl Bromide." August 22. Washington, D.C.: Office of Pesticides and Toxic Substances.

———. 1987a. *Assessing the Risks of Trace Gases that Can Modify the Stratosphere.* Washington, D.C.: Environmental Protection Agency.

———. 1987b. Protection of Stratospheric Ozone: Proposed Rule. Washington, D.C.: U.S. Environmental Protection Agency.

Etzioni, A. 1968. *The Active Society: A Theory of Societal and Political Processes.* New York: Free.

European Commission. 1987. "Meeting of National Experts: Implementation of the Montreal Protocol on Substances that Deplete the Ozone Layer." XI/III/997/87-EN. December 7–8. Brussels: European Commission.

European Communities. 1980. "Council Decision of 226 March 1980 concerning Chlorofluorocarbons in the Environment." 80/372/EEC. Brussels: European Commission.

European Report. 1992. "Environment: European Parliament Committee Votes to Phase Out CFC's." *European Report* (February 20): 453.

Evan, William, 1981. *Knowledge and Power in a Global Society.* Beverly Hills: Sage.

Farman, J. C., B. G. Gardiner, and J. D. Shanklin. 1985. "Large Losses of Total Ozone in Antarctica Reveal Seasonal ClOx/NOx Interaction." *Nature* 315 (May 16): 207–10.

Faucheux, S. and J. F. Noel. 1988. *Did the Ozone War End in Montreal?* Université de Paris, Centre Economie-Espace-Environnement, English digest. Paris: Cahiers du C.3.E.

Fay, Brian. 1987. *Critical Social Science: Liberation and Its Limits.* Ithaca: Cornell University Press.

Feyerabend, Paul. 1975. *Against Method: Outline of an Anarchist Theory of Knowledge.* London: NLB.

Fischhoff, Baruch. 1981. "Hot Air: The Psychology of CO_2-Induced Climatic Change." in J. Harvey, ed., *Cognition, Social Behavior, and the Environment.* Hillsdale, N.J.: Lawrence Erlbaum Associates.

Fischhoff, Baruch, S. Lichtenstein, Paul Slovic, S. Derby, and R. Keeney. 1981. *Of Acceptable Risk: A Critical Guide.* New Rochelle, N.Y.: Cambridge University Press.

Fischhoff, Baruch, Paul Slovic, and S. Lichtenstein. 1982. "Facts versus Fears: Understanding Perceived Risk." In Daniel Kahneman, Paul Slovic, and Amos Tversky, eds. *Judgment under Uncertainty: Heuristics and Biases.* New York: Cambridge University Press.

Fleck, Ludwig. 1979. *Genesis and Development of a Scientific Fact.* Chicago: University of Chicago Press.

Forman, Paul. 1979. "The Reception of an Acausal Quantum Mechanics in Germany and Britain" In Seymour H. Mauskopf, ed., *The Reception of Unconventional Science.* Boulder, Colo.: Westview.

Foucault, Michel. 1973. *The Order of Things: An Archaeology of the Human Sciences.* New York: Vintage.

———. 1977. *Language, Counter-Memory, Practice.* Translated by Donald Bouchard. Ithaca: Cornell University Press.

———. 1979. *Discipline and Punish: The Birth of the Prison.* New York: Vintage.

———. 1980. *Power/Knowledge: Selected Interviews and Other Writings.* Edited by C. Gordon. Translated by C. Gordon, L. Marshall, J. Mepham, and K. Soper. New York: Pantheon.

———. 1983. "Afterword: The Subject and Power." In H. Dreyfus and P. Rabinow, eds., *Beyond Structuralism and Hermeneutics.* Brighton, U.K.: Harvester.

Frederick, John E. 1986. "The Ultraviolet Radiation of the Biosphere." In James Titus, ed., *Effects of Changes in Stratospheric Ozone and Climate Change*, pp. 121–28. Washington, D.C.: Environmental Protection Agency.

Friends of the Earth (FOE). 1988. "Styro Wars Victory in United States." *Atmosphere* 1, no. 1 (Spring).

———. 1989a. "Protocol: No Protection." *Atmosphere* 2, nos. 1 and 2. (Spring-Summer).

———. 1989b. "Developing Nations Press for Ozone Fund." *Atmosphere* 2, no. 3 (Fall).

———. 1989c. "Global Action." *Atmosphere* 1, no. 4 (Winter).

———. 1990a. "Funding Change: Developing Countries and the Montreal Protocol." Washington, D.C.: FOE.

———. 1990b. "The New Montreal Protocol: FOEI Report." June 27–29. London: FOE International.

———. 1990c. *Atmosphere* 2, no. 4 (March).

———. 1990d. "Nation's Create Ozone Fund." *Atmosphere* 3, no. 2. (October).

———. 1990e. "Revised Protocol: `Too Weak.' " *Atmosphere* 3, no. 2. (October).

———. 1991a. *Atmosphere* 3, no. 3 (February).

———. 1991b. "Protocol's Ozone Fund Off to a Shaky Start." *Atmosphere* 3, no. 4 (June).

———. 1991c. *Atmosphere* 4, no. 1 (October).

———. 1991d. *Hold the Applause!* Washington, D.C.: FOE.

———. 1992a. *Atmosphere* 4, no. 2 (March).

———. 1992b. "Loopholes Mark Protocol Changes." *Atmosphere* 4, no. 3 (July).

———. 1992c. "Methyl Bromide Targetted as Ozone Destroyer." *Atmosphere* 4, no. 3 (July).

Friends of the Earth, California Action Network, Californians for Alternatives to Toxics, California Institute for Rural Studies, National Coalition Against Misuse of Pesticides, Natural Resources Defense Council, and Pesticide Action Network. 1992. *Into the Sunlight: Exposing Methyl Bromide's Threat to the Ozone Layer.* Washington, D.C.: FOE.

Gallie, W. B. 1956. "Essentially Contested Concepts." *Proceedings of the Aristotelian Society* 56 (Winter): 167–98.

Gardner, J. S. 1972. *A Study of Environmental Monitoring and Information Systems.* Iowa City: Iowa University Press.

Gaventa, John. 1980. *Power and Powerlessness: Quiescence and Rebellion in an Appalachian Valley.* Oxford: Clarendon.

George, Alexander. 1979. "Case Studies and Theory Development: The Method of Structured, Focused Comparison." In Paul G. Lauren, ed., *Diplomacy: New Approaches in History, Theory, and Policy.* New York: Free.

Gibbs, Michael and Kathleen Hogan. 1990. "Policy Options: Methane." *EPA Journal* 16, no. 2 (March/April): 22–24.

Giddens, Anthony. 1977. *Studies in Social and Political Theory.* New York: Basic.

———. 1984. *The Constitution of Society: Outline of the Theory of Structuration.* Berkeley: University of California Press.

Gilpin, Robert. 1975. *U.S. Power and the Multinational Corporation.* New York: Basic.

———. 1981. *War and Change in International Politics.* New York: Cambridge University Press.

Gilpin, Robert and C. Wright. 1964. *Scientists and National Policy-making.* New York: Columbia University Press.

Glas, Joseph P. 1989. "Protecting the Ozone Layer: A Perspective from Industry." In J. H. Ausubel and H. E. Sladovich, eds., *Technology and Environment*, pp. 137–57. Washington, D.C.: National Academy Press.

Goldhamer, Herbert. 1978. *The Adviser.* New York: Elsevier North-Holland.

Goldstein, Judith. 1988. "Ideas, Institutions, and American Trade Policy." *International Organization* 42, no. 1 (Winter): 179–217.

———. 1989. "The Impact of Ideas on Trade Policy." *International Organization* 43, no. 1 (Winter): 31–71.

Gourevitch, Peter. 1978. "The Second Image Reversed: The International Sources of Domestic Politics." *International Organization* 32 (Autumn): 881–911.

Gowa, Joanne. 1986. "Anarchy, Egoism, and Third Images: *The Evolution of Cooperation* and International Relations." *International Organization* 40, no. 1 (Winter): 167–186.

Greenberg, Daniel S. 1967. *The Politics of Pure Science.* New York: New American Library.

Gribbin, John. 1988. *The Hole in the Sky: Man's Threat to the Ozone Layer.* Toronto: Bantam.

Grieco, Joseph. 1988. "Anarchy and the Limits of Cooperation: A Realist Critique of the Newest Liberal Institutionalism." *International Organization* 42, no. 3 (Summer): 485–507.

Griffin, David R. 1988. *The Reenchantment of Science: Postmodern Proposals.* Albany: State University of New York Press.

Haas, Ernst. 1964. *Beyond the Nation-State.* Stanford: Stanford University Press.

———. 1975. "Is There a Hole in the Whole? Knowledge, Technology, Interdependence, and the Construction of International Regimes." *International Organization* 29 (Summer): 827–76.

———. 1989. "Do Regimes Matter? Epistemic Communities and Mediterranean Pollution Control." *International Organization* 43 (Summer): 349–76.

———. 1990. *When Knowledge Is Power: Three Models of Change in International Organizations.* Berkeley: University of California Press.

Haas, Ernst, M. Williams, and D. Babai. 1977. *Scientists and World Order: The Uses of Technical Knowledge in International Organizations.* Berkeley: University of California Press.

Haas, Peter. 1989. "Do Regimes Matter? Epistemic Communities and Mediterranean Pollution Control." *International Organization* 43, no. 4 (Summer): 377–404.

———. 1992a. "Banning Chlorofluorocarbons: Efforts to Protect Stratospheric Ozone." *International Organization* 46, no. 1 (Winter): 187–224.

———. 1992b. "Introduction: Epistemic Communities and International Policy Coordination." *International Organization* 46, no. 1 (Winter): 1–36.

Habermas, Jurgen. 1972. *Knowledge and Human Interests.* Boston: Beacon.

———. 1977. *Legitimation Crisis.* Boston: Beacon.

———. 1978. *Communication and the Evolution of Society.* Translated by T. McCarthy. Boston: Beacon.

———. 1981. "Modernity versus Postmodernity." *New German Critique* 22: 3–14.

———. 1984. *The Theory of Communicative Action.* Vol. 1, *Reason and the Rationalization of Society.* Boston: Beacon.

Haggard, Stephen and Beth Simmons. 1987. "Theories of International Regimes." *International Organization* 41, no. 3 (Summer): 491–517.

Hagstrom, Warren. 1965. *The Scientific Community.* New York: Basic.

Hall, Peter A. 1989. *The Political Power of Economic Ideas: Keynesianism Across Nations.* Princeton: Princeton University Press.

Hamill, P., O. B. Toon, and R. P. Turco. 1986. "Characteristics of Polar Stratospheric Clouds During the Formation of the Antarctic Ozone Hole." *Geophysical Research Letters* 13 (November): 1288–91.

Hammitt, James K., Kathleen A. Wolf, Frank Camm, William E. Mooz, Timothy H. Quinn, and Anil Bamezai. 1986. *Product Uses and Market Trends for Potential Ozone-Depleting Substances, 1985–2000.* Rand Report R-3386-EPA. Santa Monica, Calif.: Rand.

Hecht, Susanna and Alexander Cockburn. 1989. *The Fate of the Forest: Developers, Destroyers, and Defenders of the Amazon.* London: Verso.

Hiskes, Anne and Richard Hiskes. 1986. *Science, Technology and Policy Decisions.* Boulder, Colo.: Westview.

Hohnen, Paul. 1992. "The Ozone Crisis—Risk and Responsibility." Joint Statement by Greenpeace and Friends of the Earth to the Montreal Protocol Open-Ended Working Group Meeting, Geneva, Switzerland, April 8.

Holzner, Burkart. 1972. *Reality Construction in Society.* Cambridge, Mass.: Schenkman.

Holzner, Burkart and John Marx. 1979. *Knowledge Application: The Knowledge System in Society.* Boston: Allyn and Bacon.

Homer-Dixon, Thomas F. 1991. "On the Threshold: Environmental Changes as the Causes of Acute Conflict." *International Security* 16, no. 2 (Spring): 76–116.

Hopkins, Raymond. 1992. "Reform in the International Food Aid Regime: The Role of Consensual Knowledge." *International Organization* 46, no. 1 (Winter): 225–64.

Horwitch, Mel. 1982. *Clipped Wings: The American SST Conflict.* Cambridge, Mass.: MIT Press.

Ikenberry, John. 1988. "Conclusion: An Institutional Approach to American Foreign Economic Policy." *International Organization* 42, no. 1 (Winter): 219–43.

———. 1992. "A World Economy Restored: Expert Consensus and the Anglo-American Postwar Settlement." *International Organization* 46, no. 1 (Winter): 289–322.

Imperial Chemical Industries (ICI). 1990. *The Ozone Issue and Regulation.* Runcorn, Cheshire: Imperial Chemical Industries.

In Context. 1989. "Governance and Global Warming." *In Context: A Quarterly of Humane Sustainable Culture* 22 (Summer): 38–43.

Inglehart, Ronald. 1977. *The Silent Revolution: Changing Values and Political Styles Among Western Political Elites.* Princeton: Princeton University Press.

Interagency Task Force on Inadvertent Modification of the Stratosphere (IMOS). 1975. *Fluorocarbons and the Environment: Report of the Federal Task Force on*

Inadvertent Modification of the Stratosphere. Washington, D.C.: Council on Environmental Quality.

Intergovernmental Panel on Climate Change. 1990. *IPCC First Assessment Report,* vol. 1. Geneva: World Meteorological Organization and United Nations Environment Programme.

International Chamber of Commerce (ICC). 1990. *International Environmental Bureau Newsletter* 23 (May).

International Environment Reporter (IER). 1990. "India Willing to Freeze CFC Production If Given the Technology for Substitutes." *International Environment Reporter,* February 5, p. 65.

———. 1991a. "Scientists Detect Hole in Ozone Above Three Scandinavian Nations." *International Environment Reporter,* February 13, p. 68.

———. 1991b. "Ozone Depletion Occurring Twice as Fast as Previously Thought." *International Environment Reporter,* April 10, p. 187.

———. 1991c. "NASA Data Underestimate Extent of Ozone Depletion, Scientist Says." *International Environment Reporter,* April 24, p. 216.

———. 1991d. "Thai Government Taking No Steps to Curb Rapid Growth in CFC Use." *International Environment Reporter,* September 11, p. 482.

———. 1991e. "NASA Hopes Satellite Will Gather Best Information Yet on Ozone Depletion." *International Environment Reporter,* September 25, p. 504.

———. 1991f. "History of the Montreal Protocol's Ozone Fund." *International Environment Reporter,* November 20, pp. 636–40.

———. 1992a. "NASA Expedition Findings Predict Increased Ozone Depletion Over Arctic." *International Environment Reporter,* February 12, pp. 59–60.

———. 1992b. "U.K. Scientist Criticizes Early Release of NASA Data on Accelerated Ozone Loss." *International Environment Reporter,* February 26, p. 95.

Isaac, Jeffrey C. 1987. *Power and Marxist Theory.* Ithaca: Cornell University Press.

Iskandar, Ibn. 1951. *A Mirror for Princes.* Translated by Reuben Levy. New York: Dutton.

Jaafar, A. B. 1990. "Trade War by Environmental Decree." *Asia Technology* (January).

Jachtenfuchs, Markus. 1990. "The European Community and Protection of the Ozone Layer." *Journal of Common Market Studies* 28, no. 3 (March): 263–75.

Jameson, Frederic. 1981. *The Political Unconscious: Narrative as a Socially Symbolic Act.* Ithaca, N.Y.: Cornell University Press.

———. 1984. Foreword to Jean-François Lyotard, *The Postmodern Condition: A Report on Knowledge.* Minneapolis: University of Minnesota Press.

Jervis, Robert. 1988. "Realism, Game Theory, and Cooperation." *World Politics* 40, no. 2 (Spring): 317–49.

Johnston, Harold. 1971. "Reduction of Stratospheric Ozone by Nitrogen Oxide Catalysts from Supersonic Transport Exhaust." *Science* 173 (August 6): 517–22.

Journal of Commerce. 1988. "Du Pont Plans Commercial-scale Plant for Production of CFC-12 Substitute." *Journal of Commerce,* September 30.

Kahneman, Daniel, Paul Slovic, and Amos Tversky, eds. 1982. *Judgment under Uncertainty: Heuristics and Biases.* New York: Cambridge University Press.

Kaplan, Abraham. 1964. *The Conduct of Inquiry.* San Francisco: Chandler.

Kates, R. W. 1962. "Hazard and Choice Perception in Flood Plain Management." Research Paper No. 78. Chicago: Department of Geography, University of Chicago.

Katzenstein, Peter, ed. 1978. *Between Power and Plenty: Foreign Economic Policies of Advanced Industrial States.* Madison: University of Wisconsin Press.

————. 1985. *Small States in World Markets.* Ithaca: Cornell University Press.

Kavolis, Vytautas. 1970. "Post-modern Man: Psychocultural Responses to Social Trends." *Social Problems* 17 (Spring): 435–49.

————. 1972. *History on Art's Side.* Ithaca, N.Y.: Cornell University Press.

Keeley, James F. 1990. "Towards a Foucauldian Analysis of Regimes." *International Organization* 44, no. 1 (Winter): 83–105.

Keller, Evelyn Fox. 1985. *Reflections on Gender and Science.* New Haven: Yale University Press.

Kellogg, William and Robert Schware. 1982. "Society, Science, and Climate Change." *Foreign Affairs* (Summer): 1076–1109.

Kennedy, Paul. 1987. *The Rise and Fall of Great Powers: Economic Change and Military Conflict from 1500 to 2000.* New York: Random House.

Keohane, Robert O. 1980. "The Theory of Hegemonic Stability and Changes in International Economic Regimes, 1976–77." In Ole R. Holsti, Randolph M. Siverson, and Alexander L. George, eds., *Changes in the International System.* Boulder, Colo.: Westview.

————. 1984. *After Hegemony: Cooperation and Discord in the World Political Economy.* Princeton: Princeton University Press.

————. 1989. *International Institutions and State Power: Essays in International Relations Theory.* Boulder, Colo.: Westview.

Keohane, Robert and Joseph S. Nye. 1977. *Power and Interdependence: World Politics in Transition.* Boston: Little Brown.

Kindleberger, Charles P. 1973. *The World in Depression, 1929–1939.* Berkeley: University of California Press.

————. 1986. "Hierarchy versus Inertial Cooperation." *International Organization* 40, no. 4 (Autumn): 841–47.

Kleinberg, Benjamin S. 1973. *American Society in the Postindustrial Age: Technocracy, Power, and the End of Ideology.* Columbus, Ohio: Merrill.

Knorr, Klaus 1975. *The Power of Nations: The Political Economy of International Relations.* New York: Basic.

Konig, R. 1968. *The Community.* London: Routledge and Kegan Paul.

Krasner, Stephen. 1976. "State Power and the Structure of Foreign Trade." *World Politics* 28 (April): 317–47.

———. 1978. *Defending the National Interest: Raw Materials Investment and U.S. Foreign Policy.* Princeton: Princeton University Press.

———., ed. 1983. *International Regimes.* Ithaca: Cornell University Press.

Kratochwil, Friedrich V. 1990. *Rules, Norms, and Decisions: On the Conditions of Practical and Legal Reasoning in International and Domestic Affairs.* Cambridge: Cambridge University Press.

Kripke, Margaret. 1989. "Sun and Ultraviolet Ray Exposure." *Cancer Prevention* (November): 1–7.

Kuhn, Thomas. 1962. *The Structure of Scientific Revolutions.* Chicago: University of Chicago Press.

———. 1977. *The Essential Tension: Selected Studies in Scientific Tradition and Change.* Chicago: University of Chicago Press.

Kunreuther, H. 1978. *Disaster in Insurance Protection: Public Policy Lessons.* New York: Wiley.

Kyodo News Service. 1992. "Japan to Ban Making, Using Ozone Destroyers by End of '95." Japan Economic Newswire, April 30.

Lakatos, Imre. 1970. "Falsification and the Methodology of Scientific Research Programmes." In Imre Lakatos and Alan Musgrave, eds., *Criticism and the Growth of Knowledge.* Cambridge: Cambridge University Press.

Lakoff, Sanford. 1966. *Knowledge and Power: Essays on Science and Government.* New York: Free.

Lane, R. 1966. "The Decline of Politics and Ideology in a Knowledgeable Society." *American Sociological Review* 31 (October): 649–62.

Laponce, J. A. 1987. "Language and Communication: The Rise of the Monolingual State." In Claudia Cioffi-Revilla, Richard L. Merritt, and Dina A. Zinnes, eds., *Communication and Interaction in Global Politics.* Newbury Park, Calif.: Sage.

LaPorte, Todd R. 1975. *Organized Social Complexity: Challenges to Politics and Policy.* Princeton: Princeton University Press.

Lapp, Ralph. 1965. *The New Priesthood: The Scientific Elite and the Uses of Power.* New York: Harper and Row.

Latour, Bruno. 1983. "Give Me a Laboratory and I Will Raise the World." In K. Knorr-Cetina and M. Mulkay, eds., *Science Observed,* pp. 141–170. London: Sage.

———. 1988. *The Pasteurization of France.* Cambridge: Harvard University Press.

Latour, Bruno and Steve Woolgar. 1979. *Laboratory Life: The Social Construction of Scientific Facts.* Beverly Hills: Sage.

Lindblom, C. and D. Cohen. 1979. *Usable Knowledge: Social Science and Social Problem Solving.* New Haven: Yale University Press.

Linden, Mark O. and David A. Didion. 1987. "Quest for Alternatives." *ASHRAE Journal* (December): 4–7.

Lipson, Charles. 1983. "The Transformation of Trade: The Sources and Effects of Regime Change." In Stephen Krasner, ed., *International Regimes*, pp. 233–72. Ithaca: Cornell University Press.

Lloyd, Genevieve. 1984. *The Man of Reason: `Male' and `Female' in Western Philosophy*. London: Metheun.

London, J. and H. Kelly. 1974. "Global Trends in Total Atmospheric Ozone." *Science* 184: 987–89.

London Observer. 1988. "Tories Plan `Green Bill,' " October 2, p. 1.

Los Angeles Times. 1986. "Mysterious Seriousness" (editorial), November 28, p. B-8.

———. 1987. "Hodel Proposal Irks Environmentalists," May 30, p. I-2.

———. 1989a. "Greenhouse Effect Plan May Be Revived," February 17, p. I-29.

———. 1989b. "Air Gains May Be Undone by Ozone Harm," May 21, p. I-1.

———. 1989c. "Bush Proposing Talks in U.S. on Global Warming," December 6, p. A-15.

———. 1990a. "Fifty-three Nations Pledge to Ban Ozone Destroyers by 2000," June 9, p. A-1.

———. 1990b. "U.S. to Join Fund to Help Curve Ozone Depletion," June 16, p. A-27.

———. 1990c. "Chinese Delegates to Seek Beijing's Approval for Pact to Protect Ozone," June 29, p. A-8.

———. 1991. "Du Pont Will Accelerate CFC Phase-Out," October 23, p. D-1.

Los Angeles Times Magazine. 1989. "Five Weathermen of the Apocalypse," May 21, pp. 10–16.

Lovelock, James. 1973. "Halogenated Hydrocarbons In and Over the Atlantic." *Nature* 241 (January 19): 194–96.

Lowi, Theodore. 1967. "Making Democracy Safe for the World." In James N. Rosenau, ed., *Domestic Sources of Foreign Policy*, pp. 295–331. New York: Free.

Lukács, Georg. 1971. *History and Class Consciousness: Studies in Marxist Dialectics.* Cambridge: MIT Press.

Luke, Timothy W. 1989. *Screens of Power: Ideology, Domination, and Resistance in Informational Society.* Urbana: University of Illinois Press.

Lukes, Steven. 1974. *Power: A Radical View.* London: Macmillan.

Lyotard, Jean-François. 1984. *The Postmodern Condition: A Report on Knowledge. Translated by G. Bennington and B. Massumi. Minneapolis: University of Minnesota Press.*

McElroy, Michael B., Ross J. Salawitch, Steven C. Wofsy, and Jennifer A. Logan. 1976. "Agricultural Perturbations of Nitrogen Cycle and Related Impact on Atmospheric N_2O and Ozone." *Transactions of the American Geophysical Union* 57, no. 8: 600.

———. 1986. "Reductions Due to Synergistic Interactions of Chlorine and Bromine." *Nature*, June 19, pp. 759–61.

M'Gonigle, R. Michael and Mark W. Zacher. 1979. *Pollution, Politics, and International Law: Tankers at Sea.* Berkeley: University of California Press.

McKibben, Bill. 1989. *The End of Nature.* New York: Random House.

Mahlman, J. D. and S. B. Fels. 1986. "Antarctic Ozone Decreases: A Dynamical Cause?" *Geophysical Research Letters* 13 (November): 1316–19.

Makhijani, A. 1988. *Saving Our Skins: Technical Potential and Policies for the Elimination of Ozone Depleting Chlorine Compounds.* Washington, D.C.: Environmental Policy Institute.

Makhijani, A., A. Bickel, and A. Makhijani. 1990. "Still Working on the Ozone Hole." *Technology Review* 93 (May-June): 52–59.

Mandel, Ernst. 1975. *Late Capitalism.* London: New Left.

Manzer, I. E. 1990. "The CFC-Ozone Issue: Progress on the Development of Alternatives to CFC's." *Science* 249 (July 6): 31–35.

March, James. 1966. "The Power of Power." In David Easton, ed., *Varieties of Political Theory.* pp. 39–70. Englewood Cliffs, N.J.: Prentice-Hall.

Margolis, Howard. 1973. *Technical Advice on Policy Issues.* Beverly Hills: Sage.

Markandya, A. 1990. "Costs to Developing Countries of Meeting the Objectives of the Montreal Protocol." London: Metroeconomica.

Markandya, A. and H. Pargal. 1990. "Points of Agreement and Disagreement Between the Two Studies on the Costs of Developing Countries of Meeting the Objectives of the Montreal Protocol." Geneva: United Nations Environment Programme.

Marx, Karl. 1976. *The German Ideology.* Moscow: Progress.

———. 1978. In Robert Tucker, ed., *The Marx-Engels Reader. New York: Norton.*

Maynes, Charles William. 1988. "To Save the Earth from Human Ruin, Enact New World Laws of Geo-Ecology." *Los Angeles Times*, September 4, p. E-6.

Merchant, Carolyn. 1989. *Ecological Revolutions: Nature, Gender, and Science in New England.* Chapel Hill: University of North Carolina Press.

Merton, Robert. 1945. "Sociology of Knowledge." In G. Gurvitch and W. Moore, eds., *Twentieth-Century Sociology.* New York: Philosophical Library.

———. 1957. "Priorities in Scientific Discovery." *American Sociological Review* 22, no. 4: 635–59.

———. 1973. "The Ambivalence of Scientists." *Bulletin of the Johns Hopkins Hospital* (February): 77–93.

Milbrath, Lester. 1984. *Environmentalists: Vanguard for a New Society.* Albany: State University of New York.

Miles, Edward C. 1987. "Science, Politics, and International Ocean Management: The Uses of Scientific Knowledge in International Negotiations." Policy Paper in International Affairs No. 33. Berkeley: Institute for International Studies.

Miller, A. and I. Mintzer. 1986. *The Sky is the Limit: Strategies for Protecting the Ozone Layer.* Washington, D.C.: World Resources Institute.

Mills, C. Wright. 1956. *The Power Elite.* New York: Oxford University Press.

Mingst, Karen. 1981. "The Functionalist and Regime Perspectives: The Case of Rhine River Cooperation." *Journal of Common Market Studies* 20 (December): 161–73.

Mitrany, David. 1975. *The Functional Theory of World Politics.* London: Martin Robertson.

Molina, Mario and F. Sherwood Rowland. 1974. "Stratospheric Sink for Chlorofluoromethanes: Chlorine Atomic-atalysed (sic) Destruction of Ozone." *Nature* 249 (June 28): 810–12.

Monastersky, Richard. 1988. "Decline of the CFC Empire." *Science News* 133 (April 9): 234–36.

Moore, Barrington. 1950. *Soviet Politics—The Dilemma of Power: The Role of Ideas in Social Change.* Cambridge: Harvard University Press.

Morgenthau, Hans. 1946. *Scientific Man vs. Power Politics.* Chicago: University of Chicago Press.

———. 1951. *In Defense of the National Interest.* Washington, D.C.: University Press of America.

Morgenthau, Hans and Kenneth Thompson. 1985. *Politics Among Nations.* 6th ed. New York: Knopf.

Munasinghe, Mohan. 1990. "The Challenge Facing the Developing World." *EPA Journal* 16, no. 2 (March/April): 52–53.

Myers, Norman. 1979. *The Sinking Ark: A New Look at the Problem of Disappearing Species.* Elmsford, N.Y.: Pergamon.

National Aeronautics and Space Administration (NASA). 1984. *Present State of Knowledge of the Upper Atmosphere: An Assessment Report.* Washington, D.C.: U.S. Government Printing Office.

———. 1987. "Initial Findings from Punta Arenas, Chile, Airborne Antarctic Ozone Experiment." September 30. Washington, D.C.: NASA.

———. 1988. "Executive Summary of the Ozone Trends Panel." March 15. Photocopy.

National Aeronautics and Space Administration and World Meteorological Organization (NASA/WMO). 1986. *Present State of Knowledge of the Upper Atmosphere: An Assessment Report,* NASA Reference Publication 1162. Washington, D.C.: NASA.

National Research Council (NRC). 1975. *Environmental Impact of Stratospheric Flight: Biological and Climatic Effects of Aircraft Emission in the Stratosphere.* Washington, D.C.: National Academy of Sciences.

———. 1976. *Halocarbons: Effects on Stratospheric Ozone.* Washington, D.C.: National Academy of Sciences.

———. 1977. *Response to the Ozone Protection Section of the Clean Air Act Amend-*

ment of 1977: An Interim Report. Washington, D.C.: National Academy of Sciences.

―――. 1979. *Protection Against Depletion of Stratospheric Ozone by Chlorofluorocarbons.* Washington, D.C.: National Academy of Sciences.

―――. 1982. *Causes and Effects of Stratospheric Ozone Reduction: An Update.* Washington, D.C.: National Academy of Sciences.

―――. 1984. *Causes and Effects of Changes in Stratospheric Ozone: Update 1983.* Washington, D.C.: National Academy of Sciences.

Natural Resources Defense Council. 1988. "Lawsuit Seeks Full U.S. Phase-out of Ozone-Depleting Chemicals." *NRDC Newsline* (November/December): 1.

―――. 1990. "The New Montreal Protocol—Will It Close the Holes in the Ozone Treaty?" Washington, D.C.: NRDC.

Nature. 1987a. "Scientists Turn Attention to Climate," September 24, p. 422.

―――. 1987b. "Ozone Hole Deeper than Ever," October 8, p. 473.

Nelkin, Dorothy, ed. 1984. *Controversy: Politics of Technical Decisions.* Beverly Hills: Sage.

New Scientist. 1987. "Fungus Bogey Blights Ozone Layer," February 5, p. 27.

New York Times. 1986. "Chemical Process Seen in Ozone Hole," October 21, p. C-3

―――. 1987a. "Worldwide Pact Sought on Ozone," February 19, p. A-1.

―――. 1987b. "Through Rose-Colored Sunglasses"(editorial), May 31, p. E-28.

―――. 1988a. "New Compound Is Hailed as Boon to Ozone Shield," January 14, p. A-6.

―――. 1988b. "Industry Acts to Save Ozone," March 21, p. A-1.

―――. 1988c. "Behind Du Pont's Shift on Loss of Ozone Layer," March 26, p. 41.

―――. 1988d. "New Ozone Threat: Scientists Fear Layer Is Eroding at North Pole." October 11, p. C-1.

―――. 1989a. "Twelve Europe Nations to Ban Chemicals that Harm Ozone," March 3, p. A-1.

―――. 1989b. "London Talks Hear Call for '97 Ban," March 6, p. A-11.

―――. 1989c. "Talks on Ozone End in Britain Without Fixing Chemical Ban," March 8, p. A-8.

―――. 1989d. "Eighty Nations Favor Ban to Help Ozone," May 3, p. A-13.

―――. 1989e. "Large Volcanic Eruption Could Damage Ozone," May 9, p. C-4.

―――. 1990a. "The World Will Be Watching" (*Scientific American* advertisement), January 17, p. C-1.

―――. 1990b. "U.S. is Assailed at Geneva Talks for Backing Out of Ozone Plan," May 10, p. A-1

―――. 1990c. "Grappling with the Cost of Saving Earth's Ozone," July 17, p. C-1.

———. 1991. "Summertime Harm to Ozone Detected over Broader Area." October 23, p. A-1.

———. 1992a. "Pentagon Plans Move to Protect Ozone," February 15, p. A-7.

———. 1992b. "Europeans Worry About Ozone-Eating Chemicals," March 3, p. A-1.

———. 1992c. "Military is Seen Stalling on Ozone," March 21, p. A-7.

Newsweek. 1987. "An Exemplary Ozone Agreement," September 28, p. 8.

Nicholson, E. M. 1970. *The Environmental Revolution.* New York: McGraw-Hill.

Nietzsche, Friedrich. 1979. *Nietzsche,* vol. 4. Translated by M. Heidegger. San Francisco: Harper and Row.

Nitze, William. 1989. "The Intergovernmental Panel on Climate Change." *Environment* 31, no. 1 (January/February): 44–45.

Nucleus: The Magazine of the Union of Concerned Scientists. 1992–93. 14, no. 4 (Winter).

Nye, Joseph S. 1990. *Bound to Lead: The Changing Nature of American Power.* New York: Basic.

Official Journal of the European Communities. 1978. No. C 133/1- 7.6.78.

———. 1980. No. L 90/45–3.4.80.

Ohi, James M. 1985. "Science and Global Environmental Pollution Issues: A Case Study of Stratospheric Ozone Depletion by Chlorofluorocarbons." Ph.D. diss., University of Denver.

Onuf, Nicholas. 1989. *World of Our Making: Rules and Rule in Social Theory and International Relations.* Columbia: University of South Carolina Press.

Oppenheimer, Michael and Robert Boyle. 1990. *Dead Heat: The Race Against the Greenhouse Effect.* New York: Basic.

Oye, Kenneth. 1986. *Cooperation Under Anarchy.* Princeton: Princeton University Press.

Ozawa, Connie P. 1991. *Recasting Science: Consensual Procedures in Public Policy Making.* Boulder, Colo.: Westview.

OzonAction Newsletter. 1991. No.1 (November). Paris: United Nations Environment Programme and the Industry and Environment Programme Activity Center.

———. 1992. No. 2 (April). Paris: United Nations Environment Programme and the Industry and Environment Programme Activity Center.

Palm Beach Post. 1987. "Ozone Destruction May Be Advanced Too Far for Recovery, Scientist Says," March 2, p. 1-A.

Pareto, Vilfredo. 1935. *The Mind and Society.* New York: Dover.

Pargal, H. and A. Kumar. 1990. "Economic Implications for Developing Countries of the Montreal Protocol." New Delhi: Development Alternatives.

Parsons, Talcott. 1963. "On the Concept of Political Power." *Proceedings of the American Philosophical Society* 107: 232–62.

———. 1967. *Sociological Theory and Modern Society.* New York: Free.

Pell, Claiborne. 1990. "CFC Fund Decision Showed Flaws in U.S. Policy Making." *Christian Science Monitor,* June 22, p. 18.

Peterson, M. J. 1992. "Whalers, Cetologists, Environmentalists, and the International Management of Whaling." *International Organization* 46, no. 1 (Winter): 147–86.

Philp, Mark. 1983. "Foucault on Power: A Problem in Radical Translation?" *Political Theory* 11, no. 1 (Winter): 29–52.

Pirages, Dennis. 1991. "Environmental Security and Social Evolution." *International Studies Notes* 16, no. 1 (Winter): 8–12.

Polanyi, Michael. 1958. *Personal Knowledge.* Chicago: University of Chicago Press.

Popper, Karl. 1966. *The Open Society and Its Enemies.* London: Routledge and Kegan Paul.

———. 1972. *The Logic of Scientific Discovery.* London: Hutchinson.

Poster, Mark. 1984. *Foucault, Marxism, and History: Mode of Production vs. Mode of Information.* Cambridge: Polity.

Potter, William C. 1980. "Issue Area and Foreign Policy Analysis." *International Organization* 34, no. 3 (Summer): 405–25.

Prather, Michael J. and Robert T. Watson. 1990. "Stratospheric Ozone Depletion and Future Levels of Atmospheric Chlorine and Bromine." *Nature,* April 19, pp. 729–35.

Price, Don. 1964. "The Scientific Establishment." In Robert Gilpin and C. Wright, eds., *Scientists and National Policy-making.* New York: Columbia University Press.

———. 1965. *The Scientific Estate.* Cambridge: Harvard University Press.

Programme for Alternative Fluorocarbon Toxicity Testing (PAFT). 1991. "Programme for Alternative Fluorocarbon Toxicity Testing." December. Washington, D.C.: PAFT.

Pukelsheim, Friedrich. 1990. "Robustness of Statistical Gossip and the Antarctic Ozone Hole." *The IMS Bulletin* 19, no. 4 (Fall): 540–45.

Putnam, Robert D. 1988. "Diplomacy and Domestic Politics: The Logic of Two-level Games." *International Organization* 42, no. 3 (Summer): 427–58.

Ramanathan, V. 1975. "Greenhouse Effect Due to Chlorofluorocarbons: Climatic Implications." *Science* 190 (October): 50–51.

Ravetz, Jerome R. 1986. "Usable Knowledge, Usable Ignorance: Incomplete Science with Policy Implications." In W. C. Clark and R. E. Munn, eds., *Sustainable Development of the Biosphere,* pp. 415–32. Laxenburg, Austria: International Institute for Applied Systems Analysis.

Rein, Martin and Donald Schon. 1977. "Problem Setting in Policy Research." In Carol Weiss, ed., *Using Social Research in Public Policy Making.* Lexington, Mass: Heath.

Reinhardt, Forest. 1989. "Du Pont FREON Products Division: Prepared as a Harvard Business School Case." Washington, D.C.: National Wildlife Federation.

Roan, Sharon. 1989. *Ozone Crisis: The Fifteen-Year Evolution of a Sudden Global Emergency.* New York: Wiley.

Rodriguez, M. K., M. K. W. Ko, and N. D. Sze. 1986. "Chlorine Chemistry in the Antarctic Stratosphere: Impact of OClO and Cl_2O_2 and Implications for Observations." *Geophysical Research Letters* 13 (November): 1292–95.

Rorty, Richard. 1980. *Philosophy and the Mirror of Nature.* Oxford: Basil Blackwell.

———. 1986. "The Contingency of Community." *London Review of Books*, July 24, p. 10–14.

Rosecrance, Richard. 1986. *The Rise of the Trading State: Commerce and Conquest in the Modern World.* New York: Basic.

Rosenau, James N. 1973. *International Studies and the Social Sciences: Problems, Priorities and Prospects in the U.S.* Beverly Hills: Sage.

———. 1986. "Before Cooperation: Hegemons, Regimes, and Habit-Driven Actors in World Politics." *International Organization* 40, no. 3 (Autumn): 859–78.

———. 1989. "Global Changes and Theoretical Challenges: Toward a Postinternational Politics for the 1990's." In Ernst-Otto Czempiel and James N. Rosenau, eds., *Global Changes and Theoretical Challenges: Approaches to World Politics for the 1990's*, pp. 1–20. Lexington, Mass.: Lexington.

———. 1990. *Turbulence in World Politics: A Theory of Change and Continuity.* Princeton: Princeton University Press.

Rothstein, Robert L. 1984. "Consensual Knowledge and International Collaboration: Some Lessons from the Commodity Negotiations." *International Organization* 38, no. 4 (Autumn): 733–62.

Rouse, Joseph. 1987. *Knowledge and Power: Toward a Political Philosophy of Science.* Ithaca: Cornell University Press.

Rowland, F. Sherwood. 1987. "Can We Close the Ozone Hole?" *Technology Review* (August-September): 49–52.

Rowland, F. Sherwood and Mario Molina. 1976. "Stratospheric Formation and Photolysis of Chlorine Nitrate." *Journal of Physical Chemistry* 80, no. 24: 2711–13.

Ruckleshaus, William. 1983. "Science, Risk, and Public Policy." *Science* 221: 1028–29.

Ruggie, John G. 1975. "International Responses to Technology." *International Organization* 29 (Summer): 557–83.

———. 1986. "Social Time and International Policy: Conceptualizing Global Population and Resource Issues." In M. P. Karns, ed., *Persistent Patterns and Emergent Structures in a Waning Century.* New York: Praeger.

Russell, Bertrand. 1975. *Power: A New Social Analysis*. London: Allen and Unwin.

Sabatier, Paul A. 1987. "Knowledge, Policy-Orientated Learning, and Policy Change: An Advocacy Coalition Framework." *Knowledge: Creation, Diffusion, Utilization* 8, no. 4 (Fall): 64–92.

———. 1988. "An Advocacy Coalition Framework of Policy Change and the Role of Policy-oriented Learning Therein." *Policy Sciences* 21: 129–68.

Saint-Simon, Henri de. 1952. *Henri Comte de Saint-Simon: Selected Writings*. Translated and edited by F. Markham. Oxford: Oxford University Press.

San Francisco Chronicle. 1989. "Canada to Ban Ozone-Harming Chemicals," February 21, p. 2.

Sand, Peter. 1985. "The Vienna Convention is Adopted." *Environment* 27 (June): 19–23.

Schlick, Moritz. 1959. "The Foundation of Knowledge." In A. J. Ayer ed., *Logical Positivism*. Toronto: Free.

Schmidt, Rudolf. 1990. "International Financial and Other Mechanisms for Assistance to Developing Countries Under the Montreal Protocol." Nairobi: United Nations Environment Programme.

Schneider, Stephen H. 1989. "The Greenhouse Effect: Science and Policy." *Science* 243 (February 10): 771–81.

Science. 1984. "What is the Risk from Chlorofluorocarbons?" March 9, p. 1051.

———. 1986. "Taking Shots at Ozone Hole Theories." November 14, p. 817–18.

———. 1989. "Arctic Ozone Is Poised for a Fall." February 14, p. 1007.

———. 1990. "Another Deep Antarctic Ozone Hole." October 19, p. 370.

———. 1991. "Antarctic Ozone Hole Hits Record Depth," October 18, p. 373.

Science Impact. 1987. Interview with Robert Watson. *Science Impact* (September): 5–7.

Science News. 1991. "Summer Ozone Loss Detected for First Time," November 2, p. 278.

———. 1992a. "Northern Ozone Hole Deemed Likely," February 8, p. 84.

———. 1992b. "Ozone Concerns Prompt Phaseout Fury," February 15, p. 102.

Sebenius, James K. 1992. "Challenging Conventional Explanations of International Cooperation: Negotiation Analysis and the Case of Epistemic Communities." *International Organization* 46, no. 1 (Winter): 323–66.

Shapere, Dudley. 1964. "The Structure of Scientific Revolutions." *Philosophical Review* 73: 389–402.

Shapin, Steven and Simon Schaffer. 1985. *Leviathan and the Air Pump: Hobbes, Boyle and the Experimental Life*. Princeton: Princeton University Press.

Shapiro, Michael J., G. Matther Bonham, and Daniel Heradstveit. 1988. "A Discursive Practices Approach to Collective Decision-Making." *International Studies Quarterly* 32 (December): 379–419.

Sharp, Gene. 1973. *The Politics of Nonviolent Action*. Boston: Sargent.

Shea, Cynthia Pollock. 1988. "Protecting the Ozone Layer." Washington, D.C.: Worldwatch Institute.

Shrader-Frechette, K. S. 1985. *Risk Analysis and Scientific Method.* Dordrecht, Holland: Reidel.

Simon, Herbert. 1957. *Models of Man: Social and Rational* New York: Wiley.

Skolimowski, Henryk. 1983. "Power: Myth and Reality." *Alternatives* 9: 25–49.

Skowronek, Stephen. 1982. *Building a New American State: The Expansion of National Administrative Capacities, 1877–1920.* Cambridge: Cambridge University Press.

Smith, K. C. 1974. "Biological Impacts of Increased Intensities of Solar Ultraviolet Radiation: A Report to the Environmental Studies Board." Washington, D.C.: National Academy of Sciences.

Smith, V. Kerry. 1984. *Environmental Policy under Reagan's Executive Order.* Chapel Hill: University of North Carolina Press.

Snyder, Glenn and Paul Diesing. 1977. *Conflict Among Nations: Bargaining, Decision Making, and System Structure in International Crises.* Princeton: Princeton University Press.

Solomon, S., R. Garcia, F. S. Rowland, and D. J. Wuebbles. 1986. "On the Depletion of Antarctic Ozone." *Nature* 321: 755–58.

Spencer, Herbert. 1896. "The Industrial Type of Society." *Principles of Sociology,* vol. 2. New York: Appleton.

Sprout, Harold and Margaret Sprout. 1971. *Towards a Politics of the Planet Earth.* New York: Van Nostrand Reinhold.

Stein, Arthur A. 1983. "Coordination and Collaboration: Regimes in an Anarchic World." In Stephen Krasner, ed., *International Regimes,* pp. 115–40. Ithaca: Cornell University Press.

Steinbruner, John. 1974. *The Cybernetic Theory of Decision.* Princeton: Princeton University Press.

Stoel, Thomas. 1983. "Fluorocarbons: Mobilizing Concern and Action." In David Kay and Harold Johnson, eds., *Environmental Protection: The International Dimension.* Totowa, N.J.: Allanheld, Osmun.

Stoel, Thomas, Alan Miller, and Breck Milroy. 1980. *Fluorocarbon Regulation: An International Comparison.* Lexington, Mass.: Lexington.

Stolarski, Richard S. and Ralph J. Cicerone. 1974. "Stratospheric Chlorine: A Possible Sink for Ozone." *Canadian Journal of Chemistry* 52: 1610–15.

Stolarski, Richard S., A. J. Krueger, M. R. Schoeberl, R. D. McPeters, P. A. Newman, and J. C. Alpert. 1986. "Nimbus 7 Satellite Measurements of the Spring Time Antarctic Ozone Decrease." *Nature* 322: 808–11.

Stone, Clarence. 1976. *Economic Growth and Neighborhood Bias in the Urban Renewal Program of Atlanta.* Chapel Hill: University of North Carolina Press.

———. 1989. *Regime Politics: Governing Atlanta, 1946–1988.* Lawrence: University Press of Kansas.

Stone, Deborah A. 1988. *Policy Paradox and Political Reason.* New York: Harper Collins.

Stordal, Frode and Ivar Isaksen. 1986. "Ozone Perturbations Due to Increases in N_2O, CH_4 and Chlorcarbons: Two-Dimensional Time Dependent Calculations." In James Titus, ed., *Effects of Changes in Stratospheric Ozone and Global Climate,* pp. 83–120. Washington, D.C.: Environmental Protection Agency.

Storer, N., ed. 1973. *The Sociology of Science.* Chicago: University of Chicago Press.

Sundquist, James. 1978. "Research Brokerage: The Weak Link." In L. Lynn, ed., *Knowledge and Policy: The Uncertain Connection.* Washington, D.C.: National Academy of Sciences.

Taylor, Charles. 1982. "Foucault on Freedom and Truth." *Political Theory* 12, no. 2 (Spring): 152–83.

Taylor, Graham. 1984. *Du Pont and the International Chemical Industry.* Boston: Twayne.

Teramura, Alan. 1986. "Overview of Our Current State of Knowledge of UV Effects on Plants." In James Titus, ed., *Effects of Changes in Stratospheric Ozone and Global Climate,* pp. 165–74. Washington, D.C.: Environmental Protection Agency.

Terdiman, Richard. 1985. *Discourse/Counter-Discourse: The Theory and Practice of Symbolic Resistance in Nineteenth-Century France.* Ithaca: Cornell University Press.

Thatcher, Margaret. 1988. "Speech to the Royal Society." London Press Service, September 27.

Thomas, Lee. 1986. "Global Environmental Change: The EPA Perspective." In James Titus, ed., *Effects of Changes in Stratospheric Ozone and Global Climate.* Washington, D.C.: Environmental Protection Agency.

Thompson, Kenneth. 1979. *Ethics, Functionalism and Power in International Politics: The Crisis in Values.* Baton Rouge: Louisiana State University.

Tickell, Crispin. 1977. "Climatic Change and World Affairs." Cambridge: Harvard University Center for International Affairs.

Time. 1990. "A Baffling Ozone Policy," May 21, p. 20.

Titus, James, ed. 1986. *Effects of Changes in Stratospheric Ozone and Global Climate.* Washington, D.C.: Environmental Protection Agency.

Titus, James G. and Stephen Seidel. 1986. "Overview of the Effects of Changing the Atmosphere." In James Titus, ed., *Effects of Changes in Stratospheric Ozone and Global Climate,* pp. 3–20. Washington, D.C.: Environmental Protection Agency.

Tolba, Mostafa K. 1989a. "The Need to Go Further: The Montreal Protocol Nineteen Months Later." UNEP press release, May 2, Helsinki.

———. 1989b. "The Tools to Build a Global Response: Financial Mechanisms for the Montreal Protocol." UNEP Information, August 21, Nairobi.

———. 1989c. "The Montreal Protocol: The Changes Ahead." UNEP Information, August 28, Nairobi.

———. 1990. "Proposed Adjustments and Amendments to the Control Measures of the Montreal Protocol—Revised Note by the Executive Director." UNEP/OzL.Pro.WG.IV/2/Rev./1, June 20.

———.1992. "Opening Statement to the Preparatory Meeting of the Fourth Meeting of the Parties to the Montreal Protocol." UNEP Information, November 19, Nairobi.

Touraine, Alain. 1972. *The Post-Industrial Society: Tomorrow's Social History.* New York: Random House.

Trenberth, Kevin E. 1988. "Report on Reports: Executive Summary of the Ozone Trends Panel Report." *Environment* 30, no. 6 (July-August): 25–26.

Tripp, James T. B. 1988. "The UNEP Montreal Protocol: Industrialized and Developing Countries Sharing the Responsibility for Protecting the Stratospheric Ozone Layer." *Journal of International Law and Politics* 20, no. 3 (Fall): 733–52.

Tversky, Amos and Daniel Kahneman. 1981. "The Framing of Decisions and the Psychology of Choice." *Science* 211 (January 30): 453–58.

United Kingdom Department of the Environment. 1976. "Chlorofluorocarbons and Their Effect on Stratospheric Ozone." Pollution Paper Number 5. London: Her Majesty's Stationery Office.

———. 1979. *Chlorofluorocarbons and Their Effect on Stratospheric Ozone.* London: Her Majesty's Stationery Office.

———. 1990. *Stratospheric Ozone 1990.* London: Her Majesty's Stationery Office.

United Nations. 1989. *Yearbook of the United Nations.* New York: United Nations.

United Nations Conference on Environment and Development (UNCED). 1992. *United Nations Framework Convention on Climate Change.* May 9. Geneva: UNCED Secretariat.

United Nations Environment Programme (UNEP). 1978. *UNEP Compendium of Legislative Authority.* Oxford: Pergamon.

———. 1985. *Vienna Convention for the Protection of the Ozone Layer.* Nairobi: UNEP.

———. 1987a. *The Montreal Protocol on Substances that Deplete the Ozone Layer.* Final Act. Nairobi: UNEP.

———. 1987b. *The Ozone Layer.* Nairobi: UNEP.

———. 1987c. Press statement, September 22, Nairobi.

———. 1989. *Action on Ozone.* Nairobi: UNEP.

———. 1991a. *Environmental Effects of Ozone Depletion: 1991 Update.* Nairobi: UNEP.

———. 1991b. *Report of the Technology and Economic Assessment Panel.* Nairobi: UNEP.

————. 1991c. *Report of the Economic Options Committee.* Nairobi: UNEP.

————. 1992a. "Montreal Protocol Assessment Supplement: Synthesis Report of the Methyl Bromide Interim Scientific Assessment and Methyl Bromide Interim Technology and Economic Assessment," June. Washington, D.C.: NASA.

————. 1992b. "Much Progress But Still Some Problems." Press release, November 23, Nairobi.

————. 1992c. "From Montreal '87 to Copenhagen '92—An Environmental Success Story." Press release, November 26, Nairobi.

————. UNEP Press 87/42.

————. UNEP/OzL.Pro.1/2.

————. UNEP/OzL.Pro.l/5.

————. UNEP/OzL.Pro.2/3.

————. UNEP/OzL.Pro.2/L.6 ("London Revisions").

————. UNEP/OzL.Pro.3/11.

————. UNEP/OzL.Pro.4/Prep/2.

————. UNEP/OzL.Pro.4/15 ("Copenhagen Revisions").

————. UNEP/OzL.Pro.Bur.1/2.

————. UNEP/OzL.Pro.WG.I(2)/4.

————. UNEP/OzL.Pro.WG.II(1)/4 ("Synthesis Report").

————. UNEP/OzL.Pro.WG.II(1)/5.

————. UNEP/OzL.Pro.WG.II(1)/6.

————. UNEP/OzL.Pro.WG.II(1)/7.

————. UNEP/OzL.Pro.WG.II(2)/7.

————. UNEP/OzL.Pro.WG.III(1)/3.

————. UNEP/OzL.Pro.WG.III(2)/3.

————. UNEP/OzL.Pro.WG.IV/2/Rev./1.

————. UNEP/OzL.Pro.WG.IV/8.

————. UNEP/OzL.Pro.WG.1/5/3.

————. UNEP/OzL.Pro.WG.1/6/3.

————. UNEP/OzL.Pro.WG.1/6/5.

————. UNEP/OzL.Pro/WG.1/7/4.

————. UNEP/OzL.Pro/WG.1/8/2.

————. UNEP/WG.7/25/Rev.1.

————. UNEP/WG.69/3.

————. UNEP/WG.69/8.

————. UNEP/WG.78/3.

————. UNEP/WG.78/6.

————. UNEP/WG.148/2.

————. UNEP/WG.148/3.

————. UNEP/WG.151/Background 1.

————. UNEP/WG.151/Background 2.

————. UNEP/WG.151/Background 4.

————. UNEP/WG.151/L.4

————. UNEP/WG.167/INF.

————. UNEP/WG.167/2.

————. UNEP/WG.172/2.

————. UNEP/WG.172/3.

U.S. Air Force, EPA, and NATO. 1991. "The Role of the Military in Implementing the Montreal Protocol." Proceedings of a conference, Williamsburg, Virginia, September 11–13.

United States Committee on Earth and Environmental Sciences. 1992. *Our Changing Planet: The FY1992 U.S. Global Change Research Program.* Reston, Va.: U.S. Geological Survey.

United States Congress, Committee on Interstate and Foreign Commerce. 1974. *Fluorocarbons: Impact on Health and Environment.* Hearing. December 11–12.

————. Subcommittee on Human Rights and International Organizations of the Committee on Foreign Affairs. 1987a. *U.S. Participation in International Negotiations on Ozone Protocol.* Hearing. March 5.

————. Subcommittee on Health and Environment, Committee on Energy and Commerce. 1987b. *Ozone Layer Depletion.* Hearing. March 9.

————. Subcommittee on Natural Resources, Agriculture Research and Environment, Committee on Science, Space and Technology. 1987c. *Stratospheric Ozone Depletion.* Hearing. March 10.

U.S. Department of State. 1986. *Principles for an International Protocol on Stratospheric Ozone Protection.* November 3. Washington, D.C.: U.S. Department of State.

U.S. Government Accounting Office (GAO). 1990. *Global Warming: Administration Approach Cautious Pending Validation of Threat.* Washington, D.C.: U.S. Government Accounting Office.

United States Senate, Committee on Environment and Public Works. 1981. *Nominations of Anne M. Gorsuch and John W. Hernandex, Jr.* Hearing. May 1 and 4.

————. Subcommittee on Environmental Pollution, Committee on Environment and Public Works. 1986. *Ozone Depletion, the Greenhouse Effect, and Climate Change.* Hearing. June 10–11.

————. Subcommittees on Environmental Protection and Hazardous Wastes and Toxic Substances, Committee on Environment and Public Works. 1987a. *Ozone Depletion, the Greenhouse Effect, and Climate Change.* Hearing. January 28.

————. Committee on Environment and Public Works. 1987b. *Stratospheric Ozone Depletion and Chlorofluorocarbons.* Hearing. May 12–14.

————. 1987c. "U.S. Senate Resolution 226: Relating to International Negotiations to Protect the Ozone Layer," *Congressional Record,* June 5, S7759.

————. Subcommittee on Science, Technology and Space, Committee on Commerce, Science and Transportation. 1991. *New Data on Depletion of the Ozone Layer.* Hearing. April 16.

U.S. Task Force on the Comprehensive Approach to Climate Change. 1991. *A Comprehensive Approach to Addressing Potential Climate Change.* Washington, D.C.: U.S. Department of Justice.

Usher, Peter. 1989. "World Conference on the Changing Atmosphere: Implications for Global Security." *Environment* 31, no. 1 (January/February): 25–28.

Uyehara, Cecil. 1966. "Scientific Advice and the Nuclear Test Ban Treaty." In S. Lakoff, ed., *Knowledge and Power: Essays on Science and Government.* New York: Free.

Vieira, Anna da Soledade. 1985. *Environmental Information in Developing Nations: Politics and Policies.* Westport, Conn.: Greenwood.

Vogel, David. 1986. *National Styles of Regulation: Environmental Policy in Great Britain and the United States.* Ithaca: Cornell University Press.

Vogelmann, H. 1982. "Catastrophe on Camel's Hump." *Natural History* 91 (November): 8–14.

Walker, R. B. J. 1981. "World Politics and Western Reason: Universalism, Pluralism, Hegemony." *Alternatives* 7 (Spring): 196–227.

Wall Street Journal. 1975. "Earth's Ozone Shield May be Imperiled by More Fertilizer Use," November 3, p. A-4.

———. 1986. "Hard Choices Await Industry as Ozone-Layer Fears Rise," December 2, p. 4.

———. 1988a. "Firms Intensify Race to Find Substitutes for Chemicals Linked to Ozone Depletion," September 27, p. A-7.

———. 1988b. "Du Pont Plans Plant to Produce Refrigerant Harmless to Ozone," September 30, p. A-8.

———. 1989. "Ozone Chicken Littles Are at It Again," March 23, p. A-22.

———. 1990. "Chemical Giants May Be Winners in Ozone Fight," June 29, p. A-5C.

———. 1991a. "Replacement for Halons Would Damage Ozone Layer Less," May 6, p. A-7D.

———. 1991b. "Panel Sees Ozone Thinning, Intensifying Political Heat," October 23, p. B-1.

———. 1992. "Press-Release Ozone Hole," February 28, p. A-14.

Waltz, Kenneth. 1979. *Theory of International Politics.* Reading, Mass.: Addison-Wesley.

Washington Post. 1987a. "New Chemical Hole Found Over Antarctica," May 19, p. A-1.

———. 1987b. "New Theory Offered for Hole in Ozone," May 24, p. A-1.

———. 1987c. "Administration Ozone Policy May Favor Sunglasses, Hats," May 29, p. A-1.

———. 1987d. "Alternative to Ozone Pact Hit," May 30, p. A-5.

————. 1987e. "Shultz Reasserts U.S. Support for Ozone Pact," June 5, p. A-13.

————. 1987f. "The Clean McAir Act" (editorial), August 20, p. A-18.

————. 1987g. "The Ozone Treaty" (editorial), September 18, p. A-26.

————. 1987h. "Depletion Worsens: Is Linked to Man-made Gas," October 1, p. A-3.

————. 1987i. "Ozone Depletion Worsens: Hazard to Researchers Seen," October 28, p. A-9

————. 1988a. "CFCs: Rise and Fall of a Chemical Miracle," April 10, p. C-1.

————. 1988b. "Du Pont Plans to Make CFC Alternative," September 30, p. F-5.

————. 1989a. "Bush Endorses Phasing Out CFC's," March 4, p. A-20.

————. 1989b. " `Greening' of Thatcher Surprises Many Britons," March 4, p. A-20.

————. 1990a. "U.S. Intends to Oppose Ozone Plan," May 9, p. A-16.

————. 1990b. "A Serious Mistake on CFC's" (editorial), May 11, p. A-26.

————. 1991a. "The Costly Race to Replace CFC's," September 29, p. H-1.

————. 1991b. "Panel Sees Ozone Thinning, Intensifying Political Heat," October 23, p. B-1.

————. 1992. "Study Finds CFC Alternatives More Damaging Than Believed," February 23, p. A-3.

————. 1993. "Departing EPA Chief Orders U.S. Phaseout of a Popular Pesticide," January 20, p. A-3.

Waste, Robert. 1986. *Community Power: Directions for Future Research.* Beverly Hills: Sage.

————. 1987. *Power and Pluralism in American Cities: Researching the Urban Laboratory.* Westport, Conn.: Greenwood.

————. 1989. *The Ecology of City Policymaking.* New York: Oxford University Press.

Watson, Robert. 1986. "Atmospheric Ozone." In James Titus, ed., *Effects of Changes in Stratospheric Ozone and Climate Change*, pp. 69–72. Washington, D.C.: Environmental Protection Agency.

Weber, Max. 1946a. "Politics as a Vocation." In H. H. Gerth and C. W. Mills, eds., *From Max Weber: Essays in Sociology*, pp. 77–128. New York: Oxford University Press.

————. 1946b. "Science as a Vocation." In H. H. Gerth and C. W. Mills, eds., *From Max Weber: Essays in Sociology*, pp. 129–158. New York: Oxford University Press.

————. 1946c. "The Social Psychology of the World's Religions." In H. H. Gerth and C. W. Mills, eds., *From Max Weber: Essays in Sociology*, pp. 267–301. New York: Oxford University Press.

————. 1958. *The Protestant Ethic and the Spirit of Capitalism.* Translated by Talcott Parsons. New York: Scribner.

Weinberg, Alvin. 1972. "Science and Trans-science." *Minerva* 10, no. 2 (April): 209–22.

Weingart, Peter. 1982. "The Scientific Power Elite—A Chimera." In Norbert Elias, Herminio Martins, and Richard Whitley, eds., *Scientific Establishments and Hierarchies*. Dordrecht, Holland: Reidel.

Wendt, Alexander. 1987. "The Agent-Structure Problem in International Relations Theory." International Organization 41, no. 3 (Summer): 335–70.

———. 1992. "Anarchy Is What States Make of It: The Social Construction of Power Politics." *International Organization* 46, no. 2: 391–425.

Wendt, Alexander and Raymond Duvall. 1989. "Institutions and International Order." In Ernst-Otto Czempiel and James N. Rosenau, eds., *Global Changes and Theoretical Challenges: Approaches to World Politics for the 1990's*, pp. 51–74. Lexington, Mass.: Lexington.

Wetstone, Gregory. 1980. "The Need for a New Regulatory Approach." *Environment* 22, no. 5 (June): 9–14.

———. 1987. "A History of the Acid Rain Issue." In H. Brooks and C. Cooper, eds., *Science for Public Policy*. Oxford: Pergamon.

White, Hayden. 1973. *Meta-history: The Historical Imagination in Nineteenth-Century Europe*. Baltimore: Johns Hopkins University Press.

———. 1978. *Tropics of Discourse: Essays in Cultural Criticism*. Baltimore: Johns Hopkins University Press.

White, Hayden and Margaret Brose, eds. 1982. *Representing Kenneth Burke*. Baltimore: Johns Hopkins University Press.

The White House. 1992. Statement by the press secretary, February 11.

Whittemore, A. S. 1983. "Facts and Values in Risk Analysis for Environmental Pollutants." *Risk Analysis* 3: 23–33.

Wiesner, Jerome. 1965. *Where Science and Politics Meet*. New York: McGraw-Hill.

Wildavsky, Aaron. 1979. *Speaking Truth to Power: The Art and Craft of Policy Analysis*. Boston: Little, Brown.

Wittgenstein, Ludwig. 1953. *Philosophical Investigations*. Oxford: Basil Blackwell.

Wolfers, Arnold. 1962. *Discord and Collaboration*. Baltimore: Johns Hopkins Press.

Wood, Robert. 1964. "Scientists and Politics: The Rise of an Apolitical Elite." In Robert Gilpin and C. Wright, *Scientists and National Policy-making*. New York: Columbia University Press.

Wooley, Wesley T. 1988. *Alternatives to Anarchy: American Supranationalism since World War II*. Bloomington: Indiana University Press.

Woolf, Leonard. 1916. *International Government*. Westminster: Fabian Society.

World Commission of Environment and Development. 1987. *Our Common Future*. New York: Oxford University Press.

World Meteorological Organization (WMO). 1976. *Modification of the Ozone*

Layer Due to Human Activities and Some Possible Geophysical Consequences.
WMO Bulletin 25. Geneva: WMO.

————. 1982. *Report of the Meeting of Experts on Potential Climate Effects of Ozone and Other Minor Trace Gases.* WMO Global Ozone Research and Monitoring Project Report No. 14. Geneva: WMO.

WMO/NASA. 1986. *Atmospheric Ozone 1985: Assessment of Our Understanding of the Processed Controlling Its Present Distribution and Change.* 3 vols. WMO Global Ozone Research and Monitoring Project Report No. 16. Geneva: WMO.

————.. 1991. *Scientific Assessment of Ozone Depletion: 1991.* Geneva: WMO.

World Resources Institute. 1991. *World Resources 1990–91.* Washington, D.C.: World Resources Institute.

Worrest, R. C. 1986. "The Effect of Solar UV-B Radiation on Aquatic Systems: An Overview." In James Titus, ed., *Effects of Changes in Stratospheric Ozone and Climate Change,* pp. 175–98. Washington, D.C.: Environmental Protection Agency.

Wynne, Brian. 1987. "Uncertainty: Technical and Social." In H. Brooks and C. Cooper, eds., *Science for Public Policy.* New York: Pergamon.

Young, Oran. 1982. *Resource Regimes: Natural Resources and Social Institutions.* Berkeley: University of California Press.

————. 1989a. *International Cooperation: Building Regimes for Natural Resources and the Environment.* Ithaca: Cornell University Press.

————. 1989b. "The Politics of International Regime Formation: Managing Natural Resources and the Environment." *International Organization* 43, no. 3 (Summer): 349–76.

Ziman, John. 1968. *Public Knowledge: An Essay Concerning the Social Dimension of Science.* Cambridge: Cambridge University Press.

————. 1984. *An Introduction to Science Studies: The Philosophical and Social Aspects of Science and Technology.* Cambridge: Cambridge University Press.

Zimmerman, William. 1973. "Issue Area and Foreign Policy Process: A Research Note in Search of a General Theory." *American Political Science Review* (December): 1204–12.

Index